The Complexities of Police Corruption

Issues in Crime & Justice

Series Editor
Gregg Barak, Eastern Michigan University

As we embark upon the twenty-first century, the meanings of crime continue to evolve and our approaches to justice are in flux. The contributions to this series focus their attention on crime and justice as well as on crime control and prevention in the context of a dynamically changing legal order. Across the series, there are books that consider the full range of crime and criminality and that engage a diverse set of topics related to the formal and informal workings of the administration of criminal justice. In an age of globalization, crime and criminality are no longer confined, if they ever were, to the boundaries of single nation-states. As a consequence, while many books in the series will address crime and justice in the United States, the scope of these books will accommodate a global perspective and they will consider such eminently global issues such as slavery, terrorism, or punishment. Books in the series are written to be used as supplements in standard undergraduate and graduate courses in criminology and criminal justice and related courses in sociology. Some of the standard courses in these areas include: introduction to criminal justice, introduction to law enforcement, introduction to corrections, juvenile justice, crime and delinquency, criminal law, and white collar, corporate, and organized crime.

Titles in the Series

Effigy: Images of Capital Defendants, by Allison Cotton
The Prisoners' World: Portraits of Convicts Caught in the Incarceration Binge, by William Tregea and Marjorie Larmour
Perverts and Predators: The Making of Sexual Offending Laws, by Laura J. Zilney and Lisa Anne Zilney
Racial Profiling: Research, Racism, Resistance, by Karen S. Glover
State Criminality: The Crime of All Crimes, by Dawn L. Rothe
Punishment for Sale: Private Prisons and Big Business, by Donna Selman and Paul Leighton
Forensic Science in Court: Challenges in the Twenty-first Century, edited by Donald E. Shelton
Threat Perceptions: The Policing of Dangers from Eugenics to the War on Terrorism, by Saran Ghatak
Murder Stories: Idological Narratives in Capital Punishment by Paul Kaplan
Gendered Justice: Intimate Partner Violence and the Criminal Justice System, by Venessa Garcia and Patrick McManimon
Theft of a Nation: Wall Street Looting and Federal Regulatory Colluding by Gregg Barak
The Complexities of Police Corruption: Gender, Identity, and Misconduct, by Marilyn Corsianos

The Complexities of Police Corruption

Gender, Identity, and Misconduct

Marilyn Corsianos

ROWMAN & LITTLEFIELD PUBLISHERS, INC.
Lanham • Boulder • New York • Toronto • Plymouth, UK

Published by Rowman & Littlefield Publishers, Inc.
A wholly owned subsidiary of The Rowman & Littlefield Publishing Group, Inc.
4501 Forbes Boulevard, Suite 200, Lanham, Maryland 20706
www.rowman.com

10 Thornbury Road, Plymouth PL6 7PP, United Kingdom

British Library Cataloguing in Publication Information Available

Library of Congress Cataloging-in-Publication Data

Corsianos, Marilyn.
The complexities of police corruption : gender, identity, and misconduct / Marilyn Corsianos.
p. cm.
Includes bibliographical references and index.
ISBN 978-1-4422-0636-6 (cloth : alk. paper) -- ISBN 978-1-4422-0638-0 (electronic)
1. Police corruption. 2. Police misconduct. 3. Discrimination in law enforcement. 4. Sex role in the
work environment. I. Title.
HV7936.C85C67 2012
364.1'323--dc23

2012014052

The paper used in this publication meets the minimum requirements of American National
Standard for Information Sciences Permanence of Paper for Printed Library Materials,
ANSI/NISO Z39.48-1992.

Printed in the United States of America

This book is dedicated to my partner in life Spiro Vlahos, and to our children Rena and Demetre.

Contents

Acknowledgments
ix

Preface
xi

1 Police Corruption: From the Introduction of Formal Policing
Systems to Today
1

2 Interrogating Police Corruption and the Organization as Enabler
21

3 The Role of the Masculinist Police Culture in Police Corruption
59

4 Critical Dilemmas in Police Behavior
101

5 Media Constructions of Police Corruption
125

6 Increasing Police Accountability through Community Policing
153

7 Concluding Remarks
175

Bibliography
183

Index
207

About the Author
215

Acknowledgments

I would like to thank Rowman & Littlefield Publishers and especially Sarah Stanton for their support of this scholarship. Also, many thanks to Chris Basso for assisting in the final steps in the production process, and to the academic reviewers who provided helpful suggestions. I would like to extend a special thanks to the Series Editor Gregg Barak for his commitment to this project, our numerous discussions on crime and criminality, and for his helpful queries and suggestions on earlier drafts of the manuscript. I am also indebted to the many participants who were willing to share their policing experiences with me and provide invaluable insight into police corruption particularly in the kinds of behavior that were perceived to be corrupt, how commonplace many of these were, and the different police justifications for abuses. They invested time and energy in meeting with me and providing the much needed insight into the complexities of the police culture and police misconduct.

I also wish to express my appreciation to Dana Radatz for her meticulous work on the index, and for her commitment to challenging structures of inequalities and bringing gender issues to the center in her own research. Dana's work reminds us of the social changes that are desperately needed. And, to my graduate assistant, Seyed Mirmajlessi, I thank him for his timely searches and emails, and for his wonderful work on checking sources for this project and retrieving a range of articles and books. Seyed's work ethic is a model for future graduate students and his current work on the police and social media will contribute to our understanding of policing as an institution of control.

I would also like to express my gratitude to my current and former colleagues at Eastern Michigan University in the Sociology, Anthropology and Criminology, as well as, the Women's and Gender Studies departments. In particular, I would like to acknowledge, in alphabetical order, Kristine Aj-rouch, Gregg Barak, Carrie L. Buist, Margaret Crouch, Elisabeth Daeumer, Suzanne Gray, Marilyn Horace-Moore, Jess Klein, Barb Richardson, and Solange Simões. My appreciation, as always, is extended to all of the critical and feminist criminologists who have conducted invaluable research in the area of crime and justice and who continue to inspire us.

To my dear friends who are like family, I thank them for all the truly amazing moments we have shared together. I extend much gratitude to Afro-dite Triantafillou, Julia Easson-Meyer, Shawna Findlay-Thompson, Christo-pher Downer, and the entire "T.O. group" (you know who you are), Becky and Alan Turanski, and Andrea and Paul Breck. As always, my primary debt is owed to my parents Rena Corsianos and to the late Demetre Corsianos for their love, support, and encouragement. My father in particular encouraged me to ask the tough questions, to think outside the box and to make a difference. I am eternally grateful for these skills and I miss him dearly.

I also would like to thank my brothers George and Terry for their uncon-ditional love and support. George daily reminds me of the power of laughter, the importance of family, and I treasure our long conversations and endless memories of our family's journey. And, I always look forward to my inter-esting debates with Terry particularly on world politics and the economy.

Last but not least, I thank Spiro Vlahos for his constant love, patience, and commitment to creating a better world and for being my number one fan. I am grateful for his critical insight into the powers of institutions, for asking the necessary questions, and encouraging me to challenge the dominant forces that daily contribute to the construction of "knowledge". And, to our children, Rena and Demetre, no words can capture the love and joy they bring to my world, and since my last book I'm happy to report that they continue to question "authority" every chance they get!

Marilyn Corsianos

Preface

This book provides a comprehensive examination of the complexities of police corruption as they relate to hegemonic masculinity, dominant crime-control ideologies, and policing as an "institution." It posits policing as a site of contestation for officers who often must preserve and defend their actions and identities in response to public and media accounts of police behavior, and it focuses on the interconnectedness of officers' perceptions of their roles, the centrality of gender in the misconduct of officers, and the critical dilemmas confronting police in their day-to-day work.

Chapter 1, "Police Corruption: From the Introduction of Formal Policing Systems to Today," provides a brief account of the history of policing in the United States and its relationship to police corruption. As Kappeler, Sluder, and Alpert (1998:28) note, "Since the creation of the first law enforcement agencies, police have engaged in misconduct . . . To study the history of police is to study police deviance, corruption and misconduct." Examples of corruption are presented from the formative years in policing to today to provide insight into how police corruption is conceptualized by the police, and to demonstrate the dominant police image as tied to traditional crime control ideologies and hegemonic masculinity. These reveal organizational 'purpose,' how police corruption is made possible, and how and why police criminality remains a gendered enterprise.

Chapter 2, "Interrogating Police Corruption and the Organization as Enabler," examines the police organizational goals in relation to dominant masculinist crime-control practices, the internal processes within police organizations that create corruption risks, and how organizations construct and respond to particular incidents of police corruption in order to ensure organizational survival and maintain the current structure. Moreover, forms of police corruption that are not recognized as abuses or are overwhelmingly ignored by police organizations are identified.

"The Role of the Masculinist Police Culture in Police Corruption" (chapter 3) assesses the complex social world of police officers and how it maintains and defends particular police actions. More specifically, this chapter provides explanations for police corruption in the context of central police occupational themes as they relate to "hegemonic masculinity" and "the brotherhood." Attention is given to how the police culture shapes and encourages particular ideologies that officers depend on to preserve and defend police actions and why significantly fewer women are involved in police corruption despite the justifications made internally for the abusive behavior of others. Excerpts from informal interviews conducted with thirty-two former police officers regarding their experiences and perceptions of police corruption are included to illustrate the complexities of police corruption as they relate to gender constructions and hegemonic masculinity and to demonstrate how police corruption is condoned internally.

Chapter 4, "Critical Dilemmas in Police Behavior," examines the popular cultural constructions of the police as a site of contestation for officers who have to respond to public challenges to self-identities and organizational identities following publicized cases of police corruption. The moral ambiguities that exist when officers act in corrupt ways but in compliance with the popular "hypermasculine" manifestations of the police (for example, police as crime fighters and protectors) are discussed in relation to identity constructions. Police depend on the police culture to guide their reactions and to maintain dominant identities. This chapter is framed within a perspective that views policing as a gendered enterprise where hegemonic masculinity contributes to the creation and preservation of a culture of tolerance for police corruption. The gender configuring of recruitment and promotion, internal police policies, and in the division of labor "enable" officers to "see the value" associated with masculine traits, and these experiences naturalize police responses to police corruption cases in ways that condone such acts despite different individual interpretations that may exist.

Chapter 5, "Media Constructions of Police Corruption," examines the role of the mainstream media in publicly defining police corruption narrowly through the reporting of select cases deemed to be "newsworthy," and it critically evaluates the argument that police criminality is grossly exaggerated and overstated by the media. Examples of mainstream news articles on police corruption cases are provided in the second half of the chapter to highlight the kinds of behavior that are perceived to "be" corruption as well as "newsworthy," and it provides evidence of hegemonic masculinity; for instance, in how particular forms of violence are "naturalized" and the sense of entitlement, "brotherhood," secrecy, and autonomy that exists within policing.

Chapter 6, "Increasing Police Accountability through Community Policing," considers the possibilities for the Community Policing (CP) model to redefine popular constructions of the police, particularly since the majority of police departments continue to "claim" that they have embraced various tenets of the CP model. Theoretically, the CP model has the potential to minimize police corruption by making even the power relations between the police and communities as well as within organizations both structurally and ideologically. This chapter considers these possibilities in the pursuit to challenge hegemonic masculinity and patriarchal ideologies in policing and to decrease police corruption risks. At the same time, however, the chapter presents an analysis of the current challenges to integrating CP in meaningful ways.

The last chapter, chapter 7, provides some concluding remarks.

Chapter One

Police Corruption: From the Introduction of Formal Policing Systems to Today

A brief account of the early formal policing system in the United States, its relationship to police corruption, and the push by police organizations to make policing a "legitimate profession" is provided in this chapter. Examples of corruption are presented from the formative years in policing to today and demonstrate the dominant image of the police as infused with masculinist crime-control ideologies, particularly as they relate to the purpose and function of the police, how police corruption is made possible, and how police criminality remains a gendered enterprise. Examples of publicized cases of police corruption are included to provide insight into how police corruption is conceptualized by the police, and secondly, how they shape the public's perceptions of what qualifies as police corruption and how these acts are viewed by the public today as the exception and not the norm. Explanations of how these acts are made possible are provided in the subsequent chapters.

To begin, the English colonists in America introduced informal practices of social control similar to the ones they left behind; these included voluntary as well as low-paid patrol watches at night. In some jurisdictions, "watchmen" were given noise-making rattles and were expected to shout and rattle their rattles if they observed a crime or fleeing suspects. This work was undesirable and done largely by poor people. Sometimes, criminal offenders themselves were assigned to be watchmen as a form of punishment for their crimes (Trojanowicz and Bucqueroux, 1990). The Northeast (from New England to Virginia) developed into commercial and industrial centers, and after independence, scores of immigrants moved to these cities. Initially, the sheriff was the most important colonial officer, and in the villages and towns,

1

Chapter 1

marshals were common; the work of the sheriff and the marshal was done in the daytime and did not involve a patrol. But with the significant increase in the population in the northeast, the marshal was no longer able to control crime, particularly the mobs and riots and general disorder. The population explosion contributed to increases in social problems such as crime, alcoholism, overcrowdedness, homelessness, and sanitation issues. The earlier systems of control that were commonly used were now severely limited to deal with these issues. "The lack of organization made the watch incapable of controlling mobs and riots, and as the cities grew in the early 1800s, civic leaders became alarmed at the levels of crime, riot, and general disorder in the cities" (Travis and Langworthy, 2008:75).

These set the stage for the creation of a formal policing system (Travis and Langworthy, 2008). American cities had few examples of formal systems that were believed to be effective. The most appealing for some was the London Metropolitan Police, but, on the other hand, many opposed the creation of a formal policing system that could deprive individual liberty (Walker and Katz, 1983).

Policing, however, in the southern colonies took a different form. With some exceptions, southern colonies were rural, consisting of large plantations that used slave labor to produce cash crops. Social-control priorities for property owners were concentrated on creating slave patrols to prevent slave uprisings (Reichel, 1988) and to search for escaped slaves. They were also proactive in visiting plantations to ensure the safety of owners and the control of slaves (Travis and Langworthy, 2008). According to Williams and Murphy (1990), the slave patrols in the South, in many ways, can be considered the first modern police in the United States since by the middle of the 1700s, every southern colony had introduced legislation that required the creation of slave patrols. The primary law enforcement official was the county sheriff who in turn depended on the assistance of property owners in the form of a posse (Travis and Langworthy, 2008).

In the West, on the other hand, given the slow but gradual increase in population from colonial times, the need for a more formal policing system was less visible. According to Brown (1983), in many areas there was no formal law enforcement in existence. Rather, vigilantes would form to respond to a problem that arose, search for suspected offenders, and determine appropriate punishment. Over time as the population in particular areas increased, there was growing support by some for a more formal policing system.

Despite the early differences among the systems of control in the Northeast, South, and West, the initial development of formal policing took place in large cities gradually over time (Monkkonen, 1981). The model of the London Metropolitan Police was adapted by American cities, albeit independently, leading to decentralization. According to Monkkonen (1981), as their systems were improved, smaller cities incorporated these ideas into the creation of their own police agencies to meet their needs. Opposition to the creation of a police agency and the time needed for implementation gradually decreased as more and more organizations were formed and as the public started to accept the idea of a "police force" as necessary to society. Over time, however, the public began to take the existence of a formal police system for granted, assuming that the use of coercion and force on the part of the police was essential.

Monkkonen notes that the problems that first affected large cities eventually were seen in smaller cities that required a formal mechanism to reduce and deter particular crimes; the first modern U.S. police forces created in some of the largest cities reflected the organizational structure of the London Metropolitan Police, but that changed for many of the smaller police agencies that followed. "Up until the modeling of the early U.S. uniformed police on English precedents, one must maintain an Anglo-American perspective on policing, but after the establishment of the first few American departments, the paths of the police of the two countries diverged, those in American cities looking at each other rather than to London" (Monkkonen, 1981:40). In 1838, the Boston police department consisted of nine officers and is regarded by many as the first organization to patrol during the day. A few years later, New York City combined day and night patrol into a single, organized department. By 1875, nearly every major city in the United States had created a formal policing system (Platt et al., 1982; Lane, 1971).

The early formal policing system in the Northeast was presented as one based on a utilitarian philosophy; that is, that the best government action is one that provides the greatest benefit to the majority of people. It was promoted as a system that could prevent more harm (for example, by reducing crime and victimization) than the harms it caused (for example, restrictions of liberty, police surveillance of legal behavior, and police corruption). The early American police were authorized by local municipalities and lacked the central authority of the Crown to establish a unified mandate, as in the case of the English police. Local political leaders, often ward politicians, governed American police (Kelling and Moore, 1988). Kelling and Moore assert that although policing, during what they referred to as "the political era" (1840s until the 1920s), was organized as a centralized, quasi-military organization, police departments were decentralized.

> Cities were divided into precincts, and precinct-level managers often, in concert with the ward leaders, ran precincts as small-scale departments—hiring, firing, managing, and assigning personnel as they deemed appropriate. In addition, decentralization combined with primitive communications and transportation to give police officers substantial discretion in handling their individual beats. At best, officer contact with central command was maintained through the call box. (ibid., 5)

But, as Kappeler, Sluder, and Alpert (1998:28) note, "Since the creation of the first law enforcement agencies, police have engaged in misconduct . . . To study the history of police is to study police deviance, corruption and misconduct." Police corruption/misconduct should be understood as the abuse of police powers for personal and/or organizational gain. The gain can be financial, social, psychological, and/or emotional (see chapter 2).

From the 1800s to the early 1900s, the political influences in policing appear to be more obvious to people. Today, they are no less prevalent, but at times they may appear to the public as less apparent and/or less invasive. Kelling and Moore (1988) referred to the period between the 1840s and 1920s as the "political era," the period between the 1930s and 1970s as the "reform era," and the period since the late 1970s as the "community problem-solving era." But, they have been criticized, and rightly so, for suggesting that the influence of politics was eliminated or decreased in the subsequent periods following the so-called political era. Additionally, they have been criticized for excluding the relationship between police strategies and minority communities, since police strategies in minority neighborhoods have produced particular problems, and for focusing their analysis of policing largely on northeastern cities (Williams and Murphy, 1990). According to Williams and Murphy (1990:30), "Their analysis omits several crucial parts of the story of policing in America: the role of *slave patrols* and other police instruments of racial oppression; the role of the police in imposing racially biased laws; and the importance of racial and social turmoil in the creation of the first version of America's *new police*." Also, evidence of policing "reform" was seen much earlier (as in the 1880s) (Strecher, 1991), and more importantly, "reform" can take a variety of appearances that would include even some recent changes made in policing (for example, the introduction of early intervention systems, the "recording of race" by motorists stopped by police, mandatory arrest policies in domestic violence cases). For the period referred to as the "community problem-solving" era, it too has been criticized largely because some criminologists assert that even though many police departments have introduced various Community Policing (CP) initiatives, the traditional goals and crime-control function of police organizations have remained largely the same (Corsianos, 2009; Zhao, He, and Lovrich, 2003; Manning, 1997); also, evidence of CP programs were seen earlier, such as Louis Radelet's police community relations program that started in 1955 (Strecher, 1991), and, more importantly, the primary roles of the early "policewomen" were almost entirely tied to community-policing efforts (Corsianos, 2009; Martin and Jurik, 2007).

During the formative years of formal police organizations, there were distinct variations in police roles depending on the community the police served. Individual police officers were closely tied to politicians (Monkkonen, 1981; Richardson, 1974; Lane, 1971). Massive immigration to the

Northeast during the 1800s led to increased competition with established residents for scarce jobs. Immigration also led to increasingly noticeable cultural differences in urban centers that were viewed as threatening by the established residents of cities and towns. Riots and physical confrontations between members of the public increased, requiring more frequent police intervention (Kappeler, 1989). The potential for corruption was interconnected to the fact that political leaders appointed officers who were, in turn, accountable to politicians and not to the city government (Uchida, 1989), which meant that they often promoted the interests of their political leaders. Additionally, they were "often recruited from the same ethnic stock as the dominant political groups in the localities, and continued to live in the neighborhoods they patrolled" (Kelling and Moore, 1988:5). As discussed by Fogelson (1977) and Lane (1971), police protected the illegal operations of politicians, and during elections, officers used intimidation, arrest, and/or the use of excessive force to prevent supporters from opposing parties from casting their ballots. Officers also often used excessive force/beatings to extract confessions from suspects and as a form of punishment for low-level offenders in lieu of arrest (Champion, 2001). Their closeness to political leaders and the communities they policed and the organizational challenges to the supervision of patrol officers certainly did not help to limit the possibilities for police corruption.

Additionally, the police had acquired the reputation of "strikebreakers," as they were frequently called to use intimidation and/or force to break up strikes (Harring, 1983). The rampant corruption during this time is well documented. It was not uncommon for officers to accept bribes and graft on their own and to profit from the illegal operations of gambling houses, bordellos, and saloons (Champion, 2001; Fogelson, 1977; Haller, 1976; Lane, 1971). For example, in New York in 1900 the typical monthly payoff for officers protecting bordellos and gambling houses ranged from $50 to $300, and the rewards for senior officers were considerably higher. Also, officers were often involved more directly by working as money collectors for the illegal business owners seeking out those who owed gambling debts and making demands (Richardson, 1974), and at times ignored criminal activities in exchange for payoffs. Champion (2001:10–11) notes:

> The police were often used, therefore, as an instrument of social control by the politically and economically powerful interests. Their powers were diffuse, and the public was generally unfamiliar with their specific tasks. Thus, when police officers enforced the law, it was difficult to determine whether they were imposing their own standards on citizens arbitrarily or applying the law in an even-handed fashion. Most citizens acquiesced to police authority, regardless of whether it was proper or improper. Police officers had broad discretionary powers, and it was simply unacceptable to challenge the authority.

Indeed, police, at times, gained some support by operating differently in various neighborhoods in order to "appear" to represent the diverse values and needs of the public. In some poor areas, police were known to operate soup kitchens and shelters for the homeless and to help people find jobs. In wealthier areas, they were more likely to serve as security protecting the properties and businesses of the more affluent. But, on the other hand, increased conflicts among the various groups required increased police intervention, and these made the police less favorable in the eyes of some based on perceptions of whether police acted appropriately and whether they were perceived as taking sides (Monkkonen, 1981). Law enforcement was highly arbitrary given the lack of supervision of patrol officers, lack of rules to guide police behavior, the high level of discretionary powers given to individual officers, individual police biases, discriminatory practices against particular groups of people, and the diverse police roles in the different neighborhoods. At times, officers enforced unpopular laws in immigrant ethnic neighborhoods by crusading reformers who were primarily of English and Dutch background (Fogelson, 1977). In other instances, the intimate ties between the police and neighborhoods led to discrimination against strangers, particularly minority ethnic and racial groups and those who were perceived as violating neighborhood norms (Kelling, 1987a). Police were often involved in racist, sometimes genocidal policies, and the beating and torture of suspects as a form of punishment for minor crimes and to get confessions for more serious crimes was a common police approach (Kappeler, Sluder, and Alpert, 1998). The police connection to political leaders led to forms of police corruption that can be characterized as "typical," including police interference with elections that included encouraging citizens to vote for particular candidates, preventing nonsupporters from voting, and even assisting in rigging elections (Kelling and Moore, 1988; Fogelson, 1977).

Policing was largely structured around foot patrols during this time. When early automobiles became available, they were used to transport officers from one patrol area to another. Detective divisions existed but were less organized and without the recognition and status typically associated with detective work today. According to Kelling and Moore (1988), detectives were particularly important to local politicians for gathering information on individuals for political or personal reasons rather than for possible criminal offenses. For Walker (1981), the failure of the police to enforce the laws set the stage for police reform in the nineteenth century.

Several significant changes to the early formal policing system were seen throughout the late 1800s and 1900s. The wealthiest members of the public wanted the police to control the behavior of the poor and the new immigrants who were perceived as a threat to the preservation of certain "morals" and "values," and they wanted the police to serve their interests rather than those of their political opponents. At the same time, some police administrators wanted to redefine policing into a respected, professional field independent from city hall in order to have the power to define their functions and to determine appropriate practices (Kelling and Moore, 1988). Additionally, religious groups were vocal in their objections of the police protecting illegal businesses such as brothels (Uchida, 1997). The growing urban middle class was also dissatisfied with a policing system that was built on the police's loyalty to individual politicians and politicians' dependence on the bloc voting of ethnic neighborhoods for reelection.

According to Travis and Langworthy (2008:89):

> Independence for the police was expected to mean freedom from partisan political interference and the corruptions such influences bred. The elites . . . were opposed to the practice of allowing illegal operations run by political favorites to be immune from regulation. They were particularly interested in using the police to curb what they saw as dangerous behavior among the working classes, including gambling, drinking and other vice offenses. For police administrators, independence meant the freedom to control police officers and priorities without regard to political affiliation.

In addition, women's organizations during the first "wave" of the women's movement demanded the hiring of "policewomen" whose work would reflect the dominant "equal but separate" ideology relating to women and men and who they believed could more effectively respond to the changes brought about by industrialization and urbanization (Corsianos, 2009). Clearly, different groups had different intentions for wanting "reform."

SOME APPARENT CHANGES IN THE EARLY FORMAL POLICING SYSTEM

Some changes would soon follow with the passage of the Pendleton Civil Service Act by Congress in 1883, which established civil service guidelines for selecting police officers on particular qualifications rather than on their political connections (Strecher, 1995). The Progressive movement emerged in the late 1800s to advocate for reform and work toward instilling "efficiency" and "morality" into local governance (Fogelson, 1977). The International Association of Chiefs of Police founded in 1893 became the "voice of professionalism," and one of their stated goals was to remove party politics from the direct and intimate relationship they had with individual police officers.

According to Kelling and Moore (1988:9),

> Civil service eliminated patronage and ward influences in hiring and firing police officers. In some cities (Los Angeles and Cincinnati, for example), even the position of chief of police became a civil service position to be attained

through examination. In others (such as Milwaukee), chiefs were given a life-time tenure by a police commission, to be removed from office only for cause. In yet others (Boston, for example), contracts for chiefs were staggered so as not to coincide with the mayor's tenure. Concern for separation of police from politics did not focus only on chiefs, however. In some cities, such as Philadelphia, it became illegal of patrol officers to live in the beats they patrolled.

Also, some police reformers pushed for centralized, universalistic procedures and to redefine the police roles from ones focused largely on social service and order maintenance to law enforcement and controlling crime. They worked to establish hiring standards, to hire outside the local jurisdiction to increase objectivity, and to recruit chiefs from both professional and military backgrounds (Monkonnen, 1981; Walker, 1977). But these reforms were intended for male police officers since the roles of policewomen were intricately connected with more social-service types of functions, as will be discussed later.

Vollmer's Influences on Formal Policing Systems

In 1908, as the chief of police of Berkeley, California, August Vollmer established professional and educational training for "his" officers. With the help of academics, Vollmer created police training classes that included investigative techniques, fingerprinting, photography, and anatomy. Vollmer also created more effective police selection methods based on education, physical fitness, and psychological testing. In 1931, the Wickersham Commission appointed by President Herbert Hoover two years earlier issued a fifteen-volume report of the U.S. criminal justice system. One of these volumes examined police lawlessness and abuse of powers. The report also noted inconsistency throughout the country regarding the selection, training, and administration of police recruits and recommended changes that both Vollmer and Wilson supported (Champion, 2001). Vollmer believed that officers should be committed to crime control but at the same time be objective about social issues in order to maintain neutrality in their policing roles (Carte and Carte, 1975). For Vollmer, officers should be "morally committed" to their job; fighting crime was a moral commitment of service to the country's welfare, and therefore he opposed even minor forms of graft. In his view, even an officer who accepted a free cup of coffee should be fired (Carte, 1986). Additionally, in the pursuit to gain acceptance as a "legitimate profession" from the wider public, police organizations had to commit to "proving" effectiveness. For Vollmer, this meant being able to record and classify crimes. Vollmer developed and implemented a uniform system of crime classification. This later became known as the Uniform Crime Reports, which was administered by the FBI and became an integral component to police organizations' attempts to "prove" their value to the public by demonstrating "effectiveness."

In their attempts to gain legitimacy, police efforts were concentrated on promoting the image of the police as a "profession" with a specialized service, body of knowledge, and employees who were "responsible," "respectable," and "accountable" to the public. The idea of a "science of policing" was popularized and contributed to the construction of the police as a specialized area. For one, in 1893, the National Chiefs of Police Union, which became the International Association of Chiefs of Police, held annual meetings and shared information and ideas in an effort to respond to the police crisis in legitimacy. Also, the Bertillon system of identification used in France was adopted, which required officers to record descriptions of arrested persons brought to the station, take measurements of the offender's body, take photographs, note any unique features such as scars or tattoos, and take fingerprints (Bailey, 1995). Additionally, the creation of crime investigation laboratories, the development of scientific procedures for crime-scene analysis, lie detectors, and later the use of crime statistics helped promote the image of the police as having a specialized body of knowledge (Parker, 1972). According to Parker (1972:39), Vollmer was the first police administrator to use or develop "a signal system: a workable modus operandi; the use of bicycles, motorcycles, and automobiles equipped with radios; the lie detector, a scientific crime investigation laboratory, selection of college men for his police force; a police school in his department, attracting many scientists to teach his officers and encouraging many colleges to offer courses for future policemen." It appears that policewomen were not part of Vollmer's image of what a professional police force should look like.

During the late 1800s the push to narrow the roles of the police to crime control and law enforcement became more apparent, as did the push to empower police executives to use their own discretionary powers under the "guidance" of laws. According to Kelling and Moore (1988), police patrol started to become more routinized, where law enforcement became the priority. Members of the public were no longer encouraged to call their local police district for assistance. Instead, calls were directed to a central communications office. Additionally, when the 911 systems were created, the police promoted them as effective tools to improving police response time.

At the same time, specialization in police services was seen by police organizations as a necessity in promoting the image of the police as a legitimate profession. When particular problems arose, the police would form special units to deal with them; examples included vice, tactical, and drug units. Also, these units were under central command, which weakened the authority of precinct commanders (Fogelson, 1977). In fact, police organizations were hierarchical, where final authority and control was centralized and resting with members of the "brass."

In some jurisdictions officers were required to not live in the area they policed. In others, it was highly discouraged. The impersonal approach to law enforcement would separate not only individual police officers from political leaders but also the police from citizens. According to Kelling and Moore (1988), police were expected to focus on crime solving, and the role of citizens was one of "passive recipients" of police services. During this time, police reformers aggressively promoted the "new image" of the police with the help of the media and public relations campaigns. The increasing distance between police and particular communities became more obvious as the use of police cars became commonplace. Initially, moving officers from foot patrol to car patrol was presented as a tactical reason that would increase the patrol parameters of the police and put officers on a more equal playing field when trying to apprehend suspects in cars. In actuality, however, the physical separation symbolized the power disparities that existed between "the police" as instruments of state power and members of the public.

Despite some apparent changes in the early policing systems, police corruption was not discussed by police organizations in any meaningful way. The push to respond to the police crisis in legitimacy meant that police organizations had to invest time and energy in managing their appearances, particularly as they related to dominant crime-control ideologies. More specifically, they had to promote their image as "crime fighters" and as being effective in controlling crime. Also, in the pursuit to "appear" to respond to the demands of the public, gendered policing approaches were also created with the introduction of the "policewoman" position, which was distinct from the roles of "policeman" or "patrolman."

Early "Policewomen"

Criminologists who talk about reform in policing during the early and/or mid-1900s often neglect the work of policewomen and their efforts to promote the image of the police as a legitimate profession. Activists during the first wave of the women's movement in the United States fought to create the position of policewoman (Van Wormer and Bartollas, 2000; Hale and Bennett, 1995; Segrave, 1995; Feinman, 1986). They succeeded, and in 1908 Portland's Lola Greene Baldwin was sworn in to "perform police service" for the city of Portland, Oregon, making her the first woman hired by an American municipality to carry out law enforcement duties (Myers, 1995). And, two years later, Alice Stebbins Wells was appointed to the rank of detective by the Los Angeles Police Department (Van Wormer and Bartollas, 2000).

In the early 1900s in the United States, vast social changes were occurring as a result of industrialization and urbanization. The Industrial Revolution had attracted scores of immigrants and people from rural areas to the urban centers to find employment, predominantly in the vast array of factories. Significant increases in the population increased competition for jobs and other resources and often led to a series of social problems that included discriminatory policies, increased criminal activity, alcoholism, overcrowded streets, homelessness, pollution, and poor hygiene and sanitation issues (Pessen, 1989; Baltzell, 1964; Marx, 1859). Many of those representing the middle and upper socioeconomic classes blamed the poor and the new immigrants for a number of societal problems, including the spread of venereal diseases, and perceived them as "immoral" and "criminal" (Myers, 1995). Women's organizations represented largely by economically privileged women were instrumental in pushing for the creation of the policewoman position in order to proactively respond to the perceived decline of traditional values. With the dominant "separate but equal" ideology, the roles of "policewomen" were intended to be tied to work with women and children, whereas the work of "policemen" would be focused on policing men (Corsianos, 2009). But, unlike policemen, the social status and education of policewomen differed significantly. The policewomen were required to have a college education, whereas policemen had a high school diploma and overwhelmingly represented the working class (Martin and Jurik, 2007). Policewomen were also typically older, married, and were mothers with grown children (they perceived these requirements as necessary so that their police duties would not take them away from their "maternal duties") and were respected in their communities. For instance, African American women who were hired as officers in large cities to work with African American women and girls were often social workers, teachers, or ministers' wives, and their social positions provided them with "status" in their communities (Schulz, 2004).

Even though on one level policewomen's work incorporated crime-control strategies that included proactive work to identify and/or prevent crime, their work was largely considered to be more similar to social work. Policewomen's work was largely proactive; their primary goal was to prevent women and girls from committing crimes and/or becoming victims of crimes, particularly "sex crimes," and from being "sexually exploited." Policewomen worked in plainclothes visiting public places (for example, dance halls, hotels, saloons) and conducted surveillance and made arrests. Since they worked in plainclothes they could not be identified as policewomen unless they willingly disclosed their police identity verbally or showed their police badge (Martin and Jurik, 2007). But, in addition to surveillance work, they monitored local help-wanted ads that offered large wages to women and girls for questionable employment; found temporary shelter for those in need of housing; dealt with creditors to negotiate payments from debtors; helped women and girls enroll in classes to learn specific job skills; and worked to collect money from delinquent employers who refused to pay their female employees (Corsianos, 2009; Myers, 1995).

They sought to police the "morality" of females who were generally viewed as nurturing, pure, morally conservative, and civilized and were ultimately the ones who could provide moral guidance to their family members and create a nurturing family environment (Ginzberg, 1990). In fact, the privileged policewomen viewed single women searching for employment in blue-collar, white-collar, or domestic work as vulnerable in large cities since they were often away from family working with strangers who could con them or force them to engage in criminal activity. This was perceived as a serious threat to the preservation of "traditional appropriate feminine" behavior and the "traditional family unit" (Myers, 1995). Policewomen believed that it was their "moral duty" to keep a "watchful eye" over employed women who could be taken advantage of but also unemployed women who were looking for work (Myers, 1995). The early policewomen subscribed to the dominant crime-control mandate (that is, to identify specific crimes such as street prostitution, disorderly conduct, indecency in public spaces, and other street-level crimes and to make arrests), but the tools they used are reflective of the perceived innate differences between the sexes (for example, women were seen as innately nurturing, which meant they could more effectively talk to women and girls and provide support without having the "innate need" to use violent means, unlike policemen).

During the early twentieth century, the U.S. government actively promoted "cleanness," "morality," and "physical safety" as societal necessities, and the police responded by focusing their efforts on venereal disease control and vice and prostitution abatement. In fact, prostitution was defined by the government as a public health problem, which enabled the police to commit resources to fighting urban vice (Myers, 1995). But given patriarchal ideologies, the policing of "sexual delinquents" became a gendered enterprise as police work focused on females' "sexual" behavior. There was a preoccupation with policing the sexuality of girls and women (Balfour and Comack, 2006; Chesney-Lind and Shelden, 2004; Chesney-Lind, 1995; Odem and Schlossman, 1991; Brenzel, 1983; Chesney-Lind and Rodriguez, 1983; Shelden, 1981; Vedder and Somerville, 1970; Tappan, 1947). The criminal justice system aimed to enforce girls' conformity to sexual norms while ignoring the same behavior by boys (Chesney-Lind and Shelden, 2004; Chesney-Lind, 1995). In fact, the "sexual delinquent" label was attached to women and/or girls for engaging in many different types of behavior that included choices of dress, use of language, violating curfews, being a runaway, and engaging in sexual intercourse. As Myers (1995:76) states:

Although some delinquent girls literally were sex offenders, others simply offended their sex. Any outward signs of "precocious sexuality" rebuked traditional female moral standards . . . As government became involved in reform to clean up the city, it was natural that the policewoman, with her determined mission of keeping young women from prostitution and related vice, would play an enhanced role.

Furthermore, "On the basis of a mere tendency to immorality, courts could place females under indeterminate or permanent custodial care" (Myers, 1995:78).

In their attempts to secure and promote the reputation of policewomen, the early women in the field formed two professional organizations that set high entry standards and ongoing training far in excess of male officers' requirements. Policewomen did not consider themselves "the same" as policemen given their higher economic class position and education levels and perceived innate differences reflected in the prevailing "separate but equal" ideology. But policewomen chose to use the title *police* in order to ensure their legal authority and the cooperation of male officers (Schulz, 2004) and to overall improve the image of the police. Also, to avoid tension from male officers, the early Women's Bureaus were separated administratively, and sometimes physically, from the rest of the police department (Martin and Jurik, 2007). But leaders of the policewomen's movement preferred the physical separation because they believed that policewomen's services would be more accessible to women and girls if they appeared less intimidating, which could be accomplished by keeping them separate from recognized, traditional police stations (Corsianos, 2009; Myers, 1995). In other words, the popular belief was that this separation could help promote a positive image of the police by encouraging more women and girls to seek help from the police. The separate titles and accompanying roles continued until the 1960s and 1970s until changes in legislation required police organizations to hire women and men on an "equal" basis, and the gender-specific police titles were replaced with the gender-neutral "police officer" title.

REPORTS OF POLICE CORRUPTION

The public typically learns about police corruption mainly from the mainstream media but also from formal inquiries (the Knapp Commission); citizen action groups (Human Rights Watch); litigation cases involving police misconduct; and academic research. However, the abuse of police powers in maintaining control over women's and girls' lives has not been identified by the media or in the policing literature as a form of police corruption on the part of the early policewomen. Indeed, police powers were abused for social gain. The early policewomen did not work because of economic necessity but rather because they saw themselves as "moral crusaders." In some cases, women were in areas perceived by policewomen as immoral, and therefore, even though they were not breaking any laws, policewomen would force women to move from these locations by using threats of arrest. But unlike acts of corruption that are largely recognized and condemned by the public, in the case of the early policewomen, they often had the support of many in the middle and upper socioeconomic classes and, therefore, their actions were not "hidden" from the public.

Today, this form of corruption continues to take place, even though it is not conceptualized as a form of corruption by the police. The public only learns about it in a few instances when members of the "legitimate" public are involved (that is, those perceived by mainstream society to be legitimate complainants, such as the middle and upper socioeconomic classes and the formally educated). For instance, in Toronto, Canada, in January 2011, a police officer, Constable Michael Sanguinetti, spoke on crime prevention at a York University safety forum at Osgoode Hall Law School, and during his presentation he said that "women should avoid dressing like sluts in order not to be victimized" (http://en.wikipedia.org/wiki/SlutWalk).

Clearly, this officer doesn't view female victims of crime as "legitimate victims" if they dress a certain way. This statement was made by an officer who was "assumed" to be victim sensitive and aware of some of the gender, race, and class inequalities in society; the department had indeed sent him over others to represent the organization. One would assume that this person had been more carefully scrutinized internally to protect the public image of the organization. Of course, feminist and critical criminologists who have dedicated their careers to understanding gender inequalities and to bringing awareness to how certain female victims of crime are treated by police were not surprised. But the difference here was that the audience (university students) were perceived as "legitimate," which meant that when complaints were made the police organization attempted to respond quickly and engage in "damage control." (In protest, SlutWalk protest marches began on April 3, 2011, in Toronto, Ontario, and have sparked a movement of rallies across the world to challenge rape myths that include explaining rape based on a woman's appearance. See http://en.wikipedia.org/wiki/SlutWalk.)

These types of police behavior are rarely conceptualized as a form of police corruption. When one looks at the media reports on police corruption, they typically include cases in which officers abused their police powers for some sort of financial gain or used excessive force against civilians as some form of punishment. Most police corruption complaints that are reported are by victims. And the cases that often become publicized and reported by the mainstream media involve police behavior deemed to be "serious," have "sensational" appeal, involve victims who are perceived to be "credible" and/

or "legitimate," and reflect the dominant ideologies that privilege some victims over others and recognize only specific instances of abuse of powers (see chapter 5). For Beigel (1978:1) the "enormous power at the disposal of an individual police officer, therefore, makes it important to understand and identify those aspects of police fabric which develop corrupt attitudes." Recently, in June of 2011, federal judge Sam A. Lindsay sentenced a Mesquite Narcotics officer to an unusually long sentence for stealing $2,000. The veteran police officer on the Mesquite Police Department was suspected of routinely taking money from cash seized during police searches. Following a tip about Officer John David McAllister's suspected illegal behavior, the FBI conducted a "sting operation." They placed $100,000 in a bag, put it in a car, and then told McAllister to track down the "drug money." The cameras that were secretly placed in McAllister's car showed the Mesquite cop confiscating the bag and stuffing $2,000 in marked bills into his pants. The judge was "tired" of police officers (people who were sworn to uphold the law) breaking the law, and he was frustrated with the lenient sentences given to convicted officers. As a result, he sentenced McAllister to fifteen months in federal prison, hoping this would deter other officers from committing criminal activity (Lowe, 2011). This serves as a common example of the kinds of police behavior that can be considered to be "corruption" both internally within the organization and externally by the public.

Officers who witness particular forms of corruption on the part of fellow officers (for example, the abuse of powers for financial gain or the use of excessive force against "civilians" as a form of punishment) are deterred from reporting them given the various dynamics of the police culture (see chapter 3). Moreover, citizens who willingly engage in these acts of corruption with the police have no motive to report their own involvement or that of the officer. Citizens who are "less willing" participants in the corruption (for example, if the police tell them to pay a fee in exchange for not receiving a citation and they do so) or citizens who observe different forms of corruption may decide not to report these incidents because they believe the police will either not investigate or they are fearful of retribution.

Media Reports of Police Criminality: From the Early Formal Policing Systems to Today

As mentioned earlier, police corruption refers to abuses of police powers for personal and/or organizational gain—the gain can be financial, social, psychological, and/or emotional. But when we look at the public reports of police criminality since the early formal policing systems to today, they are largely comprised of abuses of police powers for financial gain, as well as excessive use of force incidents against "civilians." These behaviors were and continue to be largely gender specific. Police corruption continues to be a gendered enterprise given the disproportionate number of male officers involved in police misconduct (see chapter 3).

Reported forms of police corruption on the part of male officers during the early 1900s include police support of illegal business such as gambling, prostitution, and the manufacturing and sale of alcohol during Prohibition. According to Fogelson (1977:118):

> Despite these (professionalizing) changes most departments had only a slightly greater capacity to curtail criminal activity in 1930 than in 1890. For one reason, many policemen were not inclined to deal with crime. As the sensational scandals that erupted in Chicago, Philadelphia, and New York in the late 1920s and early 1930s indicated, some officers preferred to work with the gangsters. A few grew well-to-do from their share of the proceeds. Others preferred to pass their time eating, sleeping, and drinking, talking with buddies or visiting friends, and doing everything possible to stay away from trouble.

Between the 1940s and 1960s, reports of graft and violence on the part of policemen were frequent. Some examples included police violence against citizens during the race riots in Detroit in 1943 and the Watts riots in Southern California in 1965. In Philadelphia in the early 1950s, an investigation revealed extensive corruption among policemen who were protecting gambling and prostitution businesses. And in the early 1960s, Denver policemen were involved in a burglary ring in which their police cars were used to haul away stolen merchandise from stores and restaurants (Champion, 2001).

In the 1970s, New York police officer Frank Serpico reported widespread corruption within the New York Police Department. A special commission, the Knapp Commission, was appointed by the mayor to investigate the allegations. It held public hearings and found that corruption was widespread and bureaucratically organized, and it included police acts ranging from the exploitation of routine parking tickets, receiving gambling payoffs and other extortionate gratuities from restaurants and business owners, to those involved in narcotics trafficking (Prenzler, 2009; Champion, 2001; *Knapp*, 1972). This led to numerous indictments and convictions of police officers and a series of recommendations to prevent these types of conduct in the future. The Knapp Commission described two types of officers: "grass eaters" and "meat eaters":

> The overwhelming majority of those who take payoffs are grass-eaters, who accept gratuities and solicit $5, $10, and $20 payments from contractors, tow-truck operators, gamblers, and the like, but do not aggressively pursue corruption payments. Meat-eaters, probably only a small percentage of the force, spend a good deal of their working hours aggressively seeking out situations

they can exploit for financial gain, including gambling, narcotics, and other serious offenses that can yield payments of thousands of dollars. (*Knapp*, 1972:65)

Many of these events were further publicized in dramatized books and films such as *Serpico* (Maas, 1973) and the *Prince of the City* (Daley, 1978).

Publicized Police Corruption since the Knapp Commission

Cases of publicized police corruption following the Knapp Commission remain a common phenomenon. But the vast majority of incidents of police corruption are never identified as such or are never publicized and hidden internally within police circles. Reasons for why some cases become public versus others are discussed in later chapters. In the 1980s, "the Buddy Boys" received media attention; they were involved in corruption that ranged from stealing money and drugs from dealers to selling illegal drugs taken from the dealers. The Buddy Boys consisted of at least thirty-eight officers of the New York Police Department's 77th Precinct. In 1990, a representative sample of police agencies from cities and counties with populations of ten thousand or more was surveyed. The study found widespread police misconduct and numerous citizen complaints involving police corruption. Civil lawsuits were filed against police officers at significant costs to the cities and towns (Newell, Pollock, and Tweedy, 1992). Civil lawsuits against police officers in which misconduct is alleged account for about 40 percent of all police lawsuits (Kappeler, 1993).

Other high-profile cases of police corruption in the United States include the River Cops scandal in Miami in the 1980s, which led to the conviction or dismissal of over ninety officers for stealing cocaine from offenders and reselling it, murder, and attempted murder (Kappeler et al., 1998). In 1985, officers employed by the Key West Police Department in Florida, which included senior members of upper management such as the deputy chief, were convicted of crimes that included bribing witnesses, conspiracy, racketeering, and cocaine possession with intent to distribute ("Key West," 1984).

In the 1990s, the Mollen Commission was created to investigate drug corruption, robberies, theft, and excessive use of force committed by New York police officers (Champion, 2001). The Mollen Commission found a flawed internal police accountability system and corruption that took the form of "brutality, theft, abuse of authority and active police criminality." Some of their recommendations included improving recruitment and applicant screening, officer performance evaluations, police management, enforcement of command accountability, and internal affairs operations (Mollen Commission, 1994).

One of the most highly publicized cases of police excessive force was the Rodney King incident in Los Angeles in 1991. King led the California Highway Patrol and the Los Angeles Police Department (LAPD) on a ten-minute high-speed chase. At least twenty-seven uniformed officers (twenty-one LAPD and four California Highway Patrol) were at the scene when the chase ended (Lersch, 2002). King was tased twice and struck with officers' nightsticks and kicked by several officers for two minutes. He suffered eleven skull fractures, a broken cheekbone, a broken ankle, kidney damage, and a fractured eye socket (Kappeler, Sluder, and Alpert, 1998). He was taken to a hospital, jailed for four days, and then released without any charges filed against him. The incident was caught on video and later released for the public to see. Four male LAPD officers were indicted for their roles in the beating, but all four were acquitted in April of 1992, which led to widespread riots in Los Angeles. In August of the same year, federal prosecutors announced that the four officers were being indicted on civil rights violation charges. Two of the officers were subsequently found guilty and sentenced to thirty months in prison, whereas the other two were acquitted of all charges.

Following the police beating of Rodney King in Los Angeles, the Christopher Commission was created to investigate police behaviors and examine areas within the organization that could be improved. In 1991, the Commission identified widespread brutality in the LAPD and systematic extralegal "punishment" of suspects by police. The Commission concluded that racism and sexism were widespread, and it criticized management for their lack of leadership for failing to control these officers and for rewarding them with positive work evaluations and promotions (Christopher, 1991). The concerns identified were as follows:

1. The apparent failure to control or discipline officers with repeated complaints of excessive force.
2. Concerns about the LAPD's culture and officers' attitudes toward racial and other minorities.
3. The difficulties the public encounters in attempting to make complaints against LAPD officers.
4. The role of the LAPD leadership and civilian oversight authorities in addressing or contributing to these problems. (Independent Commission on the Los Angeles Police Department, 1991)

According to Hoffman (1993), African Americans and other minority males are singled out by the LAPD and are often targets of physical abuse and brutality, and sometimes death. Detailed accounts of police violence against African Americans have been provided by a number of sources (Burris and Whitney, 2000; Daniels, 2000; Nelson, 2000; Russell-Brown, Pfeifer, and Jones, 2000), but the abuse of powers against minorities are rarely publicized by the mainstream media and/or police unless the evidence against the involved officer becomes difficult if not impossible to conceal by the police organization (as seen in the Rodney King case).

Similar instances including excessive force and deadly force in the 1990s included Malice Green, Abner Louima, and Amadou Diallo. All of the involved officers in these cases were male. In 1992, two officers from the Detroit Police Department repeatedly kicked, punched, and bludgeoned Malice Green, who died as a result of what was officially ruled to be a homicide by "blunt force trauma to the head" (Sigelman, Welch, Bledsoe, and Combs, 1997). In 1997, Louima, a Haitian immigrant, was beaten in the back of the patrol car with fists, batons, and handheld radios and then taken to the station where he was sexually assaulted by Officer Justin Volpe, who rammed the wooden handle of a drain plunger into Louima's rectum, rupturing his bladder and colon, and then jamming it into Louima's mouth, breaking his front teeth. The day after the assault, Louima was taken to the hospital, where he spent two months and underwent several operations (Matthew, 2007; Harris, 2000).

Amadou Diallo, a twenty-three-year-old Guinean immigrant, was shot and killed in 1999 by four plainclothed New York City police officers—officers Sean Carroll, Richard Murphy, Edward McMellon, and Kenneth Boss, who were part of the Street Crime Unit, fired a total of forty-one shots. Diallo was unarmed at the time of the shooting. The officers claimed that Diallo ignored their orders to "show his hands" and ran toward his apartment house doorway. Diallo then reached for his jacket to retrieve his wallet. Believing Diallo had pulled out a gun, the officers opened fire on Diallo. The investigation into the shooting found that Diallo had a black wallet in his possession. The internal NYPD investigation ruled the officers had acted within policy, but on March 25, a Bronx grand jury indicted the officers on charges of second-degree murder and reckless endangerment. In December, a New York appellate court moved the trial to Albany, New York, stating that the defendants could not have a fair trial in New York City given the pretrial publicity. In February 2000, after two days of deliberations, a jury acquitted the officers of all charges (Fritsch, 2000).

In the 1990s, up to two hundred police officers in New Orleans were identified for their involvement in crimes that included bank robbery, drug trafficking, assault, motor vehicle theft, and murder (Kappeler et al., 1998). Between 1992 and 1999, LAPD officers working for the prestigious antigang unit, CRASH, in the Rampart Division, had committed a series of corrupt acts ranging from theft of drugs, planting of evidence on suspects, falsifying reports and evidence, to armed robbery, assault, and attempted murder (Board of Inquiry, 2000; Glover and Lait, 2000a). During the 1990s, the CRASH unit had developed a style of policing that was highly confrontational. As Cohen (2000) noted, the area had 170 murders a year in the 1960s, but by 1999, the number had dropped to thirty-three. After a series of complaints by citizens that included police assaults and shootings, stealing drugs, and planting drugs and guns on civilians, the LAPD chief, Bernard Parks, established the Rampart Corruption Task Force in 1998 to investigate the allegations. One of the guilty officers, Rafael Perez, agreed to provide details of police corruption within the unit in exchange for a five-year prison sentence. According to Glover and Lait (2000a:1), Perez reported that

> an organized criminal subculture thrived inside the Los Angeles Police Department, where a secret fraternity of anti-gang officers and supervisors committed crimes and celebrated shootings by awarding plaques to officers who wounded and killed people.

Perez gave detailed accounts of officers falsifying information and committing countless crimes. In one incident, according to Perez,

> an officer placed a gun on a dying suspect and listened to a supervisor delay an ambulance so that the officers could concoct a story to justify their shooting of the unarmed 21-year-old man. (Glover and Lait, 2000a:2)

By 2000, over seventy officers were under investigation for their involvement in committing crimes or for covering them up (Glover and Lait, 2000a).

More recently, in 2006, two retired NYPD officers, Louis Eppolito and Stephen Caracappa, were convicted of crimes that included eight murders committed between 1979 and 2005. These decorated detectives worked as informants and hired killers for the mafia Lucchese family and crime boss Anthony "Gaspipe" Casso. They used their police authority to supply information about individuals to the mafia in exchange for payments of $4,000 per month, committed murders for up to $75,000 payments, and were involved in money laundering, kidnapping, and obstruction of justice (Prenzler, 2009). All of these examples serve to illustrate the interconnectedness of police organizations with police criminality since the beginning of formal policing systems and the narrow definition of police corruption that is widely accepted. The public is typically left without a critical discussion of how police corruption is made possible, the different types of police corruption that exist (as seen in selective law enforcement and in the groups of people that are disproportionately policed), and the centrality of gender and hegemonic masculinity in police criminality.

Chapter Two

Interrogating Police Corruption and the Organization as Enabler

This chapter will set out to examine the police organizational goals in relation to dominant masculinist crime-control ideologies and how organizations construct and respond to particular incidents of police corruption as well as the organization as a vehicle to "do" corruption. In the process, this chapter will identify forms of police corruption that are not recognized as such and/or overwhelmingly ignored internally by police organizations. One cannot have an informed discussion on police corruption without first understanding police organizational goals and how organizations make corruption risks possible. These provide the necessary insight into how organizations then address corruption; specifically, how an incident is framed and how the organization responds to it. Publicized cases of police corruption are often "understood" through police organizational explanations and/or justifications.

DEFINING "POLICE CORRUPTION"

Some acts of police behavior are universally condemned while others generate disagreement and debate. Some police actions clearly violate laws while others violate internal departmental policies. Herman Goldstein (1977) defines police corruption as "the misuse of authority by a police officer in a manner designed to produce personal gain for the officer or others" (188). Similarly, Lawrence Sherman (1974:30) defines police corruption as "an illegal use of organizational power for personal gain." However, as Klockars notes (1983:336), "Some things we might well describe as police corruption may involve organizational but not personal gain. An example of organiza-

21

tional gain could include upper management directing an officer to not investigate the suspected criminal activities of an agency that has had a productive working relationship with the police organization." Langworthy and Travis (2003:414), on the other hand, define police corruption as "the intentional misuse of police power." In other words, in order for an act to qualify as police corruption it must first be shown that police powers were misused, and second, that the officer(s) misusing police powers intended to misuse them. The motive (whether it is for money or some other personal or organizational gain) is important only in establishing the intentional misuse of power. Additionally, whether the misuse of power is technically illegal (covering actions that violate criminal or civil laws as well as violations of departmental policies) is not important except to show that there was misuse of power (Langworthy and Travis, 2003). Barker and Carter (1986) define corruption as behaviors that are forbidden by some law, rule, regulation, or ethical standard. Police corruption involves the misuse of the officer's position/power, and it is done because of some actual or expected material reward or gain. For Barker and Carter, the gain can be money, goods, services, and/or discount.

However, this definition must be broadened to include psychological, social, and/or emotional gains that include vindication, recognition, sense of entitlement over others, and/or commendations. Therefore, police corruption/ misconduct should be understood as the abuse of police powers for personal and/or organizational gain where the gain is financial, social, psychological, and/or emotional. What needs to be recognized is the role of police organizations in preserving police corruption as justified police performances that are interconnected with largely masculine self-identities and organizational identities.

Police corruption can occur at different levels; they include police organizations in which officers participate in corrupt practices either on their own or with their partner, but do so independently from others, and agencies, where in addition to these, corruption can be organized and shared among many of the members within the organization or within a particular unit (Barker, 2006; Withrow, 2006; Walker, 2005, 1977; Corsianos, 2003; Burris and Whitney, 2000; Crank and Caldero, 2000; Nelson, 2000; Lynch, 1999; Delattre, 1996; Geller and Toch, 1996; Kappeler, Sluder, and Alpert, 1994; Skolnick and Fyfe, 1993; Inciardi, 1987, Stoddard, 1979; Sherman, 1974; Barker and Roebuck, 1973; Maas, 1973).

Barker and Roebuck (1973) and Barker (2006) used three elements to identify police corruption: 1. The behavior had to be forbidden by law, rule, regulation, or ethical standard; 2. The behavior had to involve the misuse of the officer's police position; and 3. The reward for committing the corrupt act had to be money or money's worth. Using these three elements, Barker (2006) provided the following typology of police corruption.

1. Kickbacks—police accept money, goods, and services by "legitimate" businesses and individuals who have something to gain from establishing a good relationship with the police.
2. Opportunistic Thefts—police steal money or other valuables from arrested persons, victims of crime, crime scenes, and unprotected property.
3. Shakedowns—police extort money or other valuables from criminal offenders or traffic violators; the officer accepts payment in exchange for not making an arrest.
4. Protection of Illegal Activities—police receive money or other valuables from vice operators (involved in gambling, prostitution, illegal drug sales, after-hours clubs, etc.) or legitimate businesses that operate illegally (for example, taxi cabs, bars, pawnshops, etc., that violate their license restrictions, or some other law). These businesses can increase profits by maintaining a good relationship with the police.
5. Fixes—an officer accepts money or other valuables to "fix" a case or traffic ticket. An officer agrees to withdraw a misdemeanor or felony prosecution or traffic ticket by failing to request prosecution, tampering with the evidence, or by providing perjured testimony in court. Additionally, officers can also have a case dismissed by saying that they did not give the suspect the Miranda warning or they failed to secure a search warrant.
6. Direct Criminal Activities—officers actively engage in crimes including burglary, robbery, and the sale and trafficking of narcotics.
7. Internal Payoffs—when officers "sell" work assignments, holidays, promotions, off days, and evidence to other officers. A police officer can offer a supervisor money in order to change his/her work assignment or holiday, or officers who work in records can sell confidential information to other officers.

Types of corrupt activities identified by Stoddard (1979) include:

1. Mooching—the acceptance of free or discount merchandise or services by officers.
2. Chiseling—making demands to be admitted to entertainment or sporting events without charge.
3. Favoritism—"giving breaks" to friends, family, other officers, or other officers' family members from arrest or citation for traffic offenses.
4. Prejudice—the differential treatment of certain groups by the police.
5. Shopping—the practice of officers taking items from a business (for example, cigarettes, sodas, sandwiches, etc.) without offering to pay.
6. Extortion—demand made by officers of citizens to buy police items by threatening to issue a citation or make an arrest.

7. Bribery—the practice of accepting cash or gifts in exchange for the officer overlooking some violation on the part of the citizen.
8. Shakedown—the taking of expensive items for personal use from crime scenes.
9. Perjury—lying as a witness, which can include lying to cover up the illegal behavior of oneself or another officer.
10. Premeditated Theft—police officers carry out a planned burglary or theft.

But, using Langworthy and Travis's (2003) definition of police corruption, mooching and premeditated theft do not necessarily qualify as police corruption. For instance, with regard to "mooching," "if merchants routinely give discounts to police officers, and if the police officers do not alter their behavior because of the discounts, then there is no misuse of authority. If officers alter their behavior to obtain the discount giving that business added police protection or service, they may be misusing the office to obtain the free or reduced-priced goods" (ibid.:448). Premeditated theft, on the other hand, is a crime and not necessarily a form of police corruption. According to Goldstein (1977:189), "If the officers involved in the crime committed it because they knew, as a result of their positions, that the owners would be absent, or that the alarm was disabled, then the crime would involve police corruption. On the other hand, if an officer or group of officers commits a crime that is not an abuse of police authority, they are criminal but not corrupt." Porter and Warrender (2009) identified three categories of police deviance, which they defined as Type A (police crime), Type B (noble cause misconduct), and Type C (corruption). This further illustrates the complexities in police criminality research but also the debate surrounding the definition of police corruption. They identified "Type B noble-cause" deviance as offenses that "were most likely to be evidence related (for example, ignoring, planting or removing evidence in order to secure a conviction)" (Porter and Warrender, 2009:85). But a limitation to this is that there may be other reasons for engaging in this behavior that would not qualify as "noble cause"; for instance, a corrupt officer may receive payment to plant evidence against an organized crime competitor.

As discussed in chapter 1, the Knapp Commission investigated the New York City corruption scandal in the early 1970s, and it identified two types of corrupt officers: the grass eaters and the meat eaters (*Knapp Commission*, 1972). Grass eaters are officers who engage in more minor forms of corruption as the opportunities arise. For example, a motorist who was drinking and driving may offer the officer money in exchange for not being arrested, and the officer accepts. Meat eaters, on the other hand, are police officers who actively seek out opportunities to engage in both minor and major forms of corruption; for example, officers who have arrangements with particular businesses to ignore legal violations on the part of the business for money, or officers who steal money or other goods from arrestees, victims, or crime scenes. Gerber and Mendelson (2008) use the term *predatory policing* to refer to officers who proactively seek out opportunities to abuse their police powers for personal gain rather than maintaining a more reactive role (for example, when someone offers an officer a bribe in exchange for not giving them a speeding ticket). For Skogan and Meares (2004), "proactive corruption" includes officers who seek out the means to engage in police criminality.

Corruption within policing, when recognized, is often associated with only a few acts of police abuse of powers (for example, abuse of power for financial gain and excessive use of force against "civilians" as a form of punishment). Other forms of corruption that are largely ignored internally include: officers using 'race' as a key factor in police decisions to stop and interrogate citizens (often referred to as racial profiling, race-based policing, or race-biased policing), unjustified shootings, selective law enforcement applied differently to "categories" of people (for example, women, racial, and ethnic minorities), and ignoring violations of the law (for example, as seen in white-collar crimes, domestic violence, and sexual assaults).

Deadly force by the police, for instance, results in an average of 373 civilian deaths each year, and they overwhelmingly involve male officers. The majority of those killed by the police are young and male, and a disproportionate number are African American (Brown and Langan, 2001). Matulia (1982) found that African Americans accounted for 60 percent of those who died in 1,428 "justifiable" shootings by police officers. Alpert (1989) found similar rates in his study of the Miami, Florida, police department, and Meyer (1980) found that officers had higher rates for shooting unarmed black citizens versus unarmed whites or Hispanics.

On the other hand, other forms of corruption/misconduct that seem to be more readily recognized by criminologists include the following: receiving payment for referring clients to attorneys, bail bondsmen, automobile service stations, and other businesses; providing additional police service to those who either pay through discounts and gifts or who have shown support for the police in different ways (for example, through advertising, displaying police memorabilia, etc.); hiring out as bodyguards or security officers to private citizens, but officers abuse their police authority to secure such employment; falsifying personnel records; and making recommendations about application for various licenses for persons outside the department (Barker, 2006; Withrow, 2006; Walker, 2005, 1977; Crank and Caldero, 2000; Geller and Toch, 1996; Skolnick and Fyfe, 1993; Inciardi, 1987; Stoddard, 1979; Sherman, 1974; Barker and Roebuck, 1973; Maas, 1973).

Using "excessive force" (for example, applying more force than required as set by "continuum-use-of-force" regulations) to effect an arrest because an officer thinks that the arrested person needs to be "taught a lesson" or because the arrested person made some derogatory comment toward the officer and the officer felt that a "good" beating would qualify as "just desserts" is not only an example of a crime but also a form of police corruption. The gain for the officer may be emotional, social, and/or psychological, which can include vindication, a sense of entitlement, and even wanting to establish a particular reputation among peers. Additionally, an unjustified shooting is a criminal act but can also be a form of corruption if the motive was for some personal or organizational gain, as seen in the actions of officers working in the Rampart Division CRASH unit or the NYPD officers who committed murders and other crimes for pay (see chapter 1). But disproportionately fewer female officers use excessive force against citizens (Schuck and Rabe-Hemp, 2005; Garner and Maxwell, 2002; National Center for Women and Policing, 2002).

The use of excessive force is often justified in the minds of many male officers who have accepted a largely masculine identity—they've been socialized to see themselves as "disciplinarians" or to have a sense of entitlement over others. Violence is characterized in Western societies as "masculine," and violent acts become the accepted means to "teach someone a lesson," especially if the other person is socially constructed as "less deserving." But how do we make sense of the fewer female officers who may choose to use illegal violent means (for example, use excessive force) to respond to civilians? As part of a police culture in which many often feel they have to prove themselves (Martin and Jurik, 2007), some level of violence may be seen as necessary for acceptance by "the brotherhood." But since risk is gendered, only small levels of violence may be applied; that is, a degree of force perceived by these women to be sufficient in signaling to male officers that they are "one of them."

Similarly, racial profiling is a form of corruption in which officers target particular groups for personal and/or organizational gain. For example, officers may be given directives to target a particular racial or ethnic group for traffic stops in the hope that the organization can later have "evidence" of drug trafficking linked to particular groups of people and/or geographic locations and advocate more government resources to proactively police these crimes and/or areas. Indeed, some types of police behavior are largely viewed as police corruption, whereas others generate more disagreement. Defining police corruption as the misuse or abuse of police powers for personal and/or organizational gain is necessary to identify the different types of harms that are caused by the police. And, as mentioned earlier, the gain can be monetary or involve some other material advantage, but it can also include social, emotional, and/or psychological "advantages." Even instances that may appear "harmless" on their face can have the potential to lead to police corruption and should be avoided. For instance, an officer may routinely accept free food from a restaurant owner. This appears to be "harmless," but if the restaurant owner assaults a patron following a disagreement, the officer, who has been accepting free food, may feel a sense of "obligation" to not arrest him/her. But in addition to recognizing the different types of police corruption/police criminality that exist, one must evaluate how police organizations respond to publicized cases of police corruption in order to gain more insight into how the organization serves as an "enabler" for officers to commit abuses, as well as the gendered differences within.

RESEARCH ON GENDER DIFFERENCES AND POLICE CORRUPTION

Gender was and continues to be the strongest indicator of police misconduct. Gender differences are seen in the different types of police corruption that include excessive force incidents and domestic violence and in citizen complaints against officers. For instance, in a content analysis of LAPD civil liability cases between 1990 and 1999, the study was intended to analyze and quantify the gender aspects of the costs of police brutality and misconduct in the LAPD (Feminist Majority Foundation and National Center for Women and Policing, 2000). The study looked at eighty lawsuits that involved the use of excessive force allegations against officers, officers who were involved in sexual assault incidents, and domestic violence cases. The findings were as follows:

1. Female officers were involved in excessive force lawsuits at rates substantially below their male counterparts, and no female officers were named as defendants in cases of police officer involved sexual assault, sexual abuse, molestation, and domestic violence. Of the $66.3 million in judgments or out-of-court settlements where the gender of the officer could be determined, $63.4 million, or 95.8 percent, was attributable to male officers' misconduct. Only $2.8 million, or 4.2 percent of total payouts, were attributable to female officers' misconduct.

2. Payouts on cases involving male officers' misconduct exceeded the payout with female officers by a ratio of 23:1. The number of male officers involved in or at the scene of an incident outnumbered the amount of female officers by a ratio of 9:1.

3. Male officer payouts for situations involving killings were higher by a ratio of 43:1 and for assault and battery with a ratio of 32:1 (Feminist Majority Foundation and National Center for Women and Policing, 2000:1–2).

The *Cincinnati Enquirer* examined civil liability payouts for excessive force against the Cincinnati Police Department between 1990 and 2000. Women accounted for 17.1 percent of officers on patrol, but they accounted for 7.7 percent of the amount paid in out-of-court settlements for excessive force and wrongful death. This translated to $358,000 out of $1,735,729. In other words, male officers accounted for 92.3 percent of the total department costs in court settlements (National Center for Women and Policing, 2002:4). The average male officer in a large police department will cost taxpayers between two-and-a-half and five-and-a-half times more than the average female officer with regard to force liability lawsuit payouts (National Center for Women and Policing, 2002).

Furthermore, female officers use less force in arrest situations with members of the public than male officers (Schuck and Rabe-Hemp, 2005; Garner and Maxwell, 2002). On the other hand, Paoline and Terrill (2004) found similar levels of force between female and male officers in police interactions with citizens. But these studies represent different "units of analysis" and differences in how "force" was operationalized. For example, both Garner and Maxwell (2002) and Schuck and Rabe-Hemp (2005) examined "arrest situations," whereas Paoline and Terrill (2004:104) assessed situations in which police displayed any "acts that threaten or inflict physical harm to citizens." Rabe-Hemp's study (2008) suggested that women were much less likely than men to use "extreme controlling behavior" such as physical restraints, threats, searches, and arrests, and that the less use of force on the part of female officers may produce safer police-citizen encounters for both the officer and the public. Rabe-Hemp (2008) asserts that these results provide support to Lonsway et al.'s (2002) argument that hiring more female officers can reduce excessive use-of-force incidents on the part of the police. Rabe-Hemp (2008:432) found that gender differences appeared under certain circumstances; for example, gender differences between male and female officers are most pronounced when the citizen is disrespectful, in low discretion situations, and when officers are encountering citizens with other officers present. Female officers displayed much less variability in their behavior and appeared to be less impacted by situational cues than male officers.

On the other hand, female officers were more likely to use "extreme controlling behaviors" when other officers were present or when a supervisor intervened in the police-citizen encounter (ibid.) This may be the result of pressure to be accepted by peers given the lack of organizational support by both peers and supervisors that is experienced by many female officers (Corsianos, 2009; Martin and Jurik, 2007; Miller, 1999; Hunt, 1990; Martin, 1980; 1990). There may be increased pressure to display "hypermasculine" traits in the presence of male peers (Martin and Jurik, 2007; Myers, Forest, and Miller, 2004; Miller, 1999). But beyond particular circumstances relating to disrespectful citizens, the presence of other officers, and low-discretion situations, Rabe-Hemp (2008) reported that male and female officers' use of "lesser controlling behaviors" were "quite similar," but overall women were much less likely to use excessive force. Also, women officers are less likely to be the subjects of citizen complaints about the use of excessive force (McElvain and Kposowa, 2004), and citizen complaints overall (Lersch, 1998); and they appear to better manage their anger and thus are less likely to use force (Abernethy and Cox, 1994). The Bureau of Justice Assistance (2001:2) reported that "research conducted both in the United States and internationally clearly demonstrates that women police officers use a style of policing that relies less on physical force. They are better at defusing and de-escalating potentially violent confrontations with citizens and are less likely to become involved in incidents of excessive force."

ARE POLICE ORGANIZATIONAL GOALS COMPROMISED WHEN INCIDENTS OF POLICE CORRUPTION BECOME KNOWN TO THE PUBLIC?

The most common statement issued by police administrators after an incident of police corruption is reported by the media is one that refers to the officer(s) involved as "bad/rotten apple(s)." According to Barker (2006:55), "Rotten apples were either weak individuals who had slipped through the screening process and succumbed to the temptations inherent in police work, or deviant individuals who continue their deviant practices in an environment of ample opportunity." Following a corruption scandal, police administrators will often point out that it is not an organizational problem but rather the result of a particular "bad officer" or a few "bad officers"; that is, "bad/rotten apples." For instance, the River Cops involved in the drug corruption scandal in Miami, Florida, in the late 1980s were identified as "rotten apples" (Delattre, 1989). Similarly, the Mollen Commission's investigation of drug corruption in the New York City Police Department (which was the sixth commission to investigate corruption in New York since 1890) concluded that "the corrupt acts were the result of small groups of rotten apples and not systematic corruption within the department" (Mollen Commission, 1994). Also, following the Los Angeles Rampart Area scandal in the 1990s, the LAPD announced that the corruption was the result of "rotten apples" working in the Rampart CRASH unit, which was a specialized gang unit (Los Angeles

Police Department, 2000). The LAPD Board of Inquiry (2000:311) reported the following: "After careful consideration of the information developed during the Board of Inquiry's work, it is the Board's view that the Rampart corruption incident occurred because a few individuals decided to engage in blatant misconduct and, in some cases, criminal behavior."

The "rotten apple" metaphor has been used to refer to the individual officer as responsible for the misconduct. O'Connor (2005) has extended this metaphor to include group nonconformity that is the result of the police culture; hence the "rotten barrel" metaphor. But others, such as Zimbardo (2007) and Punch (2003), argue that police criminality is systemic. Punch (2003) uses the metaphor "rotten orchards," and Zimbardo (2007) prefers the metaphor "bad barrel makers." For Punch (2003:172), police corruption is "in some way encouraged, and perhaps even protected, by certain elements in the system. . . . 'Systems' refers both to the formal system—the police organization, the criminal justice system and the broader socio-political context—and to the informal system of deals, inducements, collusion and understandings among deviant officers as to how the corruption is to be organized, conducted and rationalized."

"Police departments tend to use the rotten apple theory . . . to minimize the public backlash against policing after every exposed act of corruption" (O'Connor, 2005:2). This allows the police department to look no further than the guilty "individual" officers (O'Connor, 2005). Upper management will use a series of control strategies to appease the public in finding the "rotten apples" responsible for the misconduct (Fitzgerald, 1989). Attempts by police and various watchdog government agencies to discover police criminality is "by and large fragmented, episodic in nature and overly focused on an individualistic approach to dealing with police crime" (Dean, Bell, and Lauchs, 2010:219).

Although Barker (2006) argues that corruption is sometimes the result of "rotten apples," he further adds that "some police executives still use the term 'rotten apples' to deny or mask problems in their departments. They want the public to believe that a publicly identified 'corrupt,' or for that matter a 'racist' or 'brutal' cop is an aberration not a department problem. When they are gone, the problem will go away" (59).

This is not surprising, nor is it beyond the normative response by any police organization. Indeed, the goal of any public institution such as the police is to ensure organizational survival (Manning, 1997), and in the case of the police specifically, to also preserve hegemonic masculinist crime-control ideologies as they relate to law enforcement, investigative strategies, discipline, and punishment. But according to Simon (1964), the organizational goal is complex and is a multidimensional construct that both guides and restricts organizational action and that organizational decisions are directed at "satisfying a whole set of constraints." For Simon, each goal is a "constraint" because each is a "demand" on the organization that limits the possibilities in organizational action. Moreover, he asserts that not all tenets of the constraint set are equally valued; therefore, some are posited as more important than others. However, it can be argued that all elements of the constraint set require some level of organizational action (including, at times, to not act) in order to promote the image of the police as "doing its job" and "accomplishing its goals," where the majority of the public would find satisfactory and/or prevent the majority from voicing complaints against the police. Thus, the police are often expected to perform some level of law enforcement and public service and take some action to maintain community peace. If the police are perceived as not taking the necessary level of action (for example, if they are not responding to certain areas that leads to an increase in violence or police overenforcement of laws in one area leads to violent riots), then the police have not succeeded in achieving their goal.

Indeed, there may be differences in organizational priorities between police agencies (Maguire, 2001, 1997; Sanders, 1997; Zhao, 1996; Crank and Wells, 1991; Crank, 1990; Mohr, 1973; Wilson, 1968). And organizational priorities may change within particular agencies depending on the political climate and public expectations of the police. Some organizations may prioritize law enforcement over public service; others may prioritize community peace over law enforcement. This will ultimately depend on the "political culture" of the community as a constraint on the police organization (Wilson, 1968; Simon, 1964; Manning, 1997). However, most of the time police organizations promote "law enforcement" as a central goal. There is no denying the overwhelming emphasis placed on arrests as seen in the ways officers talk about and socially construct "the good pinch" and in managements' response to officers' "good" work when making arrests.

HOW DO POLICE AGENCIES ENSURE ORGANIZATIONAL SURVIVAL?

There are many tenets associated with organizational survival. For one, public institutions such as the police, which are supported via taxpayers' money, must be successful in convincing the public that they are a needed service, and secondly, that they are successful in accomplishing the goals that have, over time, become expected by the majority of the public and accepted as common sense.

1. The image of the police as a "needed service" and masculinist crime-control strategies as "necessary": How is this accomplished? This is an important question as it relates to police corruption. The degree of constructing an agency as a necessary component to social life ensures its survival despite instances of police corruption that become public. The local police as a publicly sustained entity of local government require them to engage in "image maintenance" (Manning, 1997), particularly cultivating and refining the image of the police as a necessity to our social environment. A variety of strategies have been used to accomplish this. For one, society is constructed as a "dangerous place" filled with "crime" and "criminals." Society becomes the experience of living in a world where the possibilities of "risk" are numerous and the possibilities of experiencing "criminal victimization" likely. The use of police crime statistics is a common strategy used by police administrators to secure the image of society as dangerous and risky. When crime statistics have shown an increase in crime rates, police administrators have used them as "evidence" of the need for policing in an increasingly "dangerous" world. Alternatively, when crime statistics have shown a decrease in crime rates, members of upper management have used them as evidence of how budget cuts in police resources has led to fewer arrests and thus the need for more police officers rather than them representing a drop in "actual crime." Also, McLaughlin (2007:50) asserts that, in validating their work, "the police are required to demonstrate that the rules have some meaning and that they can enforce them. They also have a vested interest in amplifying the significance of these problems."

The mainstream media has also played a key role in sensationalizing particular instances of violent crimes that leads members of the public to interpret these as commonplace (Barak, 2003). This is a good illustration of Thomas's theorem (1966:301, orig. 1931); that is, "situations that are defined as real are real in their consequences." If risk and crime are presented and accepted as "real dangers," then most people will respond to them accordingly. The majority will be more prone to view the police as a necessary service, despite publicized "limitations" or "problems" (for example, police corruption), and support the allocation of public resources in its maintenance. The continuous use of risk discourse ensures fear and anxiety by members of the public. This ensures public support of the police in controlling "crime" and "criminals" and in reducing "risk."

Risk discourse in a "civil society" guarantees the survival of police organizations. Ericson and Haggerty (1997) make a distinction between "natural risks," such as natural disasters, versus "manufactured risks" that are the result of scientific and technological intervention. "Risk is an invention based on imagined fears and on imaginative technologies for dealing with them" (Ericson and Haggerty, 1997:39), and risk discourse is the institutional construction of risk knowledge (ibid.). The role of the police in a "risk society" is to create a knowledge of risk that includes identifying and responding to "risky behaviors" and "risky populations." This exercise is another common strategy in securing the image of society as "dangerous," which strengthens public perceptions of the police as a needed service. Thus, the police are not only actors in maintaining state social control but also actors of surveillance who collect information and produce knowledge of "risky" populations that are, in turn, used to control/police them (Ericson and Haggerty, 1997; Dandeker, 1990).

The image of the police as a needed service is further validated by "civil society's" desire for security, where "dangers" are counteracted or minimized. Our pursuit for detailed and continuous risk management gives rise to new knowledge of insecurities that can move police efforts in new directions (Ericson and Haggerty, 1997). For instance, a particular population constructed as "risky" (for example, inner-city gangs) may lead to more proactive law enforcement in particular geographic locations known to police as being occupied by gang members; this in turn may lead the police to discover "new insecurities" (for example, the use of online social networks by gang members for recruitment purposes), which then leads to the creation of a special police task force for this area.

This "new knowledge of insecurities" is a political act that further strengthens the need for police organizations, despite publicized cases of police corruption. "Knowledge of insecurities" is a multidimensional construct that both guides and restricts police behavior. This knowledge is also political because it is carefully constructed in ways that perpetuate the image of crime and the criminal in both the police and public imagination as being largely that of street-level illegal activity (that is, stranger assaults, robbery, street prostitution, the sale and/or use of illegal drugs, etc.) and activity largely committed by poor or poorer people, visible minorities, younger people, and males. Knowledge of insecurities is interconnected to the politics of 'race', class, and gender in relation to securing public consensus as to who are the "risky populations" and what are the "risky behaviors."

The construction of a knowledge of insecurities allows for processes of exclusion as they become hidden within desirable rhetoric, such as "creating safe neighborhoods," "improving police-community partnerships," and "citizen empowerment." Fischer and Poland (1998) contend that processes of exclusion are emerging as crucial aspects of social control and governance in late modern societies. Public spaces become subject to surveillance and control by the public police and its allocated resources. Particular police initiatives (for example, Community Policing, see chapter 6) can be used as a tool for the removal and banning of "problem" people from particular spaces. The concern is not with fairness and social justice but with the purification of public space (Sibley, 1988). As Ericson (1994) has noted, surveillance and the management of risk factors are critical to the development of a "specialized knowledge," which is required to engineer community "safety." Emphasis is placed on the control and management of behavior and the mobility and whereabouts of "risky" individuals or populations. The exclusions of risky behaviors or individuals have become central to the operation of governance (Fischer and Poland, 1998).

The degree of public acceptance of these risks as legitimate is evinced by the willingness of many members of the public to accept the police roles as focused on law enforcement and policing "street-level" crimes and the willingness of many to overlook acts of police corruption that become known to the public, and/or dismiss them as the result of a "few bad apples" rather than to consider their relationship to what Zimbardo (2007), and others, have referred to as the "bad barrel makers." Police organizations are proactive players in constructing "corrupt officers" as "anomalies" rather than the result of multiple factors, including the organizational structure that makes corruption possible as well as the police occupational culture and the police as an institution of control (see chapters 3 and 4).

The hegemonic masculinist crime-control ideologies are accepted as necessary to ensure organizational survival. Therefore, strategies linked to law enforcement, discipline, and punishment are interconnected to the "crime control" model, which is promoted as effective and/or necessary to "fight criminals." Mainstream society socially constructs some people as "problem people" who must be proactively policed. These individuals are often perceived as lazy; people who would rather live off welfare programs rather than work for pay, who have no work ethic and no sense of responsibility to society. Therefore, "aggressive police tactics" are accepted as common sense and seen as necessary. These dominant ideologies promote an oversimplified image of society as consisting of "good" people and "bad" people, and there is no room to consider the social and structural inequalities that limit people's choices or in evaluating the kinds of behaviors that become accepted as criminal and are disproportionately policed.

2. The image of the police as "successful" in accomplishing its organizational goals: How is this accomplished? Once again, this is a central question to our understanding of organizational survival, despite widely publicized cases of police corruption. The degree of constructing an agency as "successful" in accomplishing its goals ensures its survival despite instances of police corruption that become public and where the public largely reacts negatively to it (for example, the Rampart Division incidents received less and less public support as more information was given to the public about the victims' criminal history). This is largely accomplished by police efforts to promote the appearance of the police controlling risk. Particular police policies or police initiatives have been used as ideological tools to legitimize policing to both police personnel and members of the public (Corsianos, 2009; Manning, 1997; Bayley, 1996) and to promote the police function as effective. Some contend that these are used by members of the "brass" to create the illusion that policing is somehow removed from politics (Ericson and Haggerty, 1997; Manning, 1997; Stenson, 1993; Greene and Mastrofki, 1988; Klockars, 1988). For instance, community policing initiatives have been referred to by some critics of CP as "empty rhetoric" (Manning, 1997; Greene and Mastrofski, 1988; Klockars, 1988) that create the illusion that police are concerned with operating fairly and working to foster and improve police-community partnerships. The image of the police as engaging in "law enforcement" rather than in politically and morally based ordering has been accepted as "common sense." Manning (1997) contends that this type of rhetoric is a resource used by police to justify and legitimize their actions.

External legitimation is maintained by withholding potentially damaging information from the public; maintaining complicity with the media to reveal and dramatize selectively certain stories presented in a positive "voice" or perspective; appealing to national symbols and ideologies, such as the rhetoric of crime control; and cultivating links with the legal profession and agencies and agents within the criminal justice system (Manning, 1992:34).

Indeed, the police are quick to promote investigations that lead to felony arrests as evidence of the police organization's success in controlling risk and working toward securing community safety (Fischer and Poland, 1998; Ericson and Haggerty, 1997). Police will often work with the mainstream media to report these investigations or issue an official press release (Corsianos, 2009). Evidence of success is further seen in the promotion of CP initiatives (see chapter 6). Police organizations measure success quantitatively by measuring the outcomes of masculinist crime-control practices (for example, the number of arrests made, number of officers hired, number of weapons purchased to fight "the war on crime") as well as qualitatively by sharing specific "success stories" with the public (for example, sharing video footage of police officers making an arrest after a lengthy police pursuit of an armed suspect).

ORGANIZATIONAL GOALS IN RELATION TO HOW ORGANIZATIONS CONSTRUCT AND RESPOND TO CORRUPT OFFICERS

The promotion of a knowledge of insecurities and the necessary masculinist crime-control ideologies needed to respond to them are prioritized in the public imagination and overshadow any knowledge of dangerous and/or illegal behavior on the part of the police. The construction of a knowledge of insecurities and crime-control strategies are an ongoing exercise on the part of organizations in ensuring the public's commitment to the quest for security, and these simultaneously become the tool of choice for organizations in constructing and responding to corrupt officers. According to Vicchio

(1997), traditional approaches to limiting police misconduct are based on the following beliefs: 1. People follow the rules out of fear of punishment; 2. Supervisors observe officers (even though they cannot observe them all the time); and 3. Corrupt officers will get media attention. But the level of negative public reaction toward publicized incidents of police corruption assists the police in how they carefully construct what happened, how it happened, and how they will work to ensure that it doesn't happen again. Publicized cases of police criminality are largely understood through police organizational explanations and/or justifications.

As stated earlier, police organizations have been notorious to quickly construct the corrupt officer(s) as a "bad apple(s)"; that is, that these officers are the exception and not the norm. It is not uncommon for low-ranking officers to view officers in supervisory roles as being aware of some of the different types of corruption occurring in the department and not doing anything about them, and that it would be "career suicide" for them to bring formal complaints of their peer's misconduct to their supervisors. A common perception is that if a particular incident of police corruption became public then "management would let you hang" to preserve the organization's goals. According to Kelling, Wasserman, and Williams (1988:1),

"Police chiefs continually worry about abuse of authority: brutality, misuse of force, especially deadly force over-enforcement of the law; bribery; manufacture of evidence in the name of efficiency or success; failure to apply the law because of personal interests; and discrimination against particular individuals or groups. . . . Scandals associated with abuse of authority . . . jeopardize organizational stability and continuity of leadership."

Popular cultural constructions of the police become a site of contestation for organizations attempting to respond to publicized cases of police corruption. The dominant images of the police continue to include the police as "crime fighter" and "enforcer of laws" (Corsianos, 2009; Martin and Jurik, 2007; Neugebauer, 1999, 1996; Stenson, 1993; Ericson, 1982, 1981). These are further strengthened by publicly accepted police organizational goals and wider cultural constructions of living in a "risk society" and collective efforts toward achieving security. To entertain the possibility of problems with the police occupational culture or policing as an "institution" would put the organization as a whole in jeopardy. The police as "partners" in the quest for security cannot also be part of a system that enables and condones "risky" and "dangerous" behavior among its officers. Thus, according to Walker (2005), the rotten-apple theory has powerful emotional and political appeal. "It personalizes misconduct and gives it a human face" (ibid.:14). But it also allows members of the public to "see" that this is the act of a particular person(s). This enables the public to understand corruption as something that is done by one or a few "rogue officers," while maintaining confidence in the behavior of the majority. Based on the rotten-apple theory, the department will explain the corruption as being the result of some sort of problem on the part of the guilty officer.

In the meantime, news reporters are important players in personalizing the misconduct, albeit for different reasons. The push to increase ratings, sales, and number of online "hits" ensures that journalists work to find out as much as they can about the officer's personal and professional background to keep the story in the media. The police organization, on the other hand, works to engage in "damage control," hoping to diffuse the story and bring closure to the public. The boundaries between fact and fiction are often blurred. There is manipulation of appearance in the pursuit to maintain organizational integrity and to discourage or prevent people from questioning the extent of police corruption in police organizations today, how these acts are made possible by the organization, and/or what can be done to prevent them from happening in the future.

During these instances, the police use various appearance management strategies to "dramatize the appearance of police control" (Manning, 1977). Members of upper management will remind the public that the police are the "thin blue line" standing between order and chaos. Particular "crime waves" and "moral panics" constructed by the police and/or the media serve to maintain public consensus for authoritarian policing (Belknap, 2006; Barak, 2003; Sumner, 1981; Hall et al., 1978). One of the early cultural analyses of the "authoritarian police" can be found in Hall et al.'s (1978) *Policing the Crisis*. The book examines how the "moral panic" about "mugging" came to define political debates in England in the 1970s regarding crime, law, and order. The news media reporting of this crime was strongly linked to race, and the public soon had the "knowledge" that muggers were young black men and their victims were white and vulnerable. For Hall et al., the reaction to this particular crime by both the public and state was out of proportion to the actual seriousness of the crime and the threat posed to the public. The authors could not find reliable evidence to substantiate the mugging "crime wave" claims made by the police, journalists, and politicians. "However, the organizational temptation is to amplify public anxieties and manipulate 'moral panics' because the police can benefit from them in terms of resources, empowerment, legitimacy and status. Hence, in the case of mugging, key police officers actively pronounced not only on the extent and nature of the problem but also on the solutions" (McLaughlin, 2007:64). Instances such as these further legitimize the police's position as the "thin blue line" standing between danger and security.

As a part of a society that depends on people to conform to dominant ideologies, individuals lack the cultural environment that can provide the social, political, and economic space needed to critically assess the concept of policing. Jock Young (1992:45) notes that "it is not the 'Thin Blue Line,' but the social bricks and mortar of civil society which are the major bulwarks against crime. Good jobs with a discernible future, housing estates that tenants can be proud of, community facilities which enhance a sense of cohesion and belonging, a reduction in unfair inequalities, all create a society which is more cohesive and less criminogenic." But, in working toward maintaining the appearance of control, the police remind the public about the vast variety of social problems that the police are responsible for and that there are no other agencies prepared or willing to take on these tasks. Therefore, what resonates in the public imagination is that society "needs" the police, which can be understood as "needing it in its current form," given the lack of critical reflection of policing as a whole.

THE ORGANIZATION AS "ENABLER": HOW DO POLICE ORGANIZATIONS MAKE POLICE CORRUPTION POSSIBLE?

For Walker (2005:15), "The organizational process is inseparable from the on-the-street product." But there is consistent denial by upper management about the intrinsic nature of corruption risks (Punch, 2003; Newburn, 1999; *Knapp*, 1972). For instance, the structure of policing roles and the inadequate accountability mechanisms contribute to the creation of risks for police misconduct. In terms of the structure of policing roles, officers are afforded a great deal of discretionary powers with limited supervision that give them flexibility to bend or break the laws without being discovered (Barker, 1983). Organizational rules and regulations are ambiguous and negotiable, and there is little supervisory oversight of front-line officers on patrol (McLaughlin, 2007). Many early ethnographic works found that patrol officers, once they left the station, had a great deal of discretion in what rules to enforce and where (Manning, 1978; Van-Maanen, 1973; Reiss, 1972; Bittner, 1970; Wilson, 1968; Niederhoffer, 1967).

Discretion can be understood as "the power conferred on criminal justice professionals to use their judgment to decide what action to take in a given situation. This includes the decision to take no action" (McLaughlin and Muncie, 2001:95–96). Police discretion is an integral part of police work, and policing would not be possible without police discretionary powers. There are a multiplicity of rules and laws, resulting in only a few being enforced due to available time, resources, lack of police knowledge of all rules/laws, and political influences. Moreover, at times, many laws and procedures are themselves inconsistent, if not contradictory. Hence, policing involves a high level of discretion in the application of rules (Davis, 1969; LaFave, 1965; Goldstein, 1963), and as McNamara notes, "Police work does not consist of a standardized product or service" (1967:185). It has been argued that "the source of police discretion lies with the legal powers they are given, the nature of the criminal law they have to enforce, the context within which police work takes place and limitations on resources" (McLaughlin and Muncie, 2001:96). According to Prenzler (2009), police work entails a high level of discretion in officers' day-to-day decision making, and it involves frequent contact with criminal offenders who are motivated to trade benefits for immunity from prosecution. "This *economic* demand-and-supply scenario applies to any illegal behavior coming to police attention, and may result in corruption in limited forms with individuals acting opportunistically. The scenario has also led to acute problems of long-term corruption networks, particularly where there is a high demand for illegal commerce in *vice*: drugs, liquor, prostitution, pornography, and gambling" (Prenzler, 2009:20).

Despite state laws and city ordinances that direct officers to enforce all laws all the time, and despite some department policies of full enforcement, law enforcement decisions are made mainly by individual police officers (except when there are specific policies relating to particular crimes and discretionary powers become more limited). These discretionary powers give officers access to engage in corrupt activities; that is, opportunities for corruption. This integral part of policing creates opportunities for abuse and provides access to commit misconduct. According to Prenzler (2009:21), "Detective squads are notorious for process corruption because their work is focused on the detailed investigation and prosecution of crimes. Officers in specialist licensing or vice squads are more likely to engage in organized graft. Traffic officers often have limited opportunities for regular or serious graft, but are presented with numerous low-level misconduct opportunities, especially in terms of cash payments or harassment of citizens. Officers in drug squads and armed holdup squads frequently engage in the most lucrative forms of corruption through exposure to large quantities of cash and valuables."

Hence, in relation to an organization's policing methods, there is a great deal of discretionary powers given to officers in their day-to-day decision making (for example, who to question, which motor vehicle to stop, which laws to enforce, when to make an arrest, etc.). For Davis (1975), the "overreach of the law" makes police discretion necessary (for example, laws may be too broadly worded and may include behaviors that many do not consider wrong), and therefore, officers are required to use discretion in many situations. At the same time, the level of officer discretionary powers along with the presence of illegal opportunities can create the social space for actual corrupt behavior on the part of officers. In some instances, police departments have tried to limit police discretionary powers in specific instances to try to prevent any abuse of police authority. For instance, police organizations have developed some rules to "control" police behavior. According to

Davis (1975), confining discretion involves creating policies that detail what an officer can and cannot do in particular instances. Policies can limit discretionary powers by specifying what officers can or cannot do in a set of circumstances.

Those who support limits on police discretionary practices do so primarily for three reasons (Walker, 2005; Burris and Whitney, 2000; Nelson, 2000; Kappeler, Sluder, and Alpert, 1994):

1. the power of the police to deprive an individual of his/her freedom and to use deadly force
2. the power of the police to exceed their legal authority
3. police corruption and abuse of discretionary powers have been identified

Police have detailed operating procedures as well as policy manuals that outline the rules governing police conduct. Some criminologists assert that there needs to be more organizational controls for enforcing laws. According to Goldstein (1990), some guidance in police discretion can alert officers to the alternatives available for dealing with a given situation and to the factors that should be considered in choosing from among available alternatives. Also, it is possible to be much more specific in establishing what should not be done in some specific situations.

Over the years, there have been some limitations on police discretionary powers in specific circumstances largely as a result of civil lawsuits filed against police departments as well as Supreme Court decisions. When police departments are held liable in civil courts, the courts shape and influence police policy across the country. And when the U.S. Supreme Court decides that a particular police practice is unconstitutional, that leads to the development of policies to change police behavior and limit the possibilities for misconduct. Examples of policies that attempt to limit police discretion include:

- continuum-use-of-force policies (including deadly force)
- racial profiling policies
- domestic violence policies

Deadly Force Policies

Prior to 1985, many police organizations had policies that allowed police officers to use deadly force to affect all felony arrests. This was commonly called the "fleeing-felon rule," which authorized police to use all necessary force to prevent the escape of a felony suspect. However, in 1985 the U.S. Supreme Court in *Tennessee v. Garner* held that police policies and state statutes that allowed officers to use deadly force to affect all felony arrests were unconstitutional. The Court's decision held that deadly force could only be used to prevent a dangerous felon from escaping from police custody, but the use of deadly force against a fleeing person who was believed to be unarmed violated the Fourth Amendment protections against unreasonable seizures. This decision essentially led to the rewriting of deadly force policies (Travis and Langworthy, 2008). This case began as a civil suit (*Garner v. Memphis*) brought by the father of a burglary suspect who was shot to death by a Memphis police officer while fleeing from the scene (Fyfe and Walker, 1990).

Continuum-Use-of-Force Policies

Over the years, many police organizations have developed some form of continuum-use-of-force policies that attempt to guide officers on the level of force used against private citizens and in particular situations. These policies are "intended" to confine the use of force by specifying the circumstances for when force may or may not be used. According to Walker (2005), the current standard is that an officer may use "the minimum amount of force necessary for achieving a lawful purpose" (51), but there is no consensus on what these "lawful purposes" are. However, he further adds that the Kansas Police Department reflects the current national standard for detailing four purposes: "Members may use department approved non-lethal force techniques and issued equipment to: a. Effect an arrest. b. Protect themselves and others from physical injury. c. Restrain or subdue a resistant individual. d. Bring an unlawful situation safely and effectively under control" (ibid.:51).

But nonlethal force includes a variety of actions, and there is ambiguity as to what actions constitute "force." For instance, there is no agreement on whether the handcuffing of a suspect qualifies as an example. When organizations do not have clear policies detailing the actions that qualify as "force," then this gives officers the discretionary powers to make those determinations on their own. Additionally, the extent that organizations provide clear definitions will directly impact the types of "use-of-force" reports that are completed by officers and entered in Early Intervention Systems. For instance, the Las Vegas Police Department's use-of-force policy does not require reports for the majority of instances where force is used by officers. It requires the filing of reports "only" in cases that involve "death, injury, or complaint of injury," "intentional traffic collision," or discharge of firearm" (Las Vegas Metropolitan Police Department, 2004).

In an effort to refine what is "appropriate" use of force, many organizations today have created continuum-use-of-force policies. These policies attempt to outline the degree of force (from the least to the most serious) that can be applied by officers in response to the level of force applied by the private citizen. An officer is expected to apply force that is one level above the force she or he is receiving. Certainly, these are quite vague and subjective. For instance, if a private citizen spits at or pushes an officer, what response would be considered "one level above"? But on the other hand, these policies do create *some* parameters, which in one instance a particular response by an officer could produce mixed opinions by the public but in another, there could be wide public consensus about its acceptability. For example, an incident in which an unarmed male pushes an officer and the officer responds by hitting him once with his baton, knocking him to the ground, could produce disagreement about whether the officer's action was excessive and in violation of the continuum-use-of-force policies. However, if after being pushed, the officer knocks an unarmed man to the ground where he remains motionless, and the officer continues to administer a series of blows, then we would have a situation in which more people would view this particular police response as "excessive" and in violation of the continuum-use-of-force policy.

Also, continuum-use-of-force policies are intended to respond to the U.S. Supreme Court's decision in *Garner*; that is, an unarmed fleeing felon could not be accused of demonstrating force against an officer. Thus, an officer who shoots and kills a fleeing unarmed felony suspect in the back could potentially be charged with murder. According to the U.S. Department of Justice (2001), "The levels of force that generally should be included in the agency's continuum of force include: verbal commands, use of hands, chemical agents, baton or other impact weapon, canine, less-than-lethal projectiles, and deadly force." The ACLU (1997) reports that as a result of police departments implementing restrictive policies on the use of deadly force, the number of deadly force incidents has dropped as much as 35 to 40 percent in the fifty largest cities. Barker (2006:87) notes that "this drop has been accompanied by a drop in the racial disparity in the use of deadly force." But, he adds that "most of this drop might be a direct result of the 1985 U.S. Supreme Court's decision in *Tennessee v. Garner*. This landmark decision limited the use of deadly force to only those instances where the suspect posed a threat of serious injury or death to the public or the police officer. As mentioned earlier, prior to this decision, in some states deadly force could be used to prevent the escape of all felony suspects" (ibid.).

But for Kavanagh (1994), there are no clear standards to guide police in when to apply excessive force to subdue and apprehend suspects. In other words, there is no agreement regarding what is deemed "appropriate force," and in what circumstances. And police organizations have largely condoned the use of "excessive force" as seen, for instance, in their response to citizen complaints against officers. According to Griswold (1994), three factors provide explanations of this: First, individuals who report excessive force charges are perceived by police as being less credible; second, these individuals often have been arrested before, which again undermines their credibility in the eyes of officers; and third, nonnegotiable uses of force are part of police powers, and high evidentiary requirements make citizen complaints difficult to sustain. For Cao, Deng, and Barton (2000), both the organizational characteristics of police agencies and the communities in which they operate are important correlates of the rate of citizen complaints relating specifically to the police use of excessive force. But, what is not recognized is the hegemonic masculinist crime-control ideologies that allow for abuses within the organization. The organization makes discretionary powers possible, but the abuse of these powers becomes possible because of the dominant police ideologies that support and condone "criminals getting roughed up a little" by police officers or the use of violence by police to apprehend a suspect.

Domestic Violence Policies

A series of landmark court decisions (*Scott v. Hart*, 1976; *Bruno v. Codd*, 1977; *Thurman v. Torrington*, 1984) led police organizations to create mandatory or proarrest policies in domestic violence situations to limit police discretionary powers. Prior to these policies, officers often ignored "intimate-partner abuse" because they were not perceived as "real crimes," given the relationship between the offender and victim (for example, husband and wife, common-law partners); they were perceived as a "waste" of police time and resources, and officers were often expected to "defuse" the situation and provide social service referrals and/or to serve as "peacemakers" (Buzawa and Buzawa, 1996; Goolkasian, 1986; Loving, 1981; IACP, 1967). Officers have intentionally used their police authority to ignore domestic violence crimes and not make any arrest. The lack of or limited police response to domestic violence cases was also the result of organizational directives given to officers to treat domestic violence cases as a low priority and to avoid arrests. These directives were intended to produce organizational "gains" as police resources could be focused on investigations that were deemed "serious" and prioritized by the police. In an attempt to limit police discretionary powers in this area, "mandatory arrest policies" or "proarrest" policies started to be introduced in the 1980s. Mandatory arrest policies require the police to make an arrest when there is reason to believe ("probable cause") that a felony or misdemeanor was committed. So-called proarrest policies are intended to encourage arrests, but they ultimately leave the discretion to the officer on scene to make the final decision. The officers are often required to complete a report explaining why an arrest was not warranted (Van Wormer and Roberts, 2009; Moriarty, 2002; Miller, 1997). But even recently, despite "proarrest policies," studies show that officers are more likely to arrest in domestic assaults if the victim insists on an arrest being made or if the offender is perceived by the police as acting "badly" toward them (Eigenberg, Scarborough, and Kappeler, 2001; Fyfe, Klinger, and Flavin, 1997). Once again here, dominant masculinist crime-control and patriarchal ideologies ensure that domestic violence continues to be seen as "less of a crime." Patriarchal and masculinist constructions of "intimate opposite-sex relationships" (husband and wife), privilege males and overlook abuses of power against women. Therefore, female victims of domestic violence, where the perpetrator is male, are "understood" within the police culture as less or not credible complainants, and the assault is often not seen as a criminal act. But also, male victims of domestic violence in opposite-sex relationships are also dismissed because of dominant perceptions that men cannot be seriously hurt or that "real men" shouldn't admit to being assaulted by a female partner.

Male Officers Who Commit Domestic Violence

Some studies have found that a higher rate of domestic violence perpetrators can be found among police officers in comparison to the wider public (D'Angelo, 2000; Honig and White, 1994; Neidig, Russell, and Seng, 1992). Neidig, Russell, and Seng (1992) found that nearly 40 percent of police officers in their study reported at least one episode of physical aggression in a marital conflict over the previous year. The sample included 385 male officers, 40 female officers, and 115 female spouses. Also, the Southwestern Law Enforcement Institute (1995) conducted a study that included 123 agencies and found that nearly 29 percent of the departments had experienced increases in domestic violence cases involving officers. Also, Honig and White (1994) report that domestic abuse occurs more in police families than in civilian or even military families.

Some officers have abused their positions of power for personal and/or organizational gain when victims have attempted to report the crime. Police perpetrators of domestic violence may use their police position to talk to their supervisors and ensure that the complaint is ignored. Also, patrol officers who respond to the victim's house may "cover" for the perpetrator by trying to dismiss or excuse the crime, rather than making an arrest. Most cases of domestic violence by a police officer may fall into four broad categories (Stone, 2000), which include: 1. Victims who do not report the abuse to the police, and the abuse goes undetected by the agency; 2. The abuse is known by the police, but the victim withdraws the complaint or does not cooperate; 3. Victims who report and cooperate with the investigation; and 4. Victims file false reports for retaliation or for some other gain. Stone (2000) asserts that most cases represent the first two categories, noting that when a victim refuses to cooperate then the investigation crumbles. Police know this information and can use their powers and the involvement of other officers to prevent the victim from formally reporting the abuse and/or cooperating with the investigation. Abusing one's position of power for some type of gain can also take the form of surveillance on a spouse or an intimate partner. Officers can use their resources to check the backgrounds of the friends of the spouse and/or partner or rely on other officers to do routine patrols of the spouse's/partner's place of employment and/or home.

Police perpetrators may view domestic violence as "normal" or "common" and may identify with other male abusers. This can create police hostility toward victims of domestic violence, including victim blaming (Feltgrin, 1996). Until the mid-1970s, domestic violence was treated as a family rather than criminal matter (Eigenberg and Kappeler, 2001; Jolin and Moose, 1997; Zorza, 1992; Goolkasian, 1986; Loving, 1981). The role of officer was more often that of mediator and/or peacemaker in domestic violence situations, and if officers responded to a domestic violence call and perceived the victim to be without "signs of assault," then the officers would often scold the victim for wasting their time and police resources (Zorza, 1992). It was a common perception for officers to consider domestic violence calls as a "waste of time" (Buzawa and Buzawa, 1996).

However, as a result of lawsuits filed against the police (for example, *Bruno v. Codd*, 1977; *Scott v. Hart*, 1976; *Thurman v. City of Torrington*, 1984), academic research that showed that arrest decreased the likelihood of future acts of violence (Sherman and Berk, 1984), and lobbying by women's organizations, police departments began to introduce mandatory arrest policies or some type of "hybrid" policies mandating arrest in some situations, or "proarrest" discretionary policies that encouraged officers to make an arrest but with the ultimate decision making resting with the individual officer(s) on the scene (Monk, 1993). Yet, instances of police abuse of powers in domestic violence situations have not been eliminated. Mandatory arrest policies require the police to make an arrest when there is reason to believe ("probable cause") that a felony or misdemeanor was committed (Van Wormer and Roberts, 2009). Probable cause is established by the presence of witnesses and visible injuries or property damage that suggests a crime has been committed (Renzetti and Bergen, 2005). These appear to "force" officers to make an arrest regardless of their personal views about the incident and/or perceptions of the victim. But often this has resulted in officers viewing an assault as a "dual combat" and arresting both the victim and perpetrator, which has contributed to the increase in arrests of women (Belknap, 2006). Oftentimes police officers will dismiss claims of domestic violence rather than taking the time to adequately assess the situation and determine the primary physical aggressor (Moriarty, 2002). And other studies report that officers are more likely to arrest in domestic assaults if the victim insists on an arrest being made or if the offender is perceived by the police as acting "badly" toward them (Eigenberg, Scarborough, and Kappeler, 2001; Fyfe, Klinger, and Flavin, 1997).

On the other hand, some jurisdictions have introduced some type of "hybrid" domestic violence policy that requires officers to make an arrest in certain situations (for example, if there is a third-party witness to the assault or if a weapon was used) but give them discretion to determine if an arrest is warranted in other instances. According to Moriarty (2002), only with the implementation of mandatory arrest policies is domestic violence treated as a crime. But, even with these, there still remain many police challenges as noted above, and as they relate to limited training and gender biases. The control of intimate-partner violence depends on the fundamental restructuring of gender relations and the empowerment of women (DeKeseredy and Hinch, 1991). The perceptions of many men that rationalize the subordination of women are embedded in systems of knowledge and in the processes that produce them (Humphries, 2009). When discretion is given to the individual officer, an officer can choose to make an arrest or to walk away, believing that it is not "serious enough," or claiming that there is no "evidence" to suggest a crime has occurred. Given the "naturalization" of violence against women in society, gender biases relating to the enforcement of domestic violence laws cannot be ignored.

Also, officers have chosen not to arrest in instances where they believe the victim will not appear in court to testify against the abuser. An officer may conclude that it is not worth the time to invest in an investigation where the victim is perceived to be uncooperative (Robinson and Chandek, 2000). However, the officer's job is to determine "probable cause" and not what the likelihood of victim cooperation will be in the future. Eigenberg (2001) notes several challenges in police responses to this crime: Officers' behavior reflects the values of the larger culture that has failed to view violence against women as a serious social problem, and many officers believe that a battered woman chooses to remain in an abusive relationship because she could leave if she really wanted to. Second, police work at domestic violence situations is seen as a form of social work, but the police culture promotes the crime-fighting aspect of the job; this is despite the fact that officers spend most of their time "doing" service work. Also, officers become irritated with victims who deny the abuse after the police arrive on scene or when a victim fails to appear in court to testify against the abuser. Additionally, some officers do not view domestic violence calls as a priority given the lack of organizational recognition or reward for performance in this area (Moriarty, 2002). Thus, in addition to the gender biases and sexist attitudes on the part of officers, abuse of police powers in how domestic violence situations are handled are more likely when officers assess work priority in relation to the kinds of police work they perceive are valued by the organization that can lead to rewards, promotions, and/or transfer to desired units (Buzawa and Buzawa, 1996).

The potential for abuse is further magnified when the officer responding to a domestic violence call is himself guilty of this crime (Neidig, Russell, and Seng, 1992).

Studies have also found that victims of domestic violence who kill their partners called the police many times in the past, but the police failed to arrest the abuser. In most homicide cases between partners, there were a series of "cries for help" before the killing (Bergen, Edleson, and Renzetti, 2005). The homicide records in Detroit and Kansas City showed that in 85 percent to 90 percent of the cases, police had been called to the home at least once during the two years prior to the fatal incident, and in 54 percent of the cases, they had been called five or more times (Van Wormer and Roberts, 2009). Women officers, on the other hand, view domestic violence as more serious and are more likely to involve themselves in the investigation than are male officers (Heidensohn and Brown, 2000; Feinman, 1986; Homant and Kennedy, 1985), and victims of domestic violence perceive female officers as being more involved and providing more support and care than male officers (Kennedy and Homant, 1983).

Gender remains the strongest indicator of police abuse of powers. Several studies have shown that the presence of female officers on patrol frequently decreased the number of citizen complaints and reduced overall police violence. Women tend to be perceived as presenting a less threatening image to the public, resulting in the increased avoidance of assaults as well as generating a "calming effect" on citizens (Van Wormer, 1981; Steffensmeier, 1979) and as being more comforting to women, juveniles, and especially victims of crimes (Worden, 1993). It has also been reported that female officers in female-male patrol teams are more effective in calming potentially violent situations (Corsianos, 2009; Martin and Jurik, 2007; Grennan, 1987), and female officers have typically been less likely to use excessive force (McElvain and Kposowa, 2004; Bureau of Justice Assistance, 2001; Abernethy and Cox, 1994) and be involved in deadly force incidents (Horvath, 1987).

Policies Limiting Racial Profiling

Criminal profiling can be defined as the use of a combination of physical, behavioral, or psychological factors that improve the police's probability of identifying and apprehending a suspect. Profiles can be formal (based on documented empirical evidence) or informal (represent the beliefs of the officers who use them; these are more common). Most well-known types of profiles are developed to identify serial murderers and rapists (Withrow, 2006). However, "racial profiling" refers to the use of 'race' or ethnicity as the primary factor in police decisions to stop and question citizens. Race became an important part of drug courier profiles beginning in the mid-1980s, and training programs were developed to teach officers about particular profiles, such as ones relating to drug couriers. Officers at the local level began to adopt some of the profiles developed by the Drug Enforcement Agency that focused their enforcement on source countries, since they assumed that nationals from these countries would be more likely to carry drugs. New Jersey state troopers, for instance, received training videos that led them to believe that Jamaican gangs were primarily the ones transporting drugs and could disguise themselves as professional black males in business suits. As a result, New Jersey state troopers began to target expensive cars driven by black males in business suits (Vera Institute of Justice, 2002; *Cops under Fire*, 1996).

The first major victory for critics of racial profiling came in a case brought by Robert Wilkins against the Maryland state police. Wilkins, who was an attorney, was pulled over while driving back home to Washington, D.C., with his family. The police asked to search his car, but Wilkins refused. The police then brought a narcotics dog to determine whether there were illegal drugs in the car. However, the search did not produce any drugs. Wilkins later filed a federal civil rights damage suit against the Maryland state police for violating his civil rights. He argued that he had been pulled over by the police because of his race. The case was settled, and New Jersey signed a federal court consent decree agreeing to prohibit racial profiling and to maintain a record of the race of all motorists stopped by their officers. Upon the request of the ACLU, this data would have to be turned over to them for review (Withrow, 2006).

An increasing number of police agencies now require officers to record the 'race' of the motorists they stop. Over four hundred police agencies have collected traffic-stop data either voluntarily, in response to a statutory requirement, or by court order. Twenty-three states have passed legislation requiring the collection of racial stop data or racial profiling studies (Amnesty International, 2004; McMahon et al., 2002). Some believe that these policies have succeeded in restricting police discretionary powers given officers' awareness of the possible ramifications to their careers if a formal record of discriminatory practices relating to 'race', ethnicity, and motor vehicle stops is established. But there has been no analysis of how current crime-control ideologies serve to "inform" officers of the "need" to proactively interrogate civilians in the hopes of making arrests. These police strategies cannot be separated from dominant constructions of crime as behavior that is largely synonymous with street-level crimes and racial minorities. Also, forms of resistance by police officers continue to be seen despite attempts to create accountability mechanisms through the collection of 'race' data on motorists stopped by police (for example, officers can check off "white," even though motorists may identify as Hispanic).

Moreover, police have the authority to stop motorists without probable cause or reasonable suspicion that a crime has taken place by using an observed traffic violation as a pretext for stopping motorists "suspected" of criminal activity. *Whren et al. v. United States* (1996) is an important case in relation to racial profiling. On June 10, 1993, plainclothes vice squad officers of the District of Columbia Metropolitan Police Department were patrolling a "high drug area" in the city in an unmarked car; they observed a Pathfinder with temporary license plates and "youthful occupants" waiting at a stop sign. The officers reported that the SUV remained there for an unusually long time (approximately twenty seconds), and therefore they made a U-turn and proceeded toward the SUV. They reported that the vehicle then suddenly made a right turn and "sped off" and eventually stopped behind other traffic at a red light; they pulled up next to it, and Officer Soto stepped out of his car, approached the driver's door, identified himself as a police officer, and asked the driver to put the car in park. Officer Soto observed two large plastic bags in the hands of the passenger that he thought was crack cocaine. The occupants were arrested, and quantities of several different types of drugs were found in the vehicle. The occupants were charged with violating various federal drug laws. The defendants' lawyers argued that Officer Soto's stop was not justified by probable cause or even reasonable suspicion, and that the officer's grounds to give the driver a warning concerning traffic violations was pretextual. But, the U.S. Supreme Court ruled that a traffic stop is permissible as long as a reasonable officer in the same circumstances could have stopped the car for the suspected traffic violation. The Court's decision in *Whren* did not create the practice of pretextual stops. Rather, it validated this long-standing police practice (Withrow, 2006).

Therefore, the police virtually have unlimited authority to stop anyone for any reason if a traffic violation has been observed. All evidence of possible criminal behavior that results from the stop is admissible, regardless of the officers' "true intentions" for the stop (assuming there are no constitutional violations). The officers can conduct warrantless searches using dogs, or the plain-view exception (Withrow, 2006). But given the level of discretion that officers have to determine which cars to stop and when, police policies that require officers to record the motorist's 'race' and/or ethnicity as a way to identify discriminatory patterns on the part of officers may be superficial "band-aid" attempts. This is due in part to the limitations with the forms that are intended to identify the 'race' of motorists.

PROBLEMS WITH "ACCOUNTABILITY" MECHANISMS

The intrinsic nature of corruption risks have been linked partly to the inadequate accountability mechanisms within the organization. Various scholars have advocated for the creation of multiple systems that will help to resocialize officers over time and increase accountability on the part of officers (Corsianos, 2009; Walker, 2005; Prenzler, 2009; Burris and Whitney, 2000; Champion, 2001; Barker, 2006.) According to the LAPD Board of Inquiry (2000:58), "had the Department and the Rampart management exercised more vigorous and coordinated oversight of Area operations, and its CRASH unit in particular, the crimes and misconduct that occurred may have been prevented, discouraged or discovered much earlier." Organizational structures can create opportunities for officers to commit corrupt acts.

Walker (2005) asserts that there is a failure on the part of police organizations to implement the police profession's own established standards. One example noted has been the failure to meet established standards for on-the-street supervision.

In the late 1990s and early 2000s, investigations found several police departments that allowed the ratio of sergeants to officers on the street to exceed their own recommended standard of 1:8. The examples included the Century Station in the Los Angeles Sheriff's Department; the Riverside, California, Police Department; and the Philadelphia Police Department. The police profession has long recognized that street-level supervision is a critical aspect of policing and developed a minimum standard, and yet these departments proceeded to violate that standard for extended periods of time (Walker, 2005:24–25).

Additionally,

> an observational study of activities of street sergeants identified four different styles of supervision. One that Robin Engel labeled "supportive" supervision defined its role in terms of protecting officers from discipline by upper management. In short, a common style of supervision is antithetical to principles of meaningful accountability. And it might be noted that the research was conducted in two departments implementing major community policing programs—that is, departments that were presumptively more progressive than many others. (ibid.:25)

However, given the emphasis on aggressive crime-control approaches tied to particular groups of people and behaviors, the masculinist characteristics of the police culture (see chapters 3 and 4) that, for instance, demand solidarity and loyalty to "the brotherhood" regardless of observed illegal and/or questionable behavior on the part of fellow officers, mean that increasing on-the-street supervision of patrol officers would produce little if any changes. The intrinsic organizational risks for corruption can be found in the various challenges confronted by citizens filing complaints against officers. Criticisms include difficulties in filing the complaint, not being taken seriously, complaints not investigated, and no follow-up calls to update complainants. Given the disregard for citizen complaints particularly by certain categories of people (Neugebauer, 1999, 1996; Black, 1990; Gordon, 1987), the organization enables and/or empowers officers to potentially engage in acts of corruption in certain areas or against certain groups of people if officers view the organization as rejecting or discrediting particular citizen complaints, or complaints in general.

Internal Affairs has historically been criticized for its lack of objectivity in policing its officers and for its tendency to try to conceal acts of corruption from the public in order to protect particular officers and/or prevent negative publicity about the organization (Kappeler, Sluder, and Alpert, 1994). Additionally, if acts of corruption are identified, IA moves quickly to deal with the officers involved and bring closure rather than trying to identify the extent of the corruption since it is not politically desirable to uncover its magnitude. The power dynamics within IA are such that the end goal is to protect the reputation of the organization as a whole. Their response to officers involved in corrupt acts can depend on a number of factors, including suspected officers' connections to higher-ranking officers and/or officers working in IA, their rank, their years of service and overall reputation, whether the misconduct has been leaked to the media, tangible evidence of the corrupt act beyond someone's verbal and written complaint (for example, video and/or audio recording, cell phone picture, etc.), and whether there are "legitimate" victims of police corruption (that is, victims who will be perceived as credible by the wider public). Given the lack of credibility that has been associated with police organizations' IA unit by some members of the public, various scholars have identified the need for outside agencies to monitor police behavior (Crank and Caldero, 2011; Prenzler, 2009; Walker, 2005; Champion, 2001). But external oversight of the police has not been effective largely because external agencies either cannot implement their own recommendations and ensure some level of reform or because their approach to responding to the misconduct is done on a case-by-case basis, rather than viewing police corruption as systemic.

There are two types of external oversight agencies that attempt to deal with citizen complaints against officers: the one-time, blue-ribbon commissions and permanent external oversight agencies. Blue-ribbon commissions are formed in response to perceived police problems. They typically consist of a panel of experts appointed by chief executives at the local, state, and national levels and are tasked with investigating the problem and preparing a report with policy recommendations. The Christopher Commission (Christopher, 1991) is an example of a blue-ribbon panel that was formed following the Rodney King beating in Los Angeles. But, as stated above, these commissions lack the power to implement their own recommendations (Walker, 2005).

On the other hand, citizen oversight agencies (for example, civilian review boards) have faced several challenges. Some have not had the authority to conduct independent investigations apart from the police (Walker, 2001; Terrill, 1990), whereas others have had the authority but lacked resources and personnel (New York Civil Liberties Union, 1993). Additionally, some agencies either lacked political support and/or were met with opposition from the local police union (Police Advisory Commission, 1997). More importantly, as mentioned earlier, by focusing on individual citizen complaints on a case-by-case basis, agencies fail to recognize that police corruption is, in part, the product of the organization that creates corruption risks.

Additionally, some have supported the creation of corruption units similar to the OCU (Official Corruption Unit) in New York City. New York's OCU is run by the District Attorney's office, and their mandate is to investigate complaints of corruption by government officials, including the police (http://manhattanda.org/node/174/22). The OCU consists of a team of investigators, attorneys, and paralegals. Investigators typically conduct "sting operations" to uncover acts of corruption. If they identify corrupt cops, they often will try to convince the officer to "wear wires" and assist them in identifying other corrupt cops in exchange for dropping some charges against the guilty officer or agreeing to let the officers plead guilty to a lesser charge. Unlike the IA unit, the goal of the OCU is to try to identify the extent of the corruption; that is, how many officers and units/divisions are involved and how long the corruption has been going on.

Furthermore, there have not been any reliable internal structural and systematic monitoring mechanisms for police behavior that could be used to identify police corruption or the possibility of future acts of police corruption. Over the years, there has been growing support for the creation of early intervention (EI) computerized databases that could be used to identify patterns in police behavior (Walker, 2006; Walker and Alpert, 2004). EI systems received its first important endorsement from the U.S. Civil Rights Commission (1981) in its report "Who Is Guarding the Guardians?" Early Intervention systems have been implemented by a number of police organizations over the last ten to fifteen years (Hickman, Piquero, and Greene, 2004) and consist of three basic tenets:

> The first involves the identification and selection of officers in need of formal intervention. Identification is based on an analysis of performance indicators that are entered into a computerized data base. These indicators include use of

force reports, deadly force incidents, citizen complaints, resisting arrest charges, officer involvement in civil litigation, sick leave use, and any other indicators that a department deems appropriate. (Walker and Alpert, 2004:23)

But there is no consensus regarding what the appropriate formula should be in evaluating the performance data. In the past, some organizations used a fixed-number approach relating to one specific performance indicator. For instance, three complaints within one year required a formal intervention with the officer. Given the limitations with this approach, the City of Miami Police Department (Departmental Order 2, chapter 8) introduced four categories of behavior to identify officers:

1. Complaints: A list of all officers with five or more complaints in the last two years, where the complaints were sustained or found to be inconclusive.
2. Controls of Persons (Use of Force): A list of all officers involved as principals in five or more control-of-persons incidents for the last two years.
3. Reprimands: A list of all employees with five or more reprimands for the past two years.
4. Discharge of Firearms: A list of all officers with three or more discharge of firearms in the past five years.

Walker and Alpert note (2004:25) that:

Officers who are placed on the system are informed by their supervisor who must investigate the Incidents, officer's assignment(s) reasons and write a memorandum to the Commander of Internal Affairs with a recommendation. Internal Affairs provides the supervisor with a report of each incident which must be evaluated. The supervisor must make a recommendation which may include one or more of the following:

1. Reassignment
2. Retraining
3. Transfer
4. Referral to an Employee Assistance Program
5. Fitness for Duty Evaluation or
6. Dismissal pursuant to Civil Rules and Regulations

Once this plan is agreed upon by the various supervisors and the Commander of Internal Affairs, it is the responsibility of the officer's immediate supervisor to manage and monitor the officer.

Although some EI systems may appear to be sound on their face, there are further organizational limitations. For one, there is no consensus regarding the "thresholds" for identifying officers for intervention, and, secondly, what the ratio between problem indicators and desired activity levels (for example, number of arrests) should be. Thirdly, there is no way in ensuring consistency in the delivery of interventions. Since the formal intervention phase is confidential, there is no record of the substance of the intervention placed in an officer's personnel file. The issue of confidentiality presents challenges for higher-level supervisors since they are unable to verify that the intervener (for example, officer's immediate supervisor) acted according to the agreed plan. There is no accountability, and therefore no way of knowing whether the immediate supervisor even tells the officer to "forget about it"; this is an important question given the tenets of the police culture (see chapters 3 and 4) that are often not considered in discussions on EI implementation and accountability mechanisms. Fourthly, the EI system is not built into the routine supervision of front-line officers. Sergeants do not actively use the EI to access the database, review the performance of officers, identify problems or potential problems, and take the necessary remedial steps (Walker and Alpert, 2004). Additionally, this system depends on administrators to provide consistent training on EI systems. At times, supervisors may attend one seminar and assume they have all the necessary information.

Terrill and McCluskey (2002:145) provide three scenarios regarding citizen complaints against police officers. First, citizen complaints may reveal close to nothing about the police officer's conduct. This can be rationalized by two possible explanations; that is, either "it is the citizens' view . . . that the officer acted illegally or improperly, which is unlikely to be informed by rules and procedures promulgated by police departments," or " a complaint is solely an allegation . . . and may have less to do with improper police behavior and more to do with the fact the citizen was the subject of an officer behavior." Second, complaints may actually identify problem officers in the sense that they may be "a rough indicator of an officer's 'propensity' for malpractice" (ibid.). Third, citizen complaints may indicate productiveness rather than misconduct; as Terrill and McCluskey note: "The surest way not to receive a complaint is to do little or no police work" (ibid.). Again, what is missing here is how "productivity" is conceptualized within police organizations and how masculinist crime-control ideologies allow for abuses of police powers in order to achieve desired goals. As mentioned earlier, "productivity" is often measured through crime-control functions (number of arrests, amount of drugs and other contraband seized, number of officers hired to fight the "war on crime," etc.) both quantitatively as well as qualitatively (for example, through the use of video footage to show the public the good work of the police). Also, Terrill and McClusky do not identify the class and 'race' biases on the part of the police. Complaints are rarely put forward by those representing middle and upper socioeconomic classes since they are rarely the target of law enforcement tactics and because police feel more accountable toward these civilians, which means they are more likely to take the necessary steps to ensure individual rights are not violated.

However, in examining complaints involving physical force and discourtesy, Terrill and McCluskey found high-complaint officers used a higher number of forceful tactics. Problem officers also used interrogation tactics and were more proactive. For instance, they initiated police-citizen encounters at a significantly higher rate than nonproblem officers and relied on commands and threats to perform more searches than nonproblem officers. Terrill and McCluskey assert that officers with more complaints may simply be more productive, yet they may also be more likely to resort to force. Furthermore, it is important to note that the EI implementation was conceived as something that should be done for liability concerns to ensure organizational survival and not because of some genuine commitment to improve performance evaluation mechanisms.

THE ORGANIZATION AS A "BAD BARREL MAKER"

Zimbardo (2007) argued that the crimes committed in Abu Ghraib by American soldiers were not the result of "bad apples" or even "bad barrels" but rather "bad barrel makers." In other words, the soldiers' behavior was the result of something larger; it was systemic. For Zimbardo, these soldiers were able to engage in inhumane behavior against the prisoners because of a number of factors that included socially constructing prisoners as "the enemy," which allowed soldiers to perceive them as less deserving of care, respect, and dignity; diffusion of personal responsibility; anonymity; and blind obedience to authority. But equally important for Zimbardo, the soldiers were given power without oversight, which is a "recipe for abuse," as has been seen in police corruption cases.

These demonstrate how dominant crime-control ideologies allow for these abuses. For example, socially constructing others as "the enemy" is used as justification for abuses. Also, living in a culture that glamorizes power over others instills in people the belief that this form of power is desirable; something we should strive for. Having power over individuals in some "meaningful" way becomes synonymous with having respect from others.

Additionally, the hierarchical, paramilitaristic police organizational structure as a whole represents systems that create particular power relations within the organizations that can make it difficult for officers to come forward to report a corrupt act and/or demand an investigation. These power relations can serve to put officers in a position where they feel they don't have a choice but to condone the corrupt activities of others in order to avoid being marginalized and ostracized from peers and management and suffer social, psychological, and/or financial consequences. For example, the soldier who ultimately was the "whistle-blower" in Abu Ghraib was completely ostracized for his actions, and, along with his mother and fiancé, was subjected to death threats.

Officers in upper-level administrative positions have the sociopolitical power to ensure conformity among their officers. Language is the tool often used to legitimize their position of control (Corsianos, 2001). For Gadamer (1976:3), "Language is the fundamental mode of operation of our being-in-the world, and the all-embracing form of the constitution of the world." For instance, it is not uncommon for members of upper management to use everyday rhetoric that, at the manifest level, would indicate partnership among officers relating to one another within a "collectivist, equitable police culture" and hence suggest "friendly advice," while at the latent function, they affirm respect and obedience to the chain of command and to the traditional, patriarchal police operations. Common expressions used within police departments are "the brotherhood of policing," "the blue wall," "you may win the battle but you won't win the war," "bite the bullet," "don't rock the boat," and "the old-boy's club is alive and well." These statements serve to protect and promote the paramilitaristic police structure and its traditional operations, maintain particular power relations (Corsianos, 2001), and ensure conformity. Thus officers wanting to come forward to report a corrupt act and/or demand an investigation into police misconduct are deterred in an organization where one is expected to respect the "chain of command" and accept "orders from above." Members of the "brass" who use this type of rhetoric posit themselves as trustworthy, speaking only with the best interest of the officer in mind rather than to present themselves as bureaucrats interested in preserving the agency's goals and ensuring organizational maintenance and survival. According to Itwaru (1989:13):

> Their utterance is not seen as an attempt to persuade the listener to accept being a powerless subject. It is not seen as the very condition of the absence of freedom. It is not seen as the reinforcement of inequality. But rather in a political economy which daily promises authenticity of the subject and daily denies this, this supposedly good advice takes on the persiflage of personal acceptance and concern.

Itwaru (1989:15) adds, "These 'advisors' are the legitimators of highly formalized strategies for the imprisonment of the subject. That they may not be aware of these implications in their action does not detract from the agencing role they are playing."

The hegemonizing procedures of the paramilitartic, authoritarian model of policing are operationalized through everyday rhetoric presented by members of management. Many officers will accept them and not question the intentions; this, in turn, keeps corrupt acts hidden from the public. Hegemony is a force of rule that exists within a set of ideologies that is secured through consent of the people and promoted by "common sense" (Gramsci, 1957). Therefore, everyday police rhetoric by members of management within the current police organizational structure serve as a powerful resource to maintain conformity among officers and preserve organizational goals while working to hide police actions that could put the organization in jeopardy.

For Walker (2005:15), "Changing the police organization ultimately is deeply intertwined with measures designed to control the behavior of individual officers on the street. To separate the two conceptually or in practice is to invite failure." But by focusing on the need to control the behavior of individual officers, Walker fails to recognize how the organization as a whole, and the police as an institution, create corruption risks.

The organization also creates risks of corruption as a result of the economic constraints experienced internally. For one, officers are largely identified as "blue collar workers" (Travis and Langworthy, 2008). Their pay is often considered by them to be unsatisfactory. Frustration with limited salaries can be further exacerbated when officers are unable to get paid-detail opportunities through the organization, or due to budget cuts there may be fewer or no opportunities to work overtime or make court appearances when off duty. Additionally, the pyramid structure of the organization ensures limited opportunities for advancement that compromise one's ability to increase their salary. Lower-level officers typically depend on selling their labor power to financially support themselves and any family. Their dependence on the job "naturalizes" in their overall acceptance of police corruption regardless of personal interpretations of particular instances (see chapter 4). There is a financial and emotional investment in conforming; one's job is better protected and one avoids being completely marginalized and ostracized by peers. This dependence can also contribute to a greater willingness to view police misconduct as "natural" given the "types" of people they often come in contact with, or they may even view it as "necessary" (for example, to increase their overall salary). For many officers, it appears that policing translates to a job that they depend on to make ends meet. Thus, they may at times use their discretionary powers to take advantage of criminal opportunities that arise and/or create their own "opportunities." However, these instances as discussed earlier are gendered, and women officers are significantly less likely to engage in police corruption (also see chapter 3).

Chapter Three

The Role of the Masculinist Police Culture in Police Corruption

This chapter examines the complex social world of police officers and how it overtly and covertly maintains and defends particular police actions. More specifically, this chapter provides explanations for police corruption in the context of particular police occupational themes as they relate to "hegemonic masculinity" and "the brotherhood." Attention is also given to how the police culture shapes and encourages particular ideologies that officers depend on to preserve and defend their actions and identities as they relate to police corruption and why significantly fewer women are involved in police corruption. Excerpts from informal interviews conducted with thirty-two former police officers in North America regarding their experiences and perceptions of police corruption are included in order to illustrate the complexities of police corruption as they relate to gender constructions and hegemonic masculinity. Twenty-nine of the officers were male, and three were female. To ensure anonymity and confidentiality, the geographic locations of the meetings and names of the police departments were not identified. Also, the names of specialized units/divisions/teams were omitted, along with any names or locations referred to by the participants. And at times, some of the details of particular events have been deliberately altered to avoid any possibility of being identified. Their experiences and perceptions of events provide disturbing insight into some of the corruption they witnessed while on the job and/or corrupt activities that they participated in on some level. Fourteen of the participants shared incidents of police criminality that were committed by other officers. On the other hand, eighteen provided personal accounts of their own involvement in which eleven presented themselves as the main players in the misconduct, whereas seven described "some" involvement.

Examples of corruption provided by the participants included assault, theft, perjury, extortion, kickbacks, bribery, burglary, planting of evidence, protection of illegal activities, selling illegal drugs, illegally installing spy software for the purpose of committing identity theft, and writing false ticket violations. Interestingly, other forms of misconduct in areas such domestic violence and sexual assault, racial profiling, selective law enforcement, and other types of differential treatment of particular groups of people were not discussed, which illustrate the cultural mores relating to the kinds of behavior that are or can be considered to be "corrupt."

To begin, culture refers to a shared way of life. Indeed, individuals are unique but are at the same time products of their culture (Griswold, 1986). Individuals have their own personality, which refers to the fairly consistent pattern of acting, thinking, and feeling, but personality is largely the result of socialization. As sociologists assert, nurture/socialization is humanity's nature. Without socialization, people cannot mature intellectually, socially, emotionally, and psychologically (Begley, 1995; Goldsmith, 1983; Mead, 1962, orig. 1934). People continuously "take in"/internalize what they see, hear, and read and make decisions with respect to how they should act, think, and feel about different things. To share a culture means to share a set of tenets that include a language, norms, values, ideologies, and material objects. But, admittedly, one can be part of a number of different "sub" cultures that at times can produce conflicting understandings of "self," particularly as one attempts to negotiate certain values, purposes, and belonging.

Academics have written extensively on the police occupational culture (Corsianos, 2009; Martin and Jurik, 2007; Crank, 1998; Manning, 1997, 1992, 1977; Scripture, 1997; McNulty, 1994; Fyfe, 1991; Martin, 1980; Westley, 1953). As members of the police culture officers share the dominant language spoken in the wider U.S. culture, but they also share a "police language"; that is, they frequently use official policing terms as well as everyday police jargon to refer to particular tasks and incidents and to relate to each other. This language is privileged because it signifies to other officers one's "status" and membership. Officers also share a set of material objects. Most officers today wear distinctive uniforms that identify them as police officers. Along with the uniform, officers are equipped with a firearm, utility belt, handcuffs, baton, badge, citation book, flashlight, mace or tazer, and a marked police car; these are some examples of the tangible material objects shared by members of the police culture that serve to signify to civilians the officers' positions of power and the power of the state.

The norms, on the other hand, refer to the rules that are intended to guide police behavior. Officers are expected to follow the laws as all members within the larger society but are simultaneously subject to internal rules and regulations that include directions ranging from how to conduct investigations and the relevant forms that must be completed and processed to how to wear the uniform properly and the acceptance of gifts while on the job. As discussed in chapter 2, the organizational structure creates the social space for officers to perceive their work in particular ways, but at times, to also conduct their work with more fluidity given the absence of clearly defined rules, the lack of enforcement of existing rules, as well as the level of autonomy and discretionary powers afforded to them in interpreting some of the rules. New recruits learn the rules of police work while on patrol and through socializing with peers after work (Manning, 1997, 1977; Bayley, 1996; Doig, 1978).

Additionally, values are integral to understanding any culture. In policing they are represented by patriarchal ideologies and "hegemonic masculinity" and include solidarity and "the brotherhood," loyalty to fellow officers, secrecy, autonomy, authority, particular physical strengths as they relate to crime-control functions and perceptions of danger, an "us versus them mentality," the "thin blue line" identity, and the police as distinct from other occupational cultures.

Police officers are first exposed to the police culture formally when in the academy but come to "understand" the complexities of the police culture informally when working with fellow officers and socializing with each other after work (Corsianos, 2009; Crank, 1998; Manning, 1997, 1977; Lundman, 1980; Doig, 1978). For Lundman (1980), police recruits are relatively homogeneous in terms of their class, gender, education level, and race, but the socialization they experience throughout their police training is what ultimately produces uniformity in officers' perceptions of police work and their roles as officers. More recently, the homogeneous characteristics of officers seen in the 1970s and previous decades are not as apparent in some large city police departments, but, regardless, a particular homogeneous image of the police continues to exist on many levels. In these earlier decades, the police were mainly composed of white, working-class males, and other groups were excluded through the use of height and weight restrictions, physical agility tests, and written tests. Furthermore, oral interviews and background checks on candidates' family and friends eliminated those who did not possess the highly valued "masculine traits" (Martin and Jurik, 2007). Despite the increase in diversity among officers in recent years in some organizations, the occupational culture largely remains intact to its traditional formations.

Chappell and Lanza-Kaduce (2009) examined the socialization that occurs at the police academy and found three consistent themes during their observations of recruits and instructors: 1. Recruits learned about positional authority and the command hierarchy; 2. They learned about law enforcement's emphasis on loyalty, solidarity, and reliance on fellow officers; and 3. They learned to expect stress and how to carry out roles while under stress. Additionally, the training supported the "us versus them" mentality where officers perceive the general public to be either ignorant of police work, not supportive of them, and/or in need of police surveillance. For Westley (1953), officers are in constant conflict with the community, and their experiences "give rise to a collective emphasis on secrecy, an attempt to coerce respect from the public, and a belief that almost any means are legitimate in completing an important arrest. These are for the policeman basic occupational values. They arise from his experience, take precedence over his legal responsibilities, [and] are central to an understanding of his conduct" (ibid.:53). Tiffen (2004:1175) notes that "the scope for secrecy and relatively unaccountable power is always conducive to corruption." The "code of silence" contributes to the reasons that officers largely do not report abuses of power on the part of other officers.

The police culture is on some levels similar to many other occupational cultures, particularly as it relates to both teamwork and competition, professionalism, shift work, self-discipline, productivity, the implementation of strategic methods to achieve identified organizational goals, accountability to management, and ability to measure successful outcomes. On the other hand, it can be distinct given the "nature" of policing systems. For instance, policing is perceived by officers as dangerous (Brandl, 1996; Strorch and Panzarella, 1996) given the unpredictability of the job (for example, you never know "who" you are stopping to question or "what" you are responding to and what these encounters or instances may lead to).

Officers' common perceptions of themselves making uncertain and risky decisions as well as the level of danger that is believed to be associated with their work shapes and defines police attitudes and hence the police culture (Manning, 1997; Brandl, 1996; Storch and Panzarella, 1996; Manning and Van Maanen, 1978). A common saying among officers is "complacency kills," and no common police task such as a motor vehicle stop or an alarm call should ever be perceived to be "routine." Officers "understand" that if these are accepted as "routine" then they are more likely to become complacent and put themselves at risk. Possible examples here could include officers who respond to an alarm call and park their police car in front of the house or building, assuming that it's a "false alarm," and as a result they alert robbers on the inside, making themselves direct targets; or if officers stop a motor vehicle and allow a motorist with his hands in his pockets to walk right up to the police car. The incident in Detroit, Michigan, in 2004 highlights the common police perception that "complacency kills." The two officers pulled over a motorist for a seemingly "routine" traffic stop. But "as the two officers called in the license plate information of the vehicle, while sitting in their patrol car, the suspect exited his vehicle and opened fire (Officer Down Memorial Page; www.odmp.org/officer/17238-police-officer-mathew-e-bowens). Both Officer Jennifer Fettig, twenty-six, and Matthew Bowens, twenty-one, were shot and killed. Following the incident, some officers were quick to point out that these deaths could perhaps have been prevented had the officers not allowed the motorist to approach the car either by reversing their police car back enough to create a safer physical separation between the two cars and/or to use their speaker to tell the motorist to immediately return to his vehicle, giving the officers the advantage when approaching the motorist's vehicle from behind.

Officers are trained to approach vehicles from the rear where they can observe movement in the car in front of them. And when they approach the driver from the rear, she or he has to turn her or his head around to about a ninety-degree turn to speak with the officer, putting the motorist in an awkward bodily position (Travis and Langworthy, 2008). Officers also often violate normative expectations of personal space by either standing too close with their hands up in front of their chest or too far away from the citizen. Police will typically not maintain eye contact so that they continuously scan a citizen's hands, body movement, and surrounding area (for example, inside the car). The perceived probability of dangerous instances promotes a sense of solidarity intersected with an "understanding" of police work as centered on dangerous people, events, and surroundings, where officers must protect and support each other. The intensity of the solidarity that is created is atypical in most other professions. There's a sense of connection for many officers that is tied to the belief that your fellow officer is looking out for you and will protect you. These perceptions of danger also signal to officers the "need" to be physically strong (largely understood by many officers in terms of body size, upper body strength, and male bodies more specifically). This view of "physical strength" is also seen as necessary to fulfill crime-control functions (see chapter 2).

Police perceptions of the public as ignorant or not able to understand the work of a police officer or that the public is in need of police oversight to maintain order and security posits the police as "the thin blue line" and secures the "us versus them" mentality. Citizens and the police are not equal parties in police-public interactions, and the police have the power to set the tone in the communication and dictate the events that will follow. Langworthy and Travis (2003:254) suggest that "people frequently thank an officer after receiving a traffic citation. This polite, *Thank you, officer*, symbolizes the citizen's recognition of the officer's power (and the desire not to antagonize the officer and receive any further *gifts*)." Police further view themselves as "the thin blue line" between a state of chaos and anarchy and one of peace and order. They consider the police "function" as a necessary component to living in a relatively harmonious society and that without the police, there would be a state of anarchy, conflict, and insecurity (Herbert, 2006).

As discussed in chapter 2, the structure of policing enables front-line officers to have a great deal of autonomy and authority while on patrol without direct supervision. This autonomy and authority are key tenets of police culture (Manning, 1990). Having autonomy and authority in decision making means having "power." Power is a complex, abstract concept that has explanatory value only when attached to a theory of a historically specific relationship. Critically examining the history of police-citizen relationships in various contexts is a key component to understanding police powers, particularly as they relate to patriarchal ideologies and hegemonic masculinity. For Poulantzas (1980:147), power is not "attached to a 'ciass-in-itself,' understood as a collection of agents, but depends upon, and springs from, a relational system of material places occupied by particular agents."

However, in most criminological research, feminist inquiries into the police are absent. Most mainstream criminologists do not consider the patriarchal and heterosexist aspects of the police occupational culture (Corsianos, 2009; Martin and Jurik, 2007; Miller, Forest, and Jurik, 2004) and how officers depend on these to make decisions to act illegally and/or to defend their actions and identities. Feminist and critical examinations have found that masculine characteristics are assumed to be central to policing roles, are valued and rewarded, and are often exaggerated in terms of their applicability to the job (Corsianos, 2009; Martin and Jurik, 2007). Police work embodies "hegemonic masculinity" (Connell, 1995; Messerschmidt, 1993); the centrality of masculine traits become "naturalized" and accepted as "common sense" by both the police and the wider public.

With the exception of some feminist works, the literature to date largely overlooks the effects that these have on officers' understanding of their police roles, the policing system and the communities they serve, and their relationship to police corruption. Understanding all dimensions of the police culture are key to gaining more insight into police criminality as well as the gendered aspects of these behaviors and attitudes. The occupational culture proves to be much more relevant to officers' experiences and acceptance on the job (Van Wormer and Bartollas, 2000); and, as Crank (1998:5) states, "All areas of police work have meaning of some kind to cops, and as every reformer and chief who has sought to change any organization knows, these meanings tend to bind together in sentiments and values impossible to analytically separate and individually change."

POLICE CULTURE AND "THE BROTHERHOOD"

Female officers often experience pressure to conform to the patriarchal culture that encourages machismo and are often criticized for not possessing the perceived necessary "masculine" traits of aggressiveness, rationality, objectivity, and courageousness that are assumed to guarantee effectiveness for any crime-fighting police officer (Corsianos, 2009; Miller, 1999; Haar, 1997;

Martin, 1994, 1990, 1980; Charles, 1981). Dominant constructions of police officers that emerged with the creation of formal policing systems was that of a strong, tall, fearless, crime-fighting, heterosexual male. Women, regardless of sexual orientation, and queer men threaten this constructed "masculine" and "heterosexualized" image. The privileged gender roles within the police culture are informed by what Messerschmidt (2003, 1993), Fielding (1994), Connell (1995) and others refer to as "hegemonic masculinity."

For Orban (1998), female police officers adopted a code of behavior to prove their loyalty to the patriarchal police culture while minimizing their own personal identities. Women fought for acceptance by the "brotherhood" by trying to gain the trust of male co-workers and "prove themselves" to their male peers by demonstrating capability, competency, and loyalty. There was constant pressure to "become one of the boys," keep personal challenges such as child care quiet, and keep their personal sexual lives to themselves to avoid any rumors by their male peers. And many female officers adopt the language and mannerisms of male colleagues in order to become integrated into the culture and gain acceptance (McLean, 1997). Given the interconnectedness of "masculinity" and "being male" to the police culture, women are often viewed by both male officers and the wider public as inherently less able to perform particular police tasks that reflect the crime-fighting police model and better suited for social-service type functions (Heidensohn and Brown, 2000; Breci, 1997; Heidensohn, 1992; Bell, 1982; Drummond, 1976).

Evidence of the emphasis on masculinity and "men" is further seen in the particular definition of "physical strength" and its interconnectedness to the image of the police as "crime fighters" as well as the cultural value given to aggressive crime-control tactics. Many American agencies continue to use tests that place a strong emphasis on upper body strength that disproportionately discriminate against women (for example, pushups, scaling a six-foot wall, bench press) (National Center for Women and Policing, 2005; Harrington and Lonsway, 2004). But these tests do not measure police competency in day-to-day police activities. It can be argued that many officers on the job today would probably not pass these tests, perhaps because of weight gain, lack of exercise, age, and/or injury. Yet there is no evidence to suggest that they are less effective officers. The police culture, however, accepts these tests as appropriate and/or effective measures of police officer performance (Harrington and Lonsway, 2004), given the dominant constructions of the police. Interestingly, there remains support for these tests despite the fact that many departments have written policies that prohibit some of these physical activities, such as jumping over solid walls, or indicate that they are inadvisable (National Center for Women and Policing, 2003). Also, once hired, officers are no longer subject to routine physical testing and, as mentioned above, may very well no longer be able to meet these "standards." Yet, their ability to be "effective officers" is no longer questioned. In a 2001 U.S. study, 89 percent of sixty-two large police agencies used some form of physical agility testing as a condition for hiring, but there was little standardization with regard to the actual physical tests and the measurements used to receive a pass. And given the discriminatory emphasis on upper body strength and other gender biases in some police organizations, it is not surprising to see that departments that do not require physical testing as a condition for employment have 45 percent more women serving as sworn police officers (National Center for Women and Policing, 2003).

Individual male officers are more likely to be accepted into the "brotherhood" given their perceived gender status and conformity to gender-normative behaviors. As a category, male officers experience less pressure to prove to others that they are competent and effective police officers. If one male officer makes a mistake, then the individual is held responsible. But women, because of their perceived gender status, tend to experience increased pressure to prove themselves and gain acceptance by their peers (Orban, 1998; Jackson, 1997; Wexler and Logan, 1983). It is common for female officers to cite the negative attitudes of male officers as being the most significant problems for them while on the job (Independent Commission, 1991; Martin, 1980). Corsianos (2009), on the other hand, found that when there was an obvious visible presence of female officers resulting in several female partnerships "on the road" and/or "on the beat," women were less likely to experience the intense pressure to prove themselves as some women have experienced in smaller police agencies with little female representation. But this does not negate the gendered discrimination women officers experience as a result of their perceived gender status (Corsianos, 2009). Martin and Jurik (2007:68) suggest that within the culture of policing, female officers threaten male officers primarily for four reasons:

> In one of the few remaining occupations in which strength and physical ability occasionally are useful, women's presence implies either that the men's unique asset—physical strength—is irrelevant, or that a man who works with a woman will be at a disadvantage in a confrontation. Three other less frequently articulated concerns also support men's resistance to women: the belief that women are "mentally weaker," the view that women are unable to command public respect as officers, and the concern that "moral" women will break the code of silence and expose the men's illicit activities.

The culture of policing is gendered, sexualized, and racialized. Women of color experience both sexism and racism in the occupational culture of policing. They experience a "double marginality" and are subject to both internal and external sources of stress (Pogrebin, Dodge, and Chatman, 2000; McLean, 1997; Martin, 1994; Hurtado, 1989). They are subject to exclusion from the informal channels of support and information as well as ostracism and overt racial or sexist comments by white officers (Pogrebin, Dodge, and Chatman, 2000). Forms of exclusion include poor instruction communication, peer hostility and ostracism through the silent treatment, oversupervision, exposure to dangerous situations, and inadequate backup by male officers. They are also subjected to degrading stereotypes (Pogrebin, Dodge, and Chatman, 2000). Males, on the other hand, who represent identified visible minority groups do not challenge the masculine image of the police and align themselves with the dominant majority of white male officers (Martin, 1994). Both black male officers and white female officers are viewed as trading on their racial and gender solidarity with the higher status white male officers (Martin, 1994, 1992). Women of color are further subjected to minority community resentment by citizens who perceive the police as suspicious and not trustworthy. Given these experiences, it is not surprising to see that women of African descent leave the field of policing much more frequently in comparison to all other officers; on average, they leave by their fourth year of service (Dodge and Pogrebin, 2001). Morash and Haar (1995) report that interaction in patrol units between female and ethnic minority officers and white male officers continue to remain somewhat segregated.

Miller, Forest, and Jurik (2003) found that lesbian and gay officers expressed loyalty to the police organization and were committed to many of the traditional policing goals. Like other officers, they wanted to be recognized for their hard work and achievements. But lesbian officers were more likely than heterosexual females to "downplay" their sexual orientation and perform in more "masculine" ways to gain acceptance from peers. But homosexuality is perceived as a threat to group solidarity and to the overall police culture. Gay men who hide their sexual orientation often experience the pressure to "act straight" and to exaggerate normative verbal and physical heterosexual performances in order to fit in and not risk being discovered. Lesbians who do not hide their sexual orientation are perceived as being more competent because they are assumed to be "masculine" but are still subject to harassment and hostility given their status as "women" (Miller, Forest, and Jurik, 2004). Women officers, regardless of their sexual orientation, threaten the image of the police as "doing masculinity" and celebrating "maleness." Generally, female police officers have a less aggressive style than male officers and are better at deescalating potentially violent situations (Belknap and Shelley, 1993; Belknap, 1991; Grennan, 1987; Bell, 1982); they are more effective communicators and are more likely to show emotional support to victims of violence (Feinman, 1986; Homant and Kennedy, 1985; Kennedy and Homant, 1985; Price, 1974). But the police culture overlooks and/or undermines these traits in their commitment to viewing and maintaining policing in its traditional forms.

Indeed, the number of male police officers who are supportive of women officers today has grown significantly, but these men rarely challenge the dominant attitudes (Martin and Jurik, 2007). In one study, two-thirds of female officers experienced discrimination (Miller, Forest, and Jurik, 2004):

> Women perceived continued discrimination by colleagues, supervisors, and citizens in less overt form, including derogatory comments, inappropriate behaviors, and failure to take the women seriously. In the station house, frequent pranks, jokes, and comments that call attention to women's sexuality make it clear to women that they are "outsiders." For women of color and lesbians, harassment amplifies their outsider status. For example, lesbian women may be assumed to be masculine and therefore more competent than heterosexual women on the street, but are harassed due to their gender and heterosexual male officers' curiosity and hostility.

Units that become more "feminized" given the disproportionate representation of women become synonymous with "social work" for many male officers since they conflict with the image of the police as crime fighters, and in turn they may reject opportunities to work in these units. Miller and Hodge (2004) found this to be the case with Community Policing assignments. The gendering of units legitimizes the perceived distinction between "women's work" as "feminine" and "men's work" as "masculine" (Williams, 1989). And Grant (2000) suggests that male officers worry about the impact of women officers on the public's image of the police since many in the population continue to make generalizations of women as being more emotional and weaker.

The discrimination women officers have experienced has been well documented. They range from discriminatory policies and practices; sexist, heterosexist, and/or racist comments; sexual harassment and assault; intimidation; retaliation; derogatory comments made relating to law-enforcement/crime-fighting abilities; criticism regarding their physical strength, height, and/or the ability to protect themselves and other officers in physical confrontations with members of the public; chivalrous attitudes; pressure to prove themselves and conform to the status quo; and discrimination in hiring, position assignments, and promotions (Corsianos, 2009, 2004; Martin and Jurik, 2007; Harrington and Lonsway, 2004; Gerber, 2001; Heidensohn and Brown, 2000; Van Wormer and Bartollas, 2000; Martin, 1999, 1994, 1980; Miller, 1999; Nichols, 1995; Fielding, 1994; Belknap, 1991).

The police culture continues to be male dominated, and hegemonic masculinity and patriarchal values are embraced, which presents difficulties for many women trying to "fit in" (Orban, 1998; Fletcher, 1997; Martin and Jurik, 1996; Belknap, 1995; Martin, 1990). Also, women often experience a number of conflicts that include trying to assimilate and gain acceptance by their peers and, at the same time, not violate widely accepted gender norms.

This translates into a "no win" situation as women are either seen as not competent, not "aggressive enough," "trying to be aggressive" and "less feminine," or trying too hard to prove themselves.

Indeed, gender is performative (Butler, 1989), and gender is at the same time constructed and always under construction. De Lauretis (1987) asserts that gender is the product of social technologies that include daily practices and institutionalized discourses and forms of popular culture. De Lauretis uses the Foucaudian term *technology* to explain the power dynamics in how gendered social relations are reiterated and reinforced. One can argue that policing is a technology of gender in that masculinity is reinforced and promoted in its many discursive cultural spaces. The stereotype of policing as promoting masculinity continues to be a central identity to the police culture, and "feminine" characteristics, although central to the job of policing, are not recognized, dismissed, marginalized, and/or appropriated. Traditional images and activities associated with policing are authenticated, as seen in the continued support for current police roles and discretionary powers, whereas activities and units that have become more "feminized" over the years tend to be less valued. Policing is assumed to be "masculine" and "naturalized" as "male." Police officers "perform" in masculine ways in a number of contexts, including how they talk, walk, position their body, and in the use of facial expressions, decision-making abilities, and in how they frame their conversations with others. Performing masculinity is at times obvious and direct, but it can also be subtle and insidious. One might assume that the increased visibility of women in policing since the 1970s (approximately 1 percent versus 13 percent today) might lead some to question the image of the police as innately "male," but, in actuality it has done little to change dominant images. Female officers are often "seen" as more suitable for units that bring them in contact with youth offenders or women or in roles that are believed to be comparable to "social work."

Women officers threaten to expose the artificial gender boundaries assumed to be "natural" and "fixed," and therefore, the police culture operates to maintain women's marginal status. Despite the "successes" of some female officers, including those who have become chiefs of police over the years (Harrington and Lonsway, 2004; Schulz, 2004), police culture has not been challenged in meaningful ways. In order to redefine this culture, one must be open to accepting diverse gendered meanings of policing. Women must be "seen" as a natural part of police cultures and all gender categories, including, for instance, "women," "men," "gay," "lesbian," "bisexual," "transgendered," and "queer" must be made permeable. These identity categories must be subject to constant critical evaluation. As Butler asserts, the category "woman" must be continuously scrutinized because the articulation of all women being the same "invariably produces factionalizations and exclusions" (1993:15). Additionally, the perceived interconnectedness between "masculine" performances and "men" and "feminine" performances and "women" must be recognized as conditional rather than natural and fixed.

The more "feminized" units are often understood within the police culture to be "less legitimate" and subject to budget cuts in comparison to hegemonic crime-control operations. "Feminized" units such as community policing and educational units are often denounced, and "real" men don't willingly choose to work in them. "Doing masculinity" is not fixed, but there are indeed dominant stereotypes of what "masculinity" means or should mean in policing. Additionally, male officers may identify with a number of different traits—some masculine and some feminine—although most would probably not openly admit to the latter in this way. And at times, officers may be vulnerable and show particular emotions that contrast with the more assertive celebration of masculinity (for example, being aggressive, confident, competitive). These, however, are not acknowledged as the popular image of the police remains interconnected with dominant patriarchal ideologies.

The history of police culture has been constructed around a male-centered canon. The narratives constructed to inform us about police officers contribute to one's knowledge of the police and are full of male bravado. These further serve to maintain and reinforce a sense of male comradeship. Unlike other professions, policing and the military remain overtly masculine, and this makes it more "necessary" to dominate and exclude women from gaining full membership because of the perceived threats women bring to the image and function of the police. As mentioned earlier, according to Martin and Jurik (2007:68), "In one of the few remaining occupations in which strength and physical ability occasionally are useful, women's presence implies either that the men's unique asset—physical strength—is irrelevant, or that a man who works with a woman will be at a disadvantage in a confrontation."

But what is not recognized here is that even the notion of "physical strength" is narrowly defined; it is socially constructed to reflect patriarchal ideologies relating to the "forms" of strengths that become valued and prioritized. The historical formations of policing are intertwined with dominant ideologies relating to gender as well as 'race', class, and sexuality that continue to be inscribed and reiterated in police identities today. Despite some increase in the representation of women and other minority groups, the majority of officers in most police departments continue to be white, male, heterosexual, and represent the lower middle class (Travis and Langworthy, 2008; Martin and Jurik, 2007; Hickman and Reaves, 2006; Miller, Forest, and Jurik, 2004). The degree to which gendered meanings in policing have remained intact despite some increased visibility in the diversity of the personal identities of officers illustrates the power of ideology and the processes in conforming within the police culture.

HOW DO OFFICERS DEPEND ON THE MASCULINIST POLICE CULTURE TO PRESERVE AND DEFEND THEIR ACTIONS AND IDENTITIES AS THEY RELATE TO POLICE CORRUPTION?

Particular forms of police corruption are both socially and morally controversial, but the complexities of the police culture provide insight into the interplay of social boundaries of "appropriate" police behaviors and the effects these have on how police construct their identity. Most of the officers who shared their stories of police abuses provided justifications and rationalizations for their own as well as other officers' criminal conduct.

■■■

Their narratives serve as powerful examples of how police justify their criminal behavior and/or that of other officers, particularly as it relates to the masculinist police culture where officers are expected to protect "the brotherhood" and condone corruption, particularly when victims are not perceived to be "legitimate." In the interviews some were referred to as "criminals," "scumbags," "undesirables," and "assholes" who were deserving of the officers' criminal actions against them; and, at times, evidence of "noble cause corruption" or the "Dirty Harry syndrome" can be seen in officers' justifications of the end result despite the illegal means. Their accounts further provide evidence of how hegemonic masculinity presents endless possibilities for officers to abuse their powers and act illegally, and in their level of involvement. Interestingly, the majority of male officers discussed police corruption cases that involved two or more officers working together in some capacity either by being aware of the misconduct and condoning it by keeping it to themselves (even in one case where the officer requested to be transferred out of the unit) or by participating directly in some manner. Only four male officers discussed their own criminal involvement where it was done secretly without others' awareness and/or participation. The three female officers, however, worked individually, keeping their illegal conduct to themselves as perceptions of risk were deemed too great if others were involved, particularly male officers.

At times, justifications for police abuse of powers related to helping officers gain financially and/or to maintain some level of job security. For example:

Male #2

Went to this alarm call at a jewelry store once. It was many years ago, and it was before all of the high-tech cameras and safes. My partner who was also my friend was on scene first, and I was backing him up. The place was trashed. Display cases smashed and jewelry all over the place. It was early in the morning and it would take the owner of the store some time to get there. Dispatch advised us that the owner had received a substantial amount of diamonds that day and wanted us to check to see if they were taken; they were under a hidden subfloor. Sure enough the crooks had found the hidden subfloor as well, but in their haste to flee they dropped diamonds every-where. They were all over the floor mixed in with all the broken glass. I must have counted at least a dozen of them. My friend secured the store, and I patrolled the immediate area for potential suspects. By the time I returned the owner had arrived and, naturally, he was visibly upset. My friend was doing the report and the area was secure, so I left to continue my shift. The next day when I arrived at work I looked at the previous evening's incidents. I saw the report that my friend had filed and noticed that the report stated all the diamonds were stolen. I was shocked. I know for a fact that there were at least a dozen pieces left. But I never confronted him about it. You just don't do that sort of thing. I used to hear stories and gossip about so and so doing this or so and so was on the take, but I never thought it would be somebody I called my friend. I mean he just didn't strike me as that type of guy. Oh well, shows you what a good judge of character I am. We still continued to be friends; we had to, I depended on my job. And at the end of the day it's about coming home after the shift and we all relied on each other for that.

Male #5

My partner was a real techie kind of guy. He was good with computers, software, networking and stuff like that. We became good friends and kept in touch even when he went to the XXXX for a few years but then came back. Well, he had an interesting scam going on. A lot of the burglaries occur during the day when the homeowners are at work. So somebody breaks in, the alarm goes off, and the bad guy splits. We show up on scene, enter the house, and secure the premises and wait for the homeowners to arrive, which can sometimes take up to an hour. Well, what my partner started to do was install spyware onto people's computers. The software would track and record keystrokes, passwords, and stuff like that. He was able to gather all kinds of info—banking info, account numbers, credit card information. I never asked what he did with all of that; I really didn't want to know, but he always threw money my way. You could say he wanted to make sure I was happy.

Male #17

When I was on the force the city had a contract with a couple of towing companies. When you arrived at an accident scene you were supposed to call contract towing. Well, a few of the guys were getting kickbacks from a different company to take drivers away from the city's towing companies; they towed and did body work, that's where the real money is made—it's with the auto body repair to the vehicle. The guys would get to an accident scene and call the other towing company via cell phone, and once the car owner and tow truck company had an agreement, the city's tow company could do nothing about it. We would get memos about calling city contract tow companies all the time. It got so bad that all of the city's tow companies got scanners and tried to get to the accident scenes first. It put a small dent but it wasn't enough; you see, the contracted towing companies were also used for any and all city-related towing issues. They ended up being spread too thin and couldn't respond to the accidents fast enough, even with the police scanners.

Male #18

What you might call corruption or abuse of power, I called justice. Over the years I spent my time in the XXXX where I specialized in accident investigation. Due to the nature of my work I became very familiar with some of the insurance representatives. I became close friends with this one particular fellow whose brother owned a scrap yard. I used to go to the scrap yard from time to time where we'd all just hang out and, to make a long story short, we started talking about what happens to the cars that are totaled and·written off. My friend, who was the insurance representative, told me that the vehicles' VIN is worth a lot of money if you know how to manipulate the system. You see, the VIN wasn't tracked so the insurance companies and the registration offices didn't know that the vehicles had been totaled. These databases did not interface with other databases. Let's say your car is stolen, after a certain time frame the insurance buys you another car of equal value, or your car is totaled and the insurance buys you another car. Nobody in registration knows what happened to your car, and if you go to another insurance company to insure your totaled car they won't know either. You can then say that it was stolen and have them get you a replacement or you take the cash value of the car. Unbelievable. I know, I know, what an oversight on the part of the industry this was. And when you insure a car, the insurance didn't take any pictures of the car; all they wanted was a sales slip, transfer of ownership signed over, and the vehicles' VIN. He hypothetically said that if we take one of the VINs of a scrapped car, produce a sales receipt, and have the ownership transferred we could theoretically insure that car, which really didn't exist other than the car's VIN. Then after a few months or so we could file a stolen police report and then be compensated by the insurance company. One could take the cash value or get a replacement car, whereby you then sell that car and cash in. Even though all this talk was, as my friend put it, "hypothetical," I knew what his real motives were. He wanted me in on his scheme so that I could file the police reports or run the VINs and make sure they were clean. Some time passed and basically I called him up and told him I was interested. We didn't want too many people involved so that we could ensure secrecy, so I ended up going first. We found a half decent car in the junkyard and we took the VIN and produced a sales receipt and transfer of ownership from the junkyard to me. I insured the car through my friend's insurance coverage. After a few months, I called the police and reported the car stolen. I took the replacement value and as such I was given a real car from the insurance company. I kept the car for an-other—I don't remember how many months—and then I legitimately sold it. It was unbelievable, very lucrative. This went on for some time, but more people started getting involved. I got out after a few years; I made my money and ended up retiring soon after. Well, I was getting a little uncomfortable with how big it was growing; people were getting really greedy and reckless. That's how people get caught. And management will sink you to protect themselves. Eventually, the insurance companies started to catch on, and new procedures and laws were put in place to prevent this type of fraud. I don't feel any regret over what I did. I've been screwed over so many times by insurance companies that I thought it was just payback. I know a lot of people, and I am sure you do as well, who have been screwed over by the insurance companies.

Male #9

We had this one guy who had a brother in the alarm business. His brother would install these alarms in people's homes. The area was a well-to-do area with a lot of expensive homes and businesses. So the brother had the inside scoop on when people would go on vacation and what kind of stuff they had in their homes. When they targeted a house, the alarm guy would purposely trip the alarm. His brother would respond to the call and call it in as a false alarm. Meanwhile the alarm guy, his brother, was in the house cleaning out the place. Then when he was done he would set off the alarm again. The brother, who was circling around, would respond and call it in as a legit alarm call. They were so successful that they started to expand. They had a few cops and a few other tech guys in on it. They had connections with guys who would buy all the stolen stuff as well. It went on for a few years, but then I heard they stopped because it started to get risky; a couple of people started asking some questions and you just don't need that kind of attention.

Male #10

They can have all the rules and Internal Affairs units they want; police corruption will always exist. I was a cop for a long time and saw a lot of things. The guys accepting the bribes and kickbacks were always there. Some guys couldn't handle what was going on and asked for transfers—like that's going to help—others ended up quitting. The reality is that most cops just turned a blind eye to it. They didn't want to be labeled a troublemaker or get a reputation as "not being a team player." I guess in some ways it's not that much different than other types of jobs. Each of us is tested early on in our careers. The other guys want to see how you will react in certain situations. They want to see if you're one of them; what you're made of. For me, it was early in my career. I went to a sudden death call. I was the more junior officer so I got the call assigned to me. I remember responding to an apartment complex where an elderly male had passed away. I investigated the scene and determined it to be a sudden death. I sat in the apartment preparing the report; fairly straightforward. The deceased had no next of kin and no acquaintances. As we made arrangements to have the house secured, two members of my team showed up and helped me with some of the loose ends and the report. They ended up conducting a more thorough search of the premises and discovered a couple of coffee cans full of cash totaling almost $30,000 dollars. They said that since there was no next of kin we should all split the money three ways; their reasoning was why should the government take the money, and that no one's going to miss it. I felt very uncomfortable with the whole thing and wished they hadn't shown up. But after a few minutes of going back and forth we all agreed to keep the money. I was nervous as hell, but, hey, we were talking 10,000 in one night; that was hard to walk away from.

Male #29

This cop's uncle had an auto body shop and was doing really well. Most of our guys would go to him and get our cars repaired. I heard that he used to steal cars for his uncle and then they'd ship them overseas to Russia, I think it was. The cop would pay off some of the guys at the dealerships in exchange for info about who was driving what kind of car and where they lived, and he would then make a list of a few cars and steal them. These were all high-end cars, not the cheap ones.

Male #30

I worked with a guy in the XXXX who I know was involved with some real shady people. We would go to certain areas within our boundary where he would meet people and excuse himself for a few minutes. He would then return as if nothing happened, and we'd continue walking the beat. This went on at least four to five times a shift. I thought for sure he was selling drugs or something like that. I found out later through another friend of mine that knew him that he was in fact a bookie. Apparently he was making really good money and had a reputation for collecting. He would use the police computers to track down people that owed him money. During one of our shifts, we cornered two guys that were known drug dealers. My partner arrested them even though we didn't have probable cause, handcuffed them, and searched them. We found a good quantity of cash and drugs, but I was still wondering how we were going to justify the search. Don't get me wrong, those drug dealers were going to go down one way or another. The next thing I knew my partner unhandcuffed them and told them to get lost; these clowns were stunned, as was I. He then handed me some of the drug money and said nothing. I took the money, and we finished out the night. I came to realize that he used the drug money and the cash to cover some of the bets. What's funny is that to look at him you'd never suspect this guy in a million years.

Male #3

Police corruption, sure it happens. I mean, cops are still part of the human race. It happens in many ways. I've seen kickbacks, theft, assaults, you name it. Don't get me wrong, we had a lot of good guys in all, but it happened. When you've been around as long as I had you see a lot of things. After awhile it gets confusing. You start to justify your actions. Crossing the line is a gradual thing. It's done in small increments. It happens over time. I remember how I was first slowly drawn in. I was on probation still, and because I could speak several languages I was posted in an area where my additional languages could be an asset. I was assigned to foot patrol that night. You walk the beat and talk to the locals and make inroads in the community. My training officer was also part of the XXXX and knew most of the bar owners. We went to several places that night, talking to the owners. I found out later that night that he was collecting the monthly kickback for the guys. It was all business, and essentially he said that the local bar owners were involved in local gambling, prostitution, and drugs. Our higher ups and community expect results through arrests. The criminals also expect results. Criminals want to make as much money as possible while minimizing the risks. One way they do that is they pay off the cops for protection with the understanding that the cops will make arrests from time to time. The criminals will coordinate when and where the arrests will happen. Everybody wins, my training officer used to say. We make the arrests, which satisfies the higher ups and community; the criminals get protection and stability in their operations; and we make a little extra on the side—makes sense; everybody's happy. For the guys that didn't want no part of it, you simply kept your mouth shut. You didn't want to rock the boat since you know a lot of things can happen to you if you did. Some guys had their tires slashed or their cars trashed. The biggest fear every cop has is not having backup. That can play with one's head to the point where you can't take the stress. This job was about being a team player, period. You might not like what some people do and that's fine. The unwritten code is, don't rock the boat. If you do then you're on your own. I remember when some of the guys on XXXX sent a message to one of the new guys who was causing trouble. The new guy needed backup, and the other cars would make themselves unavailable or be slow to respond. It only took a few calls to drive the message home; he eventually smartened up.

■■■

The following two excerpts were from officers who had serious concerns about the behavior they witnessed; Male #12 asked to be transferred out of the unit because he did not want to work with people who were involved in corruption, but he condoned it to the extent that he never reported it. Also, Male #4 did not approve of the misconduct but felt he had to ignore it to maintain job security. In both cases, the culture of secrecy was maintained.

Male #12

We were tasked with eliminating all the illegal gambling within our precinct. It was occurring in a lot of the so-called community coffee shops in the back rooms. We started raiding all the coffee shops in the area, and we were getting good tips on their locations and when they gambled. After a few months we pretty much cleaned house. And we were recommended for a commendation for doing such a good job. One night we headed out to celebrate after work. We ended up going to an after-hours bar that was just outside our jurisdiction. The owner, who I will call Mr. X, put us in a private backroom and provided us with food, booze, pretty ladies serving us. He treated us like we were kings. My partner and I were taken aback with what was happening, but we went along with it. Everyone else was having a good time so we didn't want to spoil it. A few hours later our supervisor wanted us to all meet at a park that we go to after work. So, we all met there. We were all a little wasted. He gave us the "good work boys" speech for all the good work closing down the gambling places, and then he handed us each an envelope with some money in it. I was confused at first. It finally dawned on me; we were closing down Mr. X's competition. I gave the money to my partner and left. I asked for a transfer the next morning and it was approved. I didn't want any part of this. I kept my mouth shut about this; I certainly wanted no trouble.

Male #4

My first day on the job and I'm with my training officer doing the night shift. We were doing radar enforcement in a less busy part of town. We were pulling cars over, and I was told to run the plates while he spoke with the drivers. I was told that if they had numerous speeding tickets to flash the headlights. We must have pulled over fifteen to twenty cars that night and most had speeding tickets, but he let them all off with a warning. Of course, I came to find out that he made several hundred dollars in the process. It was cheaper to pay off the cop than get another speeding ticket. He offered me a cut of the action, but I refused. I was still on probation, and didn't want to stir up shit. I relied on my fellow officers for backup; last thing I wanted to do was be a snitch. I wouldn't last a week on the streets without backup. So I just watched shit happen and didn't say a thing or sometimes I would just drive off and say that I wasn't there. I came to accept this stuff over the years; it was about survival.

■■■

Chappell and Piquero (2004) applied social learning theory to police misconduct in their survey of officers working for the Philadelphia Police Department and found that males and officers with more tenure were more likely to have citizen complaints, as were officers who considered misconduct to be less serious and anticipated less punishment for these types of behavior. Although Hickman's study (2008) examined the effects of officer cynicism on police problem behavior, he also found that male officers and officers with greater years of service had higher levels of police problem behavior. According to Prenzler (2009:24), "Material rewards from corruption are justified as compensation for undervalued work." But, also "victims of police abuses are characterized as deserving *social garbage*" (ibid.). Also, Goldschmidt et al. found that most officers felt that unlawful behaviors such as unlawful stops, searches, arrests, planting of evidence, false report writing and perjured testimony were a necessary part of the job, served the greated good, and/or were perceived as helping officers on a personal and/or professional level. Additionally, officers suggested that there would be negative consequences if they were completely honest in their day-to-day tasks. However, what is not discussed is how officers become part of a masculinist work culture where one is expected, for instance, to condone violent acts against "civilians" and protect "the brotherhood." For example:

Male #21

I don't think most cops have a problem with other officers roughing up criminals or adding trumped-up charges. Most of them were disillusioned with the system. They felt that criminals get off too easy. It's hard to be impartial when you deal with the victims day in and day out and know that there's not a whole lot of justice for them. Some officers resort to just giving the criminal a few extra beatings. Others might plant drugs or drug paraphernalia so that they get more jail time. Others coerce witnesses to embellish the facts so they can get him on more charges. I've seen it happen time and time again and do agree with the practice to some extent. If you are dealing with a known scumbag, who cares. They deserve what they get. Why do you think they have cameras in police booking rooms? Sure, I've heard politicians say that the cameras were installed to protect the police from being falsely accused of things, but the truth is it was to protect the criminals. The cameras were supposed to be a deterrent for what the police did. But like anything else in life people find ways around these things. Most officers just started giving the beatings before they got to the station. Whatever the reason was for the initial arrest, an additional charge of "resisting arrest" was always added. That way it muddied the waters and protected the officer from any wrongdoing; it was the officer's word against the suspect's word. And by having multiple charges you hedged your bets that he would strike a plea bargain in exchange for having some others dropped.

Male #27

I'd say most of the cops I knew had at one time or another given a criminal a tune up or did some favor for someone. It's just how things worked. We worked in close proximity to some real assholes, and once and awhile you need to play their game. If they try to assault you, well then you put them in the hospital. There are a million different ways to screw someone over; it's just that simple. Like one guy who would do vehicle stops on motorists talking to prostitutes—he would tell them that he was going to send a squad car to their residence to confirm their identity. The johns, who were family guys, always panicked and begged him not to do it. You can't imagine their fear and desperation. This guy loved tormenting them and would eventually give them a bogus ticket and demand payment that instant. And the johns would pay the so-called fine with the understanding that the ticket would go away. The officer would then take the ticket back and tell them he would take care of it.

Male #22

I responded to a call—a burglary suspect—who was being pursued by foot patrol units through this residential neighborhood. He eventually was caught by foot patrol, and the two officers needed some transportation to the station, so I gave them a ride. I knew one of the officers; we had worked on a few things together in the past. Overall, good guy, hard working. The female officer sat up front while the suspect and the officer, who I knew, sat in the back. Well, the suspect got a fairly good beating on the way to the station while in the back. I was a little worried because I didn't know the female officer really well. Just before we pulled up to the station the officer in the back "reminded" us that the guy resisted arrest, and so when the sergeant later asked about the suspect's injuries, the female officer jumped in and said, "He resisted arrest." It was a textbook answer; she didn't even flinch when she said it. I think that she was okay with it. I remember later at one of our tailgate parties she made a comment about that arrest. She said something to the effect that that will teach him from running away from us again. See what I mean, we stuck together; we had to even if we didn't always see eye to eye.

■■■

Police culture often condones police corruption, such as excessive use of force. At times, the "nature" of police work conflicts with moral ideologies and norms of behavior, thus police work can involve a transgression of socially accepted boundaries and a threat to the moral order (Dick, 2005:1368). Bittner (1970) argues police work is tainted because police officers "in the natural course of their duties inflict harm" (Dick, 2005:1367). And police concepts of "appropriate" police behavior may conflict with those of the general public. While police may have different understandings of what constitutes police corruption, they are aware of the importance of promoting and maintaining an overall positive image of the police to the public (see chapter 2), and herein exists a conflict of identity that forces police officers to constantly engage in identity protection. Officers protect their individual identity through "reframing—where the meaning attached to a specific occupation is transformed; recalibrating—where the tasks that constitute the role are re-categorized so as to emphasize the more acceptable or palatable tasks; and refocusing—where an attempt is made to shift attention to non-stigmatized aspects of the role" (Dick, 2005: 1369). Excerpts from the interviews included:

Male #7

I was in the XXXX at the time. Anyway a few of the guys were involved with protecting escorts, and over time I got involved too; it was good money on the side. The guys who weren't involved in it never said a thing. They just pretended it never happened. That's how it was. I remember Internal Affairs trying to investigate some of the allegations made against us. What a joke. We knew half the guys in Internal Affairs, and they were just going through the motions, making it look like they gave a shit. I mean what was the big deal anyway. If anything, those ladies were a lot safer with us than the losers they had before. Of course, we were the ones who arrested all of those losers. You could say we had the market cornered.

Male #13

My old partner, and a couple of others, were involved in selling drugs through an escort agency that I think he was involved in; he may have been a partner or something, and the girls would sell to the clients. The drugs came from other criminals. The guys would confiscate the drugs from arrests and not turn them in, and sometimes they would steal them from the evidence locker. They were making a ton. No, I didn't think there was anything wrong with this; they provided better job security for the girls and got paid better. It made sense, and I got a little something from time to time for helping out with some information. It made sense. Let's look at who the real crooks are really, the guys on Wall Street who steal billions from honest, hard-working Americans; they're the ones we should worry about. We were the good guys trying to make an honest living, but the public doesn't understand a lot of the time.

Male #14

One guy had a good thing going with some of the night clubs in the area. He was paid big bucks from this business guy to harass and try to close down competing night clubs. He would provide some underage street kids with false IDs and send them into the targeted clubs. Once inside, the street kids would throw away the false IDs and order a few drinks. He would then show up with a few of the other guys and do a liquor license inspection and randomly ask for people's ID and then make his way to the street kids. Of course, they didn't have it, so he'd ID and write up the night club for serving minors. A few write-ups later and the owner's license was in jeopardy. I think that he was responsible for closing down a few clubs and caused the owner of one of the buildings to go under because he couldn't lease the location to anyone. I didn't care because in my eyes it was all just business. I mean if you look at what police do on a daily basis it's just business. We would feed the criminal justice machine with criminals. Look how many people have jobs because of the police. We'd bring arrests and convict them and they'd let them out only for the system to start again. I remember how I was going to get rid of crime when I first joined; the dinosaurs used to tell me, "You aren't going to change a thing because the machine needs to be fed." I didn't understand it back then but I started to very quickly. And I also saw how the law worked against us in favor of criminals. My only concern became to finish my shift alive and go home to my family.

Male #31

I'd tag cars for tow and then call my buddies' tow truck company to come tow it, and they'd give me some cash for the business. We were required to use the contracted tow company, but if the car you needed a tow for was blocking or impeding traffic and was a safety issue you had to call for a contract tow first, but, if another tow truck arrived on scene first then you could use them. So that's how I got around using my buddies' company; I'd call them on my cell and there they'd be. This was easy money; besides, everybody I knew was doing something to make a little extra here and there. I had illegally parked cars towed and got paid for it, big deal. I didn't falsify records, didn't hurt anyone. And don't tell me that the city officials didn't get any kickbacks from the successful bidder for the city's towing contract.

■■■

Police officers have the power to redefine and contest the meaning of their behavior despite dominant external constructions, such as those by the media. Thus, following publicized cases of police corruption (for example, after the Amadou Diallo case or the Rampart Division scandal), officers often absolve themselves of any wrongdoing by framing their own actions or those of other officers within discourses of "danger" and "risk." For instance, in the Diallo case, four male officers fired their weapons forty-one times at an unarmed man who was reaching for his wallet and subsequently killed him. It was not uncommon to hear officers describe the case as "unfortunate" but to also "justify" the officers' behaviors given the "dangerous area" the officers were working in, and that the man apparently matched the description of a serial rapist whom the police were searching for at the time.

Similarly, in the Rampart Division scandal, despite the number of crimes committed by many officers (see chapter 2), in police circles these incidents were framed within similar discourses in which the officers were described as working in "dangerous," "high crime" areas with "risky" populations, and where the common perception was that officers were tired of dealing with the same "criminals" over and over again as a result of a broken system that either sent convicted persons to unsatisfactory prison terms and/or released them far too early. The interviews revealed that officers involved in drug corruption did not view themselves, or were not viewed by other officers, as corrupt because they were dealing with "criminals."

Male #15

Yeah, guys were involved in stuff, but I didn't see it as corrupt. They stole from criminals, not law-abiding citizens. Let's just say they'd pay known drug dealers and scumbags visits in the early morning and rob them and make it look like a home invasion. It was great, they didn't know who they were because they wore disguises, and they just thought they were being robbed. The boys kept the money and sold the guns and drugs. And sometimes they would pay off informants with the drugs they'd stolen; actually, their tips would sometimes lead to bigger criminals. I know some people just can't understand this, but they should walk a day in our shoes. They expected us to fight crime and criminals but sometimes we had the laws working against us. But, what's important here is that their tips sometimes led to the bigger criminals.

Male #19

We had the highest arrest rate, and the XXXX was real proud of this. He pretty much let us do what we wanted as long as we got the arrests. We would raid crack houses and keep some of the drugs we found; small-time stuff, and we'd use those drugs to pay off informants. It worked like a charm. Sometimes on a raid, if we came across a guy who was a real asshole, a criminal, we would just plant more drugs on him to up the charges. Or we'd plant some drugs on all the druggies we found in the crack house just to make the numbers look good. Sometimes we'd do vehicle stops of known drug dealers and plant drugs in their cars and arrest everyone in the car. I didn't have a problem with it at all because all of them had a record; they were what I'd call the undesirables. Sometimes, unfortunately, you had to break the rules to get results. The job was at times unpredictable; that could place you in a difficult situation leading to difficult decisions. But as far as I was concerned we were putting away criminals.

Male #20

In my opinion they were criminals and had no rights. Why should I risk my life trying to catch these guys with what they paid us? If you got hurt and ended up disabled or something like that; well, the disability benefits are just as bad. Why should anyone take those kinds of risks when the reward is minimal. I liked catching the drug dealers and sometimes ripping them off of money and drugs because they had to come up with the money and the lost revenue to their suppliers. Most of the suppliers would not believe them— that cops stole their shit. I mean, most of them probably thought that the dealer just consumed the goods for themselves, and, well, the punishment that the dealers got was more severe than what they'd get from the courts.

Male #11

Some of the guys were involved with trafficking drugs. They were in the XXXX and would shakedown the small-time dealers and steal their stuff and money. Then they'd sell it back to the drug dealers. What an operation; after awhile I heard they were on the payroll of a pretty major drug dealer in the area. The dealer would pay the cops to scare away the competition. They'd get the inside scoop on all the buys and then they'd coordinate these huge successful raids. They even got awards and commendations for their hard work. Last I heard was they retired and were living the good life.

Male #26

The worst I saw was cops planting drugs on criminals; you know, we're talking career criminals. No one worried about the criminals complaining because they were always complaining about someone, always accusing you of doing something to them. It was the same story over and over; it didn't matter how nice or how fair you were to them. It got to the point where you just expected to hear shit like that. They would say that "it's not mine" or "I don't know where that came from," "I just have no idea." I was getting sick and tired of the merry-go-round justice system and being accused of stuff I didn't even do. So some guys would plant stuff on them to get them to confess or to be an informant. Besides, no one took their accusations seriously any- way; no one really worried about someone believing them. I mean these were criminals with long records who did some really screwed-up stuff. The law can be very frustrating as most victims of crime know. I think criminals have too many rights, and the victims have no rights. I know this frustrated a lot of the guys on the force; it bothered me.

■■■

The guilty officers are often constructed by other officers as "noble" for attempting to deal with "undesirables" outside the legal system; that is, by using illegal means (Pollock, 2007; Crank and Caldero, 2004; Harrison, 1999). In the New York case involving Norman Batista and Jose Polanco, Skolnick (2002) reported the following:

> Polanco, who was given immunity to testify, said he had flushed all his drugs down the toilet when he'd heard the police pounding on the door. By doing so, he had undercut any criminal case that might be made against him or the buyer, since neither had any drugs in their possession and the police had not witnessed a sale. (After searching the apartment, the police could find only a minute amount of cocaine residue on the tip of a screwdriver.) Polanco testified that he and the drug buyer . . . were ordered to their knees and searched. Then, he testified, the police began to beat them and told them to shut up and take the beating and not to scream. Polanco, an experienced drug seller with the sturdy build of a defensive back, testified that he had complied. He also testified that he could hear loud cries of pain as the buyer, Norman Batista, was further beaten. Polanco and Batista curled into fetal positions to protect themselves; for this reason, neither could later on identify which officers had administered the blows and the kicks. After being taken into custody, Batista experienced severe pain for several hours, and the police offered to cut him loose. He refused their offer and was eventually transported to an emergency room at Metropolitan Hospital. The emergency room physician found that Batista had seven broken ribs, four on one side and three on the other, where he had been kicked while lying on the floor. Batista spent the next six days in the hospital with additional injuries to his chest, sternum, cheek, testicles, and knees. The doctor was shocked by Batista's condition. He also didn't believe that Batista had resisted arrest—no charges were ever filed—and alerted a friend who was an assistant DA in the Manhattan District Attorney's Office. . . . But, Skolnick (2002) further reported that during the verdict, police officers filled the court room to support their fellow officers. "In their view, a drug dealer and a buyer had frustrated good cops by disposing all of the drugs. Since the criminals could not legally be punished, the police had administered a well deserved beating, something the police watching from the gallery could easily imagine having done themselves."
>
> The Mollen Commission (1994) also found that police brutality was influenced by pressures for summary punishment—or, "street justice." Officers report being frustrated with the courts and public prosecutors are cynical about the legal protections made available for defendants. Officers find it acceptable to assume the roles of "judge, jury and executioner" under the utilitarian philosophy that excuses "some" harms if outweighed by "good" outcomes. (Pollock, 2007)

Examples of this were seen in the comments made by officers #15, 19, 20, 21, 22, 26, and 27. Additional examples are seen below, in which officers describe the beatings administered by another officer as a form of "street justice." The interviewed officers justified these kinds of behavior even though in the first example below the officer initially did not condone the abuse.

Male #1

I remember this one time when I was still a rookie. I was working with my training officer who was a dick. He liked to get physical with his arrests and liked being the judge, jury, and executioner, if you know what I mean. He always used to say, "They had it coming." Anyway, getting back to my story, we responded to an accident. It was Saturday night and witnesses said one of the drivers appeared to be intoxicated. We got on scene and it was a mess. Both cars were totaled. One of the cars was a minivan with four people—two of which were children. The other car had a single male occupant who was pissed out of his mind. He smelled like a brewery. Fortunately the kids weren't hurt. After talking with everyone involved and the witnesses around, the guy who was pissed crossed the center lane and hit the minivan head on. I tell you it was a miracle that no one was killed. So we arrest the driver, and we put him in the back of the car. The suspect was a repeat DUI offender— no surprise. My partner asked me to drive, and he got in the back seat with the suspect. I knew something was going down. There was no reason for my partner to be sitting in the back; our suspect was handcuffed, cooperating, and our police car had a protective Plexiglas screen. As I started to make my way to the station my partner tells me to take the side streets and to go slow. I turned into a side street, and my partner started beating on the suspect. He was hitting him everywhere, especially on his thighs. The suspect was screaming and begging him to stop. He was then begging me to stop my partner. But my partner was in a rage and kept on beating him. Anyway, it took us about ten minutes to get to the station. My partner told him that if he said anything about what just happened that he'd regret it and to say that his injuries were from the accident. The suspect agreed, and we booked him without incident. My partner never said a word to me for the rest of the shift, and I didn't say anything either. It was only when we were walking to our cars in the parking lot that he talked to me about it. He said that the suspect had it coming and that he will think twice about drinking and driving again, that the suspect could have killed that family, and that the parents would appreciate us giving him a beating. I was new at the time, and I remember being taken aback by what had happened. It bothered me for a long time. But you know, over time, I came to see what my partner meant. He really could have killed someone, and then what do you tell the family that has lost a loved one forever.

Male #6

I was assigned to the booking room; the suspects are searched here and assigned to a cell. Anyway, I was working with two other guys one evening when two of our officers brought in a suspect. And while we were going through our procedures the suspect head butted the officer in the head and broke his nose. He was subdued and taken to one of the cells. The suspect now faced additional charges of assaulting police and resisting arrest. Anyway, later that evening the officer that had his nose broken had returned to the station and wanted payback. The sergeant who I was working with asked me to get the booking tape. You see we tape all the suspects entering the station and make notations of any injuries. It's a record of their physical condition while they are in our custody. The sergeant took the VHS tape and erased all the bookings from the point where the assault occurred to the present and noted it in the journal as a defect in the tape. He let the officer in the guy's cell, and he went to town with the guy. He got hurt pretty good. The injuries he sustained were entered in the log as a result of the suspect resisting arrest after assaulting the officer. Although the evidence of assaulting police was erased on the tape the suspect was still convicted of it anyway, and he got a beating as well. I thought the suspect got what he deserved, and I had no problem with it. If it happened to me I would have done the same thing. I think it sends a message to them; it lets them know they must be respectful, we are the police. We had to protect each other because no one else would. People try to kill you, assault you, sue you, slander you, get you fired. It really was us versus them out there. The public really don't understand what we do; they think it's easy doing what we do. So we had to depend on each other, protect each other because no one else would.

Male #8

I was working with my partner one evening when we got a call for a smash and grab at a XXXX store. One of our squad cars had responded to the store and put out a description of the suspects. We were looking for two males who ran off with a few cartons of smokes and the store safe. We drove around for awhile searching the side streets and back alleys. We decided to double back when we spotted two males in the alley. They were crouched over something. So as we decided to take a look, both males walked over to us, saying they had found this safe lying in the alley. Both of them were out of breath. The safe was in rough shape and looked like it was thrown to the ground several times in an effort to open it. They said that they were trying to open it in the hopes of finding some ID and return it. But they were being real smart asses and giving us attitude, swearing—thought they were being really funny. So my partner had run their IDs and, of course, they had a lengthy criminal history. These guys didn't fit the description completely but we decided to pin it on them anyway just to teach them a lesson. They deserved what happened; I mean they were being total jackasses. They thought the whole thing was a joke . . . didn't answer our questions, kept swearing; real upstanding citizens.

■■■

Also, police powers were abused by officers to benefit/help friends and/or relatives of officers. Once again here we see evidence of hegemonic masculinity at play. Male #28 commits corruption to "protect" his then girlfriend. And Male #16 commits a series of corrupt activities because of his loyalty to a family member and the family member's business. Even when he was removed from foot patrol, he networked with other officers to continue harassing his uncle's competitor in order to protect the uncle's business.

Male #28

My wife was previously married. She was separated when we started seeing each other. But her ex-husband was a real piece of work and made her life a living hell. He would crank call her at all hours of the night and day; he even damaged her car. Of course all of this was "alleged," and we had no proof it was him. That's how I met my wife; it was through her calling the police. We started dating, and things started to get serious between us. So, one night, when I was staying the night, we woke up to the sound of glass smashing; when I ran outside I saw a car speed off. Someone had thrown a rock through the front window. My car was scratched, and my tires were slashed. Well, we called the police and they filed a report. Her ex—well, husband at the time—was questioned but since we didn't have proof nothing could be done. Well, I decided to take matters into my own hands. I found out where he worked, and I waited for him one day; he got off work and I followed him and pulled him over when we were in a more remote area and wrote him up with every traffic violation I could find. He was pissed; yelling, screaming— yelling to the point where bystanders were stopping so I arrested him for disturbing the peace and, naturally, for resisting arrest, and I brought him to the station. A few weeks later while on patrol, I waited for him again to finish work. I pulled him over, and this time told him who I was. Basically, I told him I was going to make his life a living hell if he didn't leave her alone. He had to be taught a lesson; simple as that.

Male #16

He had an uncle who had a bakery and who was also a retired cop. Well, his uncle was pissed that another bakery had opened up a few blocks down and was taking business away from him. My buddy would go by the new bakery and constantly write up parking citations in the hopes of driving customers away. This went on for weeks until the new bakery owner found out who my buddy was related to. They finally pulled XXXX from foot patrol, but it didn't change a thing. He got a couple of friends to write up the parking citations. So the harassment continued, and last I heard was the guy closed shop; moved his business someplace else.

■■■

The level of autonomy and authority given to individual officers often means that they work with little oversight from supervisors, which increases the possibility for corruption risks given organizational responses to officers' illegal conduct (see chapter 2). This is evident in the narratives above, but also apparent is the centrality of masculine traits such as the sense of entitlement they appear to have over members of the public, which is used to justify behavior that benefits themselves, friends, and/or family members, despite illegal means. This sense of entitlement and refusal to acknowledge any victims as the result of the officers' abuse of powers is also seen by Male #32.

Male #32

We had a lot of vendors, and they needed to have their permits and license and comply to the rules and regulations pertaining to their vending license. I was familiar with the bylaws for vending licenses, and I would routinely do spot checks on them in my area. The other guys used to make fun of me and thought it was a waste of time; they didn't think what I was doing was real policing. I needed to supplement my quota since I didn't ride around in a police car, which would have made reaching my quota easier. So, I was relentless with the vendors. They hated me, and I guess I didn't blame them. The fines were eating into their profits, not to mention that after so many violations they could lose their vending license and if that happened someone else could then buy the license and take their place. This went on for months, and after a while I eased up with the fines just a bit. I became very familiar with their operations and cash potential. I learned which companies had which vending locations, and I learned which vending locations were gold mines. I remember sitting in a coffee shop while I was working and I added up all of the good locations and how much money those locations were likely generating. Even after all the expenses were factored in I was astounded with the amount of money that could be made. The only weakness to this business was getting fined to the point where the city takes your license. So it got me thinking. I got my brother to incorporate a holding company that in turn created a LLC; I was the silent partner of course. The LLC purchased a couple of vending licenses from a company that I knew was struggling, but the vending locations were not in the best locations. So, I actually started to target some of the good locations and enforced the bylaws. I was writing them up so fast that some eventually lost their vending locations, which we then replaced with my LLC vendors. I didn't feel guilty about what I did to those vendors because they weren't complying with the bylaws. There's a reason for the bylaws, and business is business; it isn't always pretty, but that's just the way it goes.

■■■

Of the thirty-two participants, only four male officers discussed their own criminal involvement where it was done secretly without others' awareness and/or participation. All three of the female officers, however, acted alone. They worked individually, keeping their illegal conduct to themselves as perceptions of risk were deemed too great if others were involved, particularly male officers. The kinds of corruption they identified and the justifications for their conduct are highlighted below. Only one of the male participants (#22) discussed the involvement of any female officers in relation to abuse of powers. He described the female officer as a witness to the beating of a suspect by another police officer. As seen earlier, Male #22 was concerned with how the female officer would react, but based on her comments following the assault, he was "assured" that she was a "team player."

Female #25

I worked several years in the XXXX and became knowledgeable on checks and identity theft schemes. It was unreal the amount of money that some of these criminals were making. Most of the money schemes were run by organized crime. Anyway, stolen documents were a big thing with these gangs. They made money selling things like passports, driver's licenses, social security cards. So I got to thinking that I could do the same. The money was the driving force. My bills were piling high, and the temptation was escalating. I had access to a few key people who we knew were moving stolen IDs. I weighed the pros and cons of what I was getting into; it wasn't easy. Actually I was really freaked out about it. But, those bills, and, yet, it was so easy to get the IDs from the criminals. I got to know this one guy really well and got to trust him. I'd provide him with the goods, and he'd give me my cut. But it started to get a little more risky, where I wasn't feeling comfortable anymore. I was never totally comfortable, but something felt wrong. I felt like I was being watched; I was losing sleep, having a hard time sleeping actually, getting really anxious. So, I ended up getting out. The gravy train was good for the time it lasted. No, I never felt bad about this because all the documents I sold were from hardcore criminals anyway; so for me it was fighting fire with fire and I made some money in the interim.

Female #23

I did some small-time stuff over the years, always on my own. I never was really exposed to any misconduct by the other guys because I think they didn't trust me or that I might rat them out or something. It's actually kind of funny now that I look back at it all. I knew through the grapevine who was doing what, but the guys did a good job shielding me from it. It pissed me off sometimes though, especially when a new guy would show up and he was instantly on the inside and there I was—there much longer—but still on the outside. I think that's why I was cautious and distant with some of the guys. I saw over the years how a few of them supplemented their incomes; I heard things, but, didn't know for sure, and really, didn't want to know. I guess the one thing I did from time to time was take a few things; you know when a home was burglarized and here I was sitting around waiting for the homeowner. Well, sometimes I'd help myself to a few items; nothing too big, but, you know, the odd cash lying around, or sometimes, small things like a watch. I worked in a fancy area; the houses had insurance so it's not like I felt bad about it. First of all, the stuff was insured; these people were loaded; and third, stuff had already been stolen.

Female #24

I used to drive around and pull over johns with the girl in the car. I would wait until I pretty much caught them in the act. It was easy pickings. I would tell the girl to split; run the guy and make sure he was not wanted. If the guy checked out I would then go to work on him. I would tell him stuff like how everyone is going to find out and that we have to call his wife to verify who he is. And I'd tell him that I had to give him a citation and that all of this costs money and we the police could be serving the public better if we didn't have to deal with solicitation. I'd say things like I didn't care about his personal life but I had to do my job. This is usually when he'd say something like, "Officer what can I do to make this go away," "Can I pay just a fine?" "Please officer, please, give me a break." So, I'd tell them to "donate" some money to me and I would let them go, and if I saw them again I'd arrest them.

It always worked and, well, I'd do it a few times here and there. I guess it was risky, but they would never complain. They had too much to lose over a couple of hundred bucks. For them it was the cost of doing business. They got caught and paid a personal fine to me versus the alternative. I came up with the idea by accident you could say. This guy I arrested begged me not to take him in. He begged and begged and offered money in exchange for letting him go. He said something like, "It's a win win for both of us." So many things went through my head at that moment. But, I ended up taking the money and off he went; he was so relieved, I think he thanked me about a thousand times.

■■■

Examples of corruption provided by the participants included assault, theft, perjury, extortion, kickbacks, bribery, burglary, planting of evidence, protection of illegal activities, selling illegal drugs, illegally installing spy software for the purpose of committing identity theft, and writing false ticket violations. Interestingly, other forms of misconduct, including ignoring violations of the law (for example, with regard to white-collar crimes, domestic violence, and sexual assaults), racial profiling, and selective law enforcement that disproportionately focuses on marginalized populations were not discussed, which illustrate the cultural mores relating to the kinds of behavior that are, or can be considered, to be "corrupt."

Also, police corruption is understood in the context of particular police occupational themes as they relate to "hegemonic masculinity" and "the brotherhood." The police culture shapes and encourages particular ideologies that officers depend on to preserve and defend their actions and identities as they relate to police corruption. But why are significantly fewer women involved in police corruption?

WHY ARE FEWER WOMEN OFFICERS INVOLVED IN CORRUPTION?

First, it is important to examine the gendered differences in criminal offending in the wider population before focusing specifically on women police officers.

Early Feminist Criminology

For the most part, prior to the 1970s, biology-causes crime arguments were used to "explain" the differences in criminal behavior between women and men (Pollack, 1950; Thomas, 1923; Lombroso and Ferrero, 1895). Klein (1973) criticized the androcentric theories of the late nineteenth and twentieth centuries, which pathologized the bodies and minds of female criminal offenders. These early works failed to make the significant distinction between sex and gender, rather depicting women in sexist and stereotypical ways without the necessary evidence to support their claims. And they failed to see the social constructions of gender that led to the differences in the experienced realities of "women" versus "men." This is despite the fact that gender was and continues to be the strongest indicator of one's likelihood to commit a criminal offense (Belknap, 2006).

In addition to supporting the biology-causes crime argument, Pollack (1950) argued that chivalry contributed to the differences in crime rates between women and men. Pollack's paternalism thesis assumed that chivalry on the part of male criminal justice agents showed leniency toward women from the initial police-citizen encounter through prosecution. Chivalry assumes that males were protective of women who were often perceived as weak and dependent. But as feminist scholars since the 1970s have pointed out, Pollack assumed that all female offenders were given leniency, without examining the relevance of factors such as class, race, and type of crime in officers' treatment; all of which contribute to differences in police responses (Comack, 2007; Reiman and Leighton, 2007; Corsianos, 2004, 2003, 2001; Chesney-Lind and Shelden, 2004; Koons-Witt and Schram, 2003; Barak, Flavin, and Leighton, 2001; Visano, 1998).

In the late 1960s some feminist criminologists were publishing works that criticized mainstream criminology for ignoring women in their research on crime, ignoring the relevance of gender in people's behavior, and/or falsely assuming that the research findings that included male-only samples could be applied to women and girls (Bertrand, 1969; Heidensohn, 1968; Reckless, 1961).

Betty Friedan's book *The Feminine Mystique* (1963) was a call to arms and was intended to get women to realize that they were being denied equal treatment. The book made the case that women in the United States in the 1900s had been subordinated as a result of patriarchal ideologies and controls. In order to live a life where meaningful choices became the reality, these dominant controls would have to change. She states, "It is my thesis that as the Victorian culture did not permit women to accept or gratify their basic sexual needs, our culture does not permit women to accept or gratify their basic need to grow and fulfill their potentialities as human beings, a need which is not solely defined by their sexual role." Feminist criminologists, on the other hand, worked to inform the public that certain types of behavior on the part of women and/or girls, such as prostitution and engaging in sexual relations while under the legal age and noncriminal status offenses such as curfew violations and running away from home, largely comprised the "criminal" acts of women and girls that mainstream criminologists studied (Morris, 1987; Heidensohn, 1985; Smart, 1976; Millman, 1975; Chesney-Lind, 1973; Klein, 1973; Temin, 1973).

By the 1970s, "liberation theorists" assumed that "increases in female offending" reported by the "official" U.S. crime statistics were the result of "emancipated" women who were now beginning to act "like men" as they were freed from their traditional roles as women. For instance, Rita Simon (1975) argued that more women were committing property crimes because as more women entered the workplace they had more opportunities to participate in committing property crimes such as fraud and embezzlement. Freda Adler (1975), in her book *Sisters in Crime*, claimed that women were surpassing men in the rate of increase for almost every crime category, and like Simon, she argued that this was the result of women's liberation in society. Adler (1975:7) referred to the perceived changes as "a new breed of women criminals." She did not specifically indicate that the change in women's behavior was the result of "liberation"; rather, it was inferred by connecting the new "female crime wave" to the same conditions that produced the women's movement (Faith, 1993; Adler, 1975). Rita Simon (1975) argued that as women gained access to higher-paid occupations they would also gain access to white-collar crimes. But contrary to Simon's assertion, reported increases in women's property crimes were the result of petty thefts from women who were not gainfully employed (Gimenez, 1990).

As stated by Faith (1993:65):

> Women in the late 20th century who steal, write bad cheques or cheat on their welfare claims—the most common offences for which women in North America are convicted . . . do so not because they have gained independence but because they have not. Women who are dependent on the state are subjected to an infantilizing form of *parens patriae*, as if they were children. For such women, the state takes the place of the absent husband or father as protector and punisher, master of women's lives; society shifts from familial patriarchy to a form of state patriarchy, within an abidingly gendered ideological framework.

Despite early "liberation" theories that linked female criminal activity to the women's movement (Adler, 1975; Simon, 1975), many studies found that the rate of female offenders remained steady, with the exception of less serious property crimes (Steffensmeier and Allan, 1988; Naffine, 1987; Leonard, 1982; Steffensmeier and Cobb, 1981). Carol Smart (1976:xv) critically challenged "the emerging moral panic over the relationship of women's emancipation to increasing participation by women in criminal activity." Others examined the discriminatory responses by criminal justice agents. For example, Chesney-Lind (1973) reported different legal responses to girls' "delinquent" behavior in comparison to boys. Girls, for instance, were placed in detention facilities for violating "status offenses," such as having sex while underage. And others found that women were granted leniency by the criminal 'justice' system only to the extent that they could be shown to be "good mothers" (Daly, 1987a, 1987b; Eaton, 1987).

Indeed, there has been a significant increase in the number of women incarcerated over the last four decades. But it appears that this increase is largely the result of changes in policies and practices rather than in drastic changes in the behavior of women (Belknap, 2006). Some of these changes include the introduction of mandatory sentencing policies that have taken away the discretion of judges, "three-strike" laws, the "war on drugs," the mainstream media's portrayal of "violent women," and changes in criminal justice agents' attitudes and overall perceptions of female criminal offenders. The "war on drugs" and the "get tough on crime" climate led to the introduction of new legislation and police policies that increased law enforcement's focus on drug violations. This has directly resulted in significantly higher arrests and incarceration rates. If one looks at the crime category that most people were arrested for in the United States in the early 1900s, we find that being intoxicated in a public place was the most common (Belknap, 2006). The fact that few people are arrested for this type of crime today does not necessarily suggest that fewer people consume alcohol in public in relation to the early 1900s, but rather it illustrates the change in political climate where this particular type of crime is no longer perceived as important as it once was. Similarly, mandatory arrest policies in domestic violence situations have also played a role. Domestic violence calls constitute the majority of police calls in many police departments across the country, and with the introduction of mandatory arrest policies in many jurisdictions, there has been an increase in the number of women arrested. Oftentimes in domestic violence calls, there are no outside witnesses to the assault, which creates a situation in which it is one person's word against another, with both parties saying they were assaulted by the other. With mandatory arrest policies, this verbal statement of victimization is often enough to qualify as "probable cause"; that is, "evidence" that both parties assaulted each other, leading to the arrest of both. This unfortunately creates situations where victims of assault are arrested based on false allegations or for hitting back in self-defense (Malloy et al., 2003; Martin, 1997; McMahon and Pence, 2003; Melton and Belknap, 2003; Miller, 2001; Dasgupta, 2001).

Feminist research has made profound contributions to our understanding of gender and criminology, focusing initially on female offenders and female victims of crime and subsequently on women working as criminal justice agents (Smart, 1990; Daly and Chesney-Lind, 1988; Rafter, 1985; Chesney-Lind and Rodriguez, 1983; Freedman, 1981; Silbert and Pines, 1981; James and Meyerding, 1977). And feminist research on the police has challenged previous dominant ideologies relating to police work and culture (Corsianos, 2009; Martin and Jurik, 2007; Miller, 1999; Martin, 1994, 1990, 1980). However, the role of gender, hegemonic masculinity and patriarchal ideologies in police corruption has been largely overlooked until now.

Female Officers and Corruption

Just as "women," as a category, are significantly less likely to commit crimes in the wider population, female officers are less likely to commit corruption in comparison to male officers. There are different motivating factors for officers to engage in police corruption. For some it may be for financial gain; for others it may be for psychological gain, such as the "need" to have "power" over others (see chapter 2). But regardless of the different motivating factors, the complexities of the police culture along with the police organizational structure create corruption risks; that is, opportunities for misconduct are made possible. For Moran (2005:62),

> corruption may develop in an organization simply to gain monetary and other advantages for the officers concerned. Officers are pressured initially or over time into accepting bribe money or the proceeds of illegal activities. Further, the "twilight world" of intelligence gathering, general policing and criminal investigation presents ample opportunities for officers to become enmeshed in corrupt networks. Whether in the areas of the use of informants or policing illicit economies the structural context will be reinforced by existing networks of corrupt officers, informants, private detectives, solicitors and so forth.

However, perceptions of "risk" are gendered and, therefore, opportunities for misconduct vary along gender lines. The average male officer in a large police department will cost taxpayers between two-and-a-half and five-and-a-half times more than the average female officer with regard to force liability lawsuit payouts (National Center for Women and Policing, 2002). Also, female officers use less force in arrest situations with members of the public than male officers (Garner and Maxwell, 2002; Schuck and Rabe-Hemp, 2005). Rabe-Hemp's study (2008) suggested that women were much less likely than men to use "extreme controlling behavior," such as physical restraints, threats, searches, and arrests, and that the less use of force on the part of female officers may produce safer police-citizen encounters for both the officer and the public. Rabe-Hemp (2008) asserts that these results provide support to Lonsway et al.'s (2002) argument that hiring more female officers can reduce excessive use-of-force incidents on the part of the police. Women are significantly less likely to commit corruption and receive fewer complaints by citizens (Martin and Jurik, 2007; McElvain and Kposowa, 2004; Lersch, 1998); and appear to better manage their anger and thus are less likely to use force (Abernethy and Cox, 1994). The Bureau of Justice Assistance (2001:2) reported: "Research conducted both in the United States and internationally clearly demonstrates that women police officers use a style of policing that relies less on physical force. They are better at defusing and de-escalating potentially violent confrontations with citizens and are less likely to become involved in incidents of excessive force."

Differences in socialization between the sexes is central to our understanding of why women continue to commit fewer crimes. Differences in behavior, ideas, and beliefs between people representing the category "women" and "men" have been well documented. These differences are not biologically determined but rather ascribed by society. West and Zimmerman (1987:137) note that "doing gender means creating differences between girls and boys and women and men, differences that are not natural, essential, or biological. Once the differences have been constructed, they are used to reinforce the 'essentialness' of gender." Gender roles are learned through socialization from infancy. The beliefs that many people have about people appearing to belong to a particular sex are the result of dominant historical, socioeconomic, and political forces. When one says, "he's acting like a girl" or "she's a tomboy," these serve as illustrations of normative conceptions of sex-appropriate behavior that many falsely assume to be the product of biology. Women overall have been largely socialized to be nurturers, caretakers, emotional providers for their children, more passive and dependent, and to conform to the normative standards set by society and take less risks.

By applying a feminist perspective of labeling theory (Becker, 1966), Morris (1987) asserted that girls and women run the risk of being further stigmatized if labeled "deviant/criminal" given their minority, less privileged social status. They have more to lose socially and financially if labeled a "criminal," which contributes to our understanding of why fewer women and girls commit crimes. In relation to men, economic opportunities for women are disproportionately fewer, as seen in the "feminization of poverty" (U.S. Census Bureau, 2008), but they become significantly more scarce, almost nonexistent, for women with criminal records. Similarly, women in policing have more to lose if labeled "corrupt" and/or associated with particular instances of police misconduct as a result of their gender status. For Faith (1993:70), "Females are commonly subject to many more private forms of social control than are males, and the female *deviant* is deemed more deviant than her male equivalent. She suffers greater social stigmatization when she breaches idealized gender standards." Indeed, female officers on one level challenge the gender normative standards by seeking a career that continues to be male dominated and "hypermasculinized." But, on the other hand, a disproportionate number of female officers are represented in gender-specific units that can be perceived as more "feminized." So even though they become part of a patriarchal, masculinist work environment, differences in socialization lead officers to "choose" or be given assignments that are more gender specific. And, as noted by Corsianos (2009), these "feminized units" tend not to produce the high arrests and the police chases, and they do not reflect the crime-fighting aspects that have been traditionally associated with policing and that are highly valued, recognized, and rewarded internally. Once again, we see similar patterns in the choices of many women officers to conform to the norms as seen in the larger population (for example, that fewer women commit crimes in comparison to men). They are less likely to take on "risks" that could label them "corrupt" or "deviant" within police circles. Dominant constructions of "masculine traits" as both desirable and necessary and as overwhelmingly attached to "being male" ensure that women are without full membership. Therefore, female officers who choose to engage in corrupt activities often must rely on themselves in order to maintain control over the situation and to limit the possibilities of being exposed. This was seen with all three female participants (#23, #24, and #25) who engaged in illegal behavior, but on their own.

Understanding why women are less likely to be involved in forms of police corruption is tied to social constructions of gender and risk. Perceptions of risk are gendered. "Risk" can be understood as being in a position of danger where physical, social, emotional, psychological, and/or financial harms may result. Women officers are less likely to assume the types of risk associated with the various forms of police corruption given the occupational and organizational challenges they have had to overcome to become officers and the challenges they confront as police officers. Also, the "risk" of "being made an example of" by the organization (often depending on the perceived seriousness of the incident, "strength" of the evidence against the officer, and public knowledge of the case) may mean termination or even criminal charges, depending on the type of act committed. This risk may be too great for particular officers who do not have "full membership" given the continued existence of gendered experiences within the culture. The seriousness of these risks may be further exacerbated by external realities that can include, for instance, officers who are single mothers raising young, dependent children and where policing provides some level of financial security in the form of pay and benefits. In assessing gendered risk, one must also examine the level of trust one has in relationships with colleagues. Since women often see themselves as the "outsiders within the station" (Martin, 1994), and given the gendered challenges experienced within the culture, they may be less likely to trust male peers and may perceive them to be more likely to protect each other while leaving female colleagues exposed. Interestingly, the three female officers included in this chapter engaged in corrupt acts individually, contrary to the collective experiences of most of the male officers. In fact, one of the female officers talked about feeling as if she was "on the outside" because of her gender and perceived the male officers as not trusting her and how this in turn made her not trust them, which led her to be "cautious" and "distant."

Another factor to understanding why fewer women officers are involved in corruption is the relationship between gender and support for the community policing philosophy. Women officers continue to be more supportive of community policing and view it as an important model in working with communities and improving police-citizen relationships (Corsianos, 2009; Miller and Hodge, 2004; Miller, 1999). The community-policing model has been described as a more collectivist approach to working with communities to identify and respond to concerns and together build healthier communities. Crime control is presented as a collective enterprise representing the efforts of both the police and the public, and more "feminine" traits become central in accomplishing the goals of the organization (see chapter 6). Lonsway (2000) found that women police possessed better communication skills than male officers and were more competent in using the necessary tools to instigate community-policing initiatives.

One can make the argument that those who are committed to introducing CP initiatives in the hope of creating better police services and improving police-community relationships and changing the internal police operations and power dynamics will be less likely to engage in illegal behavior. Women's stronger support and commitment to CP (Miller and Hodge, 2004; Miller, 1999) can also provide insight as to why fewer women are involved in police corruption.

On the other hand, one must consider the level of "access" for women considering corrupt activities because perceptions of "risk" are gendered. Women and girls historically have not had opportunities to commit certain crimes in comparison to their male counterparts given the differences in socialization, social controls, and organizational challenges for women and girls. These have made "having access" less possible. For instance, when looking at youth crime, parents are more likely to set stricter curfews for their daughters, and police disproportionately arrest girls for curfew violations in comparison to boys (Chesney-Lind and Shelden, 1997; Chesney-Lind, 1973). This in turn decreases the level of "access" girls may have in committing certain types of crimes.

Similarly, women officers may have different motivating factors to commit misconduct (for example, officers who are single mothers are often the primary caretakers of their children) but may lack "access"/the opportunity to engage in such behavior as a result of who she is partnered with on patrol or by the nature of her assignment/position. She may feel that she is without the necessary support to act due to her gender status. She may mistrust her fellow officer, feel that she's an "outsider within" (Martin, 1994), and/or believe that the illegal conduct on the part of herself and male partner, if discovered, will lead to her alone, where she will suffer the consequences given her lack of full membership into "the brotherhood." Or, if she acted alone and was discovered, she may feel that the department will make an example out of her and apply punitive measures. Also, as mentioned above, "access" may not be possible due to her work assignment; that is, her position in the organization may make access difficult. Policing remains gendered not only in terms of the few women working in the field, which is 13 percent (U.S. Department of Labor, 2008; National Center for Women and Policing, 2003) but also in the disproportionate number of women found in particular units. Women are disproportionately represented in units centered around domestic violence and sexual assault, juveniles, community policing, education, and court services (Corsianos, 2009). Alternatively, a disproportionate number of male officers are often found in homicide units, vice, specialized tactical units, fraud, and antigang and motorcycle units (Martin and Jurik, 2007; Schulz, 2004; Heidensohn and Brown, 2000; Boni, 1998; Ness and Gordon, 1995), that often present more opportunities for corruption that produce, for instance, material gains.

Furthermore, some sources show that police officers who hold a college degree are less likely to participate in acts of police corruption and are more likely to be fair and honest (Hoover, 1995; Lynch, 1976). They are also less likely to receive citizen complaints and are more likely to have fewer disciplinary problems (Carter, Sapp, and Stephens, 1988). Similar to the early policewomen, female officers today tend to have higher educational achievements and come from higher socioeconomic backgrounds in comparison to their male counterparts (Corsianos, 2009). One can argue that since women are less likely to be involved in police corruption, this can be partly explained by the fact that women are more formally educated, many with a four-year degree, and recognize they have a lot to lose given the time and money they invested in pursuing a "career" in policing. However, the current reality is that gender remains the strongest indicator of criminal offending at all education and class levels, and this is also the case with police corruption (National Center for Women and Policing, 2002, 2000).

Chapter Four

Critical Dilemmas in Police Behavior

This chapter will assess the popular cultural constructions of the police as a site of contestation for officers who often have to navigate through public challenges of self-identities and organizational identities following publicized cases of police corruption and who depend on the police culture to guide their reactions to these incidents and protect police identities. Also, it will critically evaluate the moral ambiguities that exist when officers act in questionable and/or illegal ways but in compliance with the popular "hypermasculine" manifestations of the police (for example, police as crime fighters and protectors, police put their lives at risk, police respond when others won't), and the impact these have on identity constructions. This chapter will be framed within a perspective that views policing as a gendered enterprise where hegemonic masculinity contributes to the creation and preservation of a culture of tolerance for police corruption. The gender configuring of recruitment and promotion, internal police policies, and in the division of labor enable officers to see the "value" associated with "masculine" traits, and these experiences naturalize police responses to police corruption cases in ways that condone such acts despite possible variations in individual officers' interpretations of these incidents.

The subjective component in police corruption is often neglected in most criminological research. There has been an overreliance on empirical studies that attempt to measure police corruption. But the lack of a clear operationalization of variables such as "police corruption," "excessive force," or "problem officers" renders the empirical studies open to interpretation. Studies have included citizen complaints, surveys, observational methods, and official use-of-force reports and often present the findings as the result of objective measurements. But each of these approaches leads to ambiguous data for a variety of reasons; for example, the researchers may vary in the definition of what types of police behavior qualify as "police corruption," official use-of-force reports represent only the reported incidents, and citizens may file baseless complaints against officers (Lersch and Mieczkowski, 2005). Regardless of the innate limitations in social research, both quantitative and qualitative research can be helpful in understanding the complexities of police corruption. However, qualitative studies on officers' experiences with police corruption have been largely overlooked by mainstream criminologists, even though invaluable insight can be gained about police behavior. By examining the subjective element of people's actions, more insight is gained on the larger social constructs and the shifting roles of people within these constructs. And by evaluating the meanings and interpretations of police corruption on the part of officers, one can better understand the intersections in identity politics with the various social boundaries as they relate to how officers construct their identities.

Cases of police corruption that are reported by the mainstream media are typically considered serious and often include "legitimate" victims. For instance, in the Rampart scandal (see chapter 2), media reports focused on the vast array of police corruption that included extortion, bribery, perjury, and excessive use of force. But once details of the victims' criminal histories were reported, the public seemed to be less interested and ultimately the media reports became less frequent (*Cops under Fire*, 1996). Indeed, officers' responses to publicized cases of police corruption frequently conflict with those of the public. Individual officers may vary in the types and degree of corruption they deem "appropriate" or "more" versus "less appropriate," but they are aware of how the public generally views publicized cases of police misconduct and recognize the importance in protecting themselves within the culture and protecting the public image of the organization as a whole. Even the most ethical police officers seem to be uncomfortable with public accounts of police misconduct because of the negative picture that is typically attached to the entire organization by members of the public despite the officers' perceived "good work" performed by the "majority of cops." These officers are often relieved to see and hear the media move on to other news stories after days or weeks of negative publicity.

Interpretations and understandings of police corruption by individual officers are influenced by both their perceptions of how they are viewed internally within the police culture as well as externally by the public. Officers are constantly defining and redefining their work experiences to protect their identities, which includes responding to instances of officers' "questionable" behavior, but in compliance with the popular "hypermasculine" manifestations of the police. Dick (2005) uses the term *dirty work* to refer to the less-desired aspects of policing, including activities that may be physically revolting (for example, searching a decayed body for identification), but also to actions that "run counter to the more heroic of our moral conceptions" (Dick,

2005:1364). These have the potential to stigmatize people who participate in them. The current nature of police work can, at times, conflict with moral ideologies and normative behavior, and therefore police work can involve a transgression of socially accepted boundaries that, at times, can challenge the popular constructions of the police. However, oftentimes officers who abuse their powers for some type of gain do so in compliance with the popular manifestations of the police.

Bittner (1970) asserts that police officers "in the natural course of their duties inflict harm." But, as discussed above, the interpretations and understandings of police misconduct by individual officers are related to their perceptions of how they are viewed both internally and externally, and these "force" officers to constantly redefine and protect their identities and preserve hegemonic masculinity as central to the police identity.

According to Dick (2005:1369), protecting individual identity can be achieved through "reframing—where the meaning attached to a specific occupation is transformed; recalibrating—where the tasks that constitute the role are re-categorized so as to emphasize the more acceptable or palatable tasks; and refocusing—where an attempt is made to shift attention to non-stigmatized aspects of the role." But questionable police behavior regardless of differences in the degree of acceptance or interpretations of events by individual officers is often excused by these same officers following public criticism against the police department as they come together to defend police work as expressed in their "heroic imagination." Common police rhetoric following public attacks of the police resulting from a reported incident of police corruption include versions of "the public don't understand what we do"; "they should walk a day in our shoes"; "they think it's easy doing what we do"; "they expect us to fight crime and criminals but sometimes we have the laws working against us"; "the job is at times unpredictable, which can place you in a difficult situation leading to difficult decisions"; and "management will sink you in order to protect themselves" (see chapter 3).

Also, by avoiding or minimizing discussions regarding the incident with peers and rather centering communication on the media representations and the public's reaction, a culture of tolerance for this behavior is preserved. For Hughes (1962), by the unwillingness to consider the "dirty work" that has been done, "good people" are able to remove intolerable knowledge from their consciousness. He further adds that silence protects the group solidarity, where open discussion would threaten the group identity and be considered a sort of treason and betrayal. This creates silent compliance and acceptance through ignorance and secrecy cultivated by fear and terror of retribution. Admittedly, workers generally need a relatively fixed image of the kind of work they do and the purpose for it. Ashforth and Kreiner (1999) argue that "individuals need a relatively secure and stable sense of self-definition of who they are—within a given situation to function effectively," and occupational identity is a major part of self-identification. For Ashforth and Kreiner, workers seek to enhance their self-esteem through their social identities and have a strong desire to view them in positive ways, but these perceptions are at least partly grounded in the perceptions of others. People, to some extent, come to see themselves and/or act in ways that are influenced by their perceptions of how they think others see them (Cooley, 1964, orig. 1902; Mead, 1962, orig. 1934). And these can, at times, create an internal conflict and a crisis of identity. Self-identities are fluid and always subject to change, and people are always engaged in identity construction.

Factors influencing perceptions of self include daily encounters with others, the introduction of new experiences and information, as well as a reprocessing of old experiences and knowledge construction. According to Boham and Haley (2005), the police self-image reflects officers' feelings of self-worth. That is, if officers feel they are respected for their work and that their roles are important, then they will perform better; they will be more productive and will be more likely to experience a higher level of job satisfaction. But in instances of public attacks against officers as a whole and/or the police organization following publicized cases of police misconduct, officers tend to reject the social stigma placed on all officers, including themselves, and often absolve the actions of the officers involved in the "questionable" acts by focusing on the public's inability to "understand" the complexities of police work generally, and "police corruption" more specifically. This is not surprising given contemporary constructions of the police that include police as "protectors," "crime fighters," and "heroes."

As noted by Ashforth and Kreiner (1999), some writings have acknowledged that police officers prefer to communicate with criminal offenders rather than victims because an offender is perceived as having the ability to appreciate the officers' investigative work in apprehending him/her. Also, the arrest of a criminal offender serves as validation to the officers' identity as one of "crime fighter." Thus, the potential for a crisis of identity here is minimized given the prioritization of the "collective identity," particularly in times of conflict.

The collective identity "addresses the *we-ness* of a group, stressing the similarities or shared attributes around which group members coalesce" (Cerulo, 1997). Cerulo (1997) also suggests that it is from these collective social units that a construction of self is developed. Taylor and Whittier (1992) construct and map a step-by-step process in the collective identity scheme of boundaries that both insulate and separate the group. These include the emergence of a shared consciousness and set of goals and a politicization of the group's status.

HEGEMONIC MASCULINITY IN POLICE IDENTITY CONSTRUCTIONS

The internal police culture embodies "hegemonic masculinity." According to Connell (2005:236), "Hegemonic masculinity can be defined as the configuration of gender practice which embodies the currently accepted answer to the problem of the legitimacy of patriarchy, which guarantees (or is taken to guarantee) the dominant position of men and the subordination of women." Popular constructions of the police allow officers to construct their identities in ways that celebrate masculinity, including incidents of police corruption such as police excessive use of force and even deadly force; ignoring violations of laws (for example, in domestic violence) where disproportionate numbers of victims are female and perpetrators are male; and engaging in sexist enforcement of laws (for example, in prostitution). Masculine characteristics are accepted as "common sense" and are "naturalized" in policing methods.

Physical force is expected, condoned, preferred, and even celebrated. These particular masculine-constructed performances are constructed as necessary to "fight criminals" and "protect the community." They are also promoted as "heroic" given dominant societal constructions of "danger," the use of violence as a means to accomplish identified goals, and the role of police in perceived dangerous situations that are avoided by others in society. Since "crime fighting" is seen as being entirely done by police officers, police organizations actively construct the heroic identity in both the public and police imagination with strategic rhetoric, such as the police are the "thin blue line" between a state of peace and order and one of anarchy and chaos; the police protect the public; police control crime; police put away the "bad guys" who may be lurking in your neighborhoods; and "the police are always available to assist in times of need." In addition to using this rhetoric for organizational maintenance and survival (see chapter 2), they are also used by the police to remind the public of what the police "do." These popular manifestations of the police are further used by individual officers to remind themselves of their value in society and to excuse police behavior that is believed to be in compliance with these popular constructions of the police, despite "questionable" tactics used.

The police frequently use the phrase *us versus them* to mark their social separation from the public and position themselves above the public at large. This "us versus them" mentality shapes and influences police work on a daily basis (Young, 1993, 1991; Smith and Gray, 1985), and members of the public who are investigated by the police are often dehumanized and police misconduct may become justified. For McLaughlin (2007), this separation directly reflects the social stratification of a given society. Police posit themselves as "the law" and, at times, "above the law," where they should be afforded privileges given the "nature" of their work. On the other hand, particular categories of people who are disproportionately policed are placed on the opposite side of the legal spectrum and viewed as less deserving of police attention.

Masculine characteristics that include crime fighting; physical discipline; applying subjective justice, particularly in the absence of grounds for arrest; warlike mentality; emotional separation from victims; and a sense of entitlement over "civilians" as well as "police knowledge" are prioritized and highly valued internally by police organizations. Skolnick and Fyfe (1993) assert that abuses of coercive force are encouraged in an environment where there has been both a political and police declaration of a "war against crime." Policing further becomes entrenched in masculinist militaristic approaches and language that further posit those investigated by police as the "others"; that is, the "them" in the "us versus them" dynamic, and "the enemy" who break the laws and put society in "danger." The militaristic approach enables a tougher stance on dealing with and controlling "enemies."

Workers without supportive outsiders are likely to both socially and psychologically withdraw and move closer internally to their occupational cohort, where it is safer and where affirmation can be found (Ashforth and Kreiner, 1999). But, when the public criticizes the police for engaging in brutality or for violating human rights, and the evidence against the officers is considered strong within the agency, the police organization will engage in "damage control," constructing the involved officers as "bad apples" as discussed in chapter 2. And individual officers among themselves will often dismiss the media and public as being ignorant of police work, despite the various interpretations and understandings of the reported misconduct. By critically evaluating the media and public accounts of the incident, a culture of tolerance for police corruption is maintained.

Even in "high profile" cases that include police misconduct, evidence of this culture of tolerance is undeniable. For instance, in Corsianos (2003), officers chose to act differently in particular "high profile" cases in order to protect self-identities and organizational identities in compliance with the popular cultural constructions of the police. In these investigations, officers responded differently in the time, resources, and priority given to the case, depending on a number of factors, which included the "status" of the accused and/or the victim (for example, if they were affluent and/or well known by the public or whether they were relatives of police officers, etc.); the role of the media; police wanting to conceal any questionable and/or illegal police conduct from the public; cases that were perceived to have serious political implications; and the public's reaction to a case and/or their expectations of the police. Police decision making often moved up the hierarchy, involving members of upper management, where they could take the necessary steps to control and manage police appearances to the larger public including the media since negative publicity could hurt the image of the police. Officers believed that in these "high profile" cases, their actions could be scrutinized more carefully by "outsiders," and therefore they wanted to avoid making mistakes and/or decrease the possibilities of police misconduct becoming public. As a result, police accountability increased; more time, energy and police resources were used in these investigations; and, at times, decision making moved up the hierarchy, involving final investigative decisions being made by management personnel (Corsianos, 2003). These are deemed acceptable and necessary to preserve self-identities and organizational identities in a positive light.

Dick (2005) used Goffman's (1959) concepts of "front stage" and "back stage" to explain identity construction. Dick claims that "dirty workers'" identity operates in two spheres; that is, "front region" and "back region." The "front region" is where the worker may feel the need to present to an audience the appearance of control; that is, that the tasks are being performed and are performed well. The worker may feel morally obligated to do this to avoid disapproval of the task and the worker by the audience. But beyond Dick's (2005) assertion of a moral obligation, there is the need for a constant management of appearances by police organizations to ensure support by the public and ultimately organizational survival. The "back regions," on the other hand, are considered to be dominated by "work with colleagues, or at home with supportive friends and family, the individual can relax; the audience is absent, and the boundaries of professional ideology will go unchallenged" (Goffman, 1959; Dick, 2005). It is in the "back regions" where police are more likely to criticize public and media accounts of the police and defend police work regardless of their interpretations and understanding of specific instances of police misconduct. But the police culture as discussed in chapter 3 provides the "means" for the particular understandings of police misconduct on the part of officers.

POPULAR CONSTRUCTIONS OF THE POLICE AND THE CULTURE OF TOLERANCE FOR CORRUPTION

The occupational culture creates a system of beliefs that shapes officers' interpretations and understandings of police corruption, but, more importantly, it enables officers to protect the dominant popular constructions of the police that embody masculinist behavior and rhetoric and tolerate police misconduct. By focusing on the public and/or media representations of the police following a publicized incident of police misconduct, officers dismiss the experiences of possible victims who often represent marginalized populations. Privileged police positions are protected, which include the image of the paramilitaristic police organizational structure that operates continuously to legitimize policing to the public.

Members of marginalized populations who are victimized by police are typically dismissed or overlooked by officers as a whole regardless of the possibility of having experienced emotional or psychological harm, physical injury, or having been killed. Criminal laws define certain behaviors as illegal and hence criminal. However, criminal behavior that officers are expected to police and ultimately apply their discretionary powers in terms of which laws to enforce and when to challenge a particular historically socially constructed social order. Therefore the policing of "criminal" behavior is an inquiry into power relationships and cultural controls (Corsianos, 2009; Kappeler, Sluder, and Alpert, 1998). Police organizations are structured to largely apply selective law enforcement to the less privileged (Ericson, 1982), protect the economically powerful (Neugebauer, 1999, 1996; Gordon, 1987), and protect police interests by maintaining a positive police image to the public (Corsianos, 2003; Manning, 1997). And popular constructions of the police incorporate the above as most people in the population come to "know" that "poor people are more likely to commit crimes" or "most crimes are committed by minorities." In the United States, the poor are often dismissed and/or overlooked given the cultural emphasis on individual work ethic and its perceived relationship to economic success. The poor are typically held personally responsible for their economic situations, and there is an assumption that economic failure on the part of an individual reflects some sort of personal shortcomings and/or laziness (Wilson, 1996). And officers' perceptions of the public are influenced by their personal experiences largely with poorer people who are overwhelmingly more likely to deal with the police (willingly or unwillingly) given the "nature" of policing, laws, and preoccupation with street-level and/or blue-collar crimes.

Masculine traits are posited as desirable, positive, and necessary for the tasks of "law enforcement" agents. Officers' perceptions of "criminals" (for example, what constitutes criminality), appropriate responses to suspects (for example, the continued emphasis on use of force versus effective communication), and assumptions of suspects' guilt are used to overlook or dismiss cases of police misconduct. Police work is presented as incorporating egalitarian ideals, but, in actuality, police culture reflects and maintains structures of dominance (Manning, 1997; Shearing, 1981). The social construction of "criminals" reflects the class, race, ethnicity, and gender inequalities in society (Barak, Flavin, and Leighton, 2001). And language is an important "tool" used to protect self-identities and organizational identities and to create and maintain a culture of tolerance for police corruption.

Language is strategically used within the police culture to secure group identity and to construct the public as ignorant of policing. The need for tactical language becomes heightened in times of conflict. Officers produce a number of illusions through the use of language in order to legitimize their roles (Corsianos, 2001), despite publicized cases of police misconduct. For Gadamer (1976:3), "Language is the fundamental mode of operation of our being-in-the-world, and the all-embracing form of the constitution of the world." A series of defenses that can be heard among officers following an incident of police corruption include versions of the following: "the public don't understand"; "it can happen to anyone"; "we're the good guys"; "he (i.e., the victim) was deserving of what happened to him"; "the law sometimes works against us in favor of criminals" (see chapter 3). These suggest a sense of shared understanding and interpretation of events, but, at the same time, they affirm a total disregard for the possibility of a victim who has experienced direct harm by the police. This level of insensitivity is also demonstrated in the language used to promote a collective identity that posits the police as an elite group separate from the public; for example, "we're a brotherhood"; "we're the blue wall"; "there exists an us versus them"; and "criminals get more protections." These serve to protect and promote the paramilitaristic police structure and its traditional operations, maintain dominant power relations, and preserve hegemonic masculinity (Corsianos, 2009).

The hegemonizing procedures of domination are operationalized through language. Hegemony is a force of rule that exists within a set of ideologies that is secured through consent of the people and promoted by "common sense" (Gramsci, 1957). Language serves as a powerful tool for police organizations to create the illusion that they are committed to policing ethically and fairly. And language is used to present policing as demonstrating a collective policing approach (i.e., policing by consent). Language is also used within the police culture to unify officers and shift priorities to preservation of "self" by protecting popular constructions of police identities rather than considering the possibilities of police corruption. Additionally, it sustains the current policing model as a gendered enterprise that preserves dominant masculine characteristics emphasizing, for instance, aggressive crime control, selective law enforcement that serves to privilege positions of power, emotional separation from victims, the promotion of physical strength (defined narrowly), a sense of entitlement over "civilians" and "policing knowledge," and the police as the "experts" on criminal activity and communities.

Externally, however, police organizations may use language differently to convey a service-oriented model of policing that serves all citizens equally. Rhetoric such as "justice for all," "community policing," "to serve and protect" are promoted to connote that every person has equal access to police service and to the quality of service. These are intended to be "understood" as the police providing equal protection and an equal voice for all. At the manifest level, this use of language indicates more "feminine" traits, such as sensitivity and respect for all citizens. But at the latent level, it affirms confirmation to the social, economic, and political order; exploitation; discrimination; and police self-legitimization (Corsianos, 2001), and it exemplifies patriarchal ideologies and hegemonic masculinity.

Internally, the police culture creates a system of beliefs that provide officers with a means for interpreting and understanding "police corruption," but more importantly, it provides the means to effectively respond to these incidents and protect identity constructions of the police. Dominant ideologies of the police as "the good guys" who "catch the bad guys," for instance, become shared among members and foster security and validity in what they "do." These hegemonic constructions enable officers to perhaps downplay or overlook officers' misconduct or to "see" the incident in a number of possibilities contrary to mainstream media representations and/or public accounts. More importantly, they allow officers to focus attention on the "ignorance" of the public at large. Police work may be seen as "dirty" (Dick, 2005) due, for instance, to the moral ambiguities produced and the categories of people that officers disproportionately police and/or apply excessive force to (for example, the poor and racial and ethnic minorities) (Kappeler, Sluder, and Alpert, 1998). But despite elements of the occupation that undermine the organizational goals and may be considered "dirty," crime control remains one key tenet of the police function that is highly valued as both a means and an end. Crime-control ideologies maintain the heroic positive self-image in officers while rendering other less desirable and/or controversial aspects of the job as "less important."

The moral ambiguities within policing are commonplace but are largely overlooked within the culture. For instance, these ambiguities are often seen in officers' assumptions of "guilt" in their "suspects." Under the law, a person is "innocent until proven guilty." But Klockars (1980) argues that there are four commonly held contradictory assumptions of guilt on the part of officers. First, there is the "operative assumption of guilt" where "guilt" is assumed given the nature of police work; that is, they assume some level of deviant behavior in order to question someone, stop a motor vehicle, and/or make an arrest. Second, "the worst of all possible guilt" refers to the assumption of guilt that is made when a person is "dangerously guilty." Third is "the great guilty place assumption," where an officer may develop an "ecology of guilt," where assumptions of guilt are made based on personal characteristics such as age, race, and sex. Fourth, "the not guilty (this time) assumption," which occurs when even illegal means fail to provide evidence of guilt. The officer concludes that the individual (who has been victimized by police) is not innocent but rather is innocent "this time." Police often assume that they are dealing with people who are factually if not legally guilty (Klockars, 1980). Despite legal protections, the assumption of guilt is evidence of the moral ambiguities within policing that are relegated to the margins of culturally and organizationally given police priorities in securing positive identities by making arrests and "controlling" crime.

For Klockars (1980), the moral ambiguities are seen in the judgment call made by the officer in determining, for instance, to use illegal means to police illegal behavior; this would include deciding to use coercive force as well as the degree of force. This is often referred to as the "noble-cause" corruption (Pollock, 2007; Heffernan, 1985) or the "Dirty Harry" problem (Klockars, 1980), named from the 1971 Warner Brothers film, *Dirty Harry*. In the film, the assumed "good cop" acts illegally and immorally in order to bring "criminals to justice." The moral dilemma seen here are the justifications for questionable and illegal behavior on the part of the police. According to Skolnick (1975), support for officers' actions comes from peers, the department, and the wider community. Therefore, even "dirty tactics" may at times be deemed acceptable given the "ends." This, however, denies the contradiction in the use of "dirty means" being in the "same moral class of wrongs" as those used to fight crime. Furthermore, in instances where the "ends" are very desirable for the police organization, a failure on the part of an officer to achieve those "ends" may compromise his/her abilities and reputation as an officer. Thus, "dirty means" may be used to avoid shame and/or feelings of inadequacy or incompetence (Klockars, 1980).

Policing, like other occupations, produces "guilty knowledge." "Although all professions publicly protest their virtue, social value, and personal sacrifice, private talk is often of occupational tricks and shortcuts, of the dubious maneuvers that make the socially required performance possible or provide private satisfactions that conflict with public expectation" (Tiffen, 2004:1175–76). This would include "noble cause corruption," where the police secretly justify the use of illegal means to arrest those who violate the laws. As Moore (1997:63) notes, noble-cause corruption is based on the idea that "yes, I did something wrong, but justice demanded it, not tolerated it but demanded it, because I could put the guy away who otherwise wouldn't be successfully prosecuted." The police condone these actions in order to obtain a conviction in a criminal justice system that they frequently perceive as benefiting the "criminals." In 1931, the Wickersham Commission was the first presidential commission to examine the American Criminal Justice system, and it devoted two of its fourteen volumes to illegal police conduct. In one of the volumes Ernest Jerome Hopkins described the police as operating under a "War Theory of Crime Control" that he described as follows:

This criminal is the enemy: he is to be defeated by being quelled. Being the enemy, he has no rights worthy of the name. He is to be met by the weapons of war. Individual rights, including those of noncombatants in wartime, are subject to evasion like the rights of noncombatants in wartime. The policeman is a peacetime soldier. If the bullets go astray, if civil rights are suspended, those are accidents in warfare that is waged in crowded cities. (Hopkins, 1972:319)

Dick (2005) asserts that officers are able to "reframe" the meaning of questionable police conduct by absolving their actions in a broader, legally defined social order, thereby neutralizing potential accusations. She states that "when a society requires a group to hold ambiguous roles, the persons in that group are often credited with the potential to wield uncontrolled, dangerous and disapproved power" (Dick, 2005). But police acceptance of the knowledge that, at times, they must operate "above the law" or that the laws, at times, work against them in favor of "criminals" allow officers to prioritize particular police functions regardless of the means. For Sherman (1980), the police culture values violence as a necessary means and allows police to misuse their violence license to accomplish particular "ends." The misuse of violence is justified with a manufactured need to fight violence (Barak, 2003).

Despite the popular police as "good guys" identity who "catch criminals" in both the police culture and public imagination, ethnographic researchers verify that the exact function of policing is difficult to define, and, for the most part, is unrelated to "fighting crime and criminals" and making arrests (Corsianos, 2009; McLaughlin, 2007; Martin and Jurik, 2007). As Manning notes (1997:158–59), typical policing "is boring, tiresome, sometimes dirty, sometimes technically demanding but it is rarely dangerous." But what becomes promoted in both the police and public imagination are the atypical instances such as shootings, hot pursuits, and dramatic arrests of "wanted criminals."

MAINTAINING HEGEMONIC MASCULINITY

There are also cultural differences within the organization as seen in how gender, race, ethnicity, sexual orientation, age, level of education, officer's rank, and position assignment (patrol officer versus management) create police subjectivities (Corsianos, 2009; Miller, Forest, and Jurik, 2004; Miller, 1999; Martin, 1994). Indeed, through socialization officers reenact police culture, but they also renew it as they bring with them their subjective life experiences. Personal experiences resulting from socially constructed identity categories (such as gender, race, etc.) allow individuals to "see" and/or "understand" police work in particular ways. But despite the increase in diversity among officers in recent years, evidence of assimilation to the dominant police culture has been well documented. For instance, in their examination of the relationship between race, ethnicity, and police culture, the National Research Council (2004) found little evidence that African American and Hispanic officers interacted differently in their dealings with the public compared to white officers. And despite the number of male officers who are today supportive of female officers, male officers still rarely challenge the dominant ideologies and attitudes (Martin and Jurik, 2007).

Despite the slow but gradual increase in the representation of women working as police officers since the 1960s, female officers continue to threaten the image of the police as "doing masculinity" and promoting "hegemonic masculinity." For instance, the feminization of certain areas in policing (for example, domestic violence and sexual assault units, community policing) has led some male officers to perceive these areas as less important than traditional crime-control approaches and identified priorities. These units are less valued, whereas policing assignments where women are either nonexistent or comprise only a small number are perceived as more important and more valued and typically include aggressive crime-control methods and the promotion of narrow definitions of physical strength (Tactical Units, Homicide, and Vice) (Corsianos, 2009; Miller, 1999). The culture of policing is gendered (Corsianos, 2009; Martin and Jurik, 2007; Martin, 1999, 1980; Miller, 1999), racialized (Dodge and Pogrebin, 2001; Pogrebin, Dodge, and Chatman, 2000; Morash and Haar, 1995; Martin, 1994), and sexualized (Miller, Forest, and Jurik, 2004; Messerschmidt, 1997). Women, regardless of their sexual orientation and/or gender identity, and queer men threaten this constructed "masculine" and "heterosexualized" police image. For instance, Miller, Forest, and Jurik (2004) found that lesbian officers expressed loyalty to the police organization and were committed to many of the traditional policing goals but were more likely than heterosexual females to "downplay" their sexual orientation and display particular "masculine" traits to gain acceptance from fellow officers.

"Hegemonic masculinity" (Messerschmidt, 1997, 1993; Connell, 1995) is challenged by the presence of more women because most women are largely constructed as "feminine" and/or "not masculine." Even lesbian officers who are open about their sexual orientation and may perform and present themselves in more masculine ways also threaten "hegemonic masculinity" because ultimately they are still seen as women. Also, gay men are perceived as a threat to group identity within the police culture. For Connell (2005:237), "Oppression positions homosexual masculinities at the bottom of a gender hierarchy among men. Gayness, in patriarchal ideology, is the repository of whatever is symbolically expelled from hegemonic masculinity . . . Hence, from the point of view of hegemonic masculinity, gayness is easily assimilated to femininity." Gramsci's (1957) concept of "hegemony" refers to the power relations by which a group claims and sustains a dominant position in society, and in turn, others accept it as "common sense," as it is presented as "natural." The successful claim to positions of dominance is evidence of hegemony. For Connell, as stated earlier (2005:236), hegemonic masculinity is "the configuration of gender practice which embodies the currently accepted answer to the problem of the legitimacy of patriarchy, which guarantees (or is taken to guarantee) the dominant position of men and the subordination of women."

Indeed, personal subjectivities help officers renew police culture in a multitude of ways, but at the same time the dominant police culture is maintained given the hegemonic acceptance of particular organizational and individual characteristics. This is evident in the culture of tolerance that is maintained after a publicized incident of police corruption. Regardless of officers' understandings and interpretations of events, the priority often becomes one of protecting both self-identities and organizational identities in compliance with organizational goals and popular constructions of police.

Also, officers consider the possibilities of misuse and abuse of police powers as inevitable given the complexity of tasks police officers perform on a daily basis. Seasoned officers know that policing translates to a "high risk" profession, given all the possibilities for mistakes, opportunities for abuse of powers, and the diverse interpretation of events by different groups. Evidence of the profession as risky has also included the actions of management. Low-ranking officers have at times been critical of members of upper management for moving quickly to label officers involved in publicized cases of police corruption as "bad apples," even though front-line officers identified with and/or condoned the actions of the accused officers. This construction of policing as a "high risk profession" also contributes to the promotion of group solidarity and the tendency to dismiss or overlook the existence of possible "legitimate victims" in identified police misconduct cases as mentioned earlier. Officers view policing as a "high risk" profession beyond perceived physical dangers; that is, that there are "endless possibilities" for "serious mistakes" to be made and that diverse interpretations of "mistakes" can be made by different groups with competing political interests. The perception of policing as "high risk" is shared by seasoned officers who have experienced firsthand the ambiguous nature of police work that can at any time put officers' livelihood at risk. This information is shared with new recruits who begin to "understand" the complexities of their work through their own experiences and ultimately "see" it as fact. And this magnifies their support for police autonomy in order to deal with the various ambiguous situations in their day-to-day interactions. The socialization process conditions officers to view policing as risky and dangerous. Police begin to understand the complexities of their work from training within and through exposure to the unique demands of their profession (Skolnick, 1994). Also, police instructors who are responsible for disseminating "police knowledge" to new recruits at police academies often present material that reinforces dominant masculinist police ideologies, including perceptions of dangers on the job

(Murphy and Caplan, 1993; Cohen and Feldberg, 1991). Most police training overemphasizes the potential for death and injury, and instructors spend a great deal of time teaching "officer survival" skills (Kappeler et al., 1996). Skolnick (1994) notes that danger is one of the most important facets in the development of a police working personality. The police learn the potential for danger through "war stories" and field training by seasoned officers after the police academy. For instance, Kraska and Paulsen (1997:263) describe the intense preoccupation with danger for officers in tactical units:

> The military weapons, tactics, training, and drug-raids generate an intense feeling of "danger" among the officers. There exists of course a universal fear of being victim of violence among regular police officers . . . However, the preoccupation with danger in this special operations team, and the fear of being a victim of violence, is heightened. All the PPU officers expressed an extreme fear of the worst happening to them, emphasizing the "real possibility" that every call-out could end in tragedy . . . The perception of danger and death serves to create a military-like camaraderie among PPU officers. Just as the fear of danger involved in the PPU is more intense than in normal policing, the camaraderie formed is also more intense. Officers emphasize that they must rely on fellow officers more, and their close bonding functions to protect each other's "backsides."

The militaristic training and emphasis on aggressive crime-control tactics and warlike ideologies condition officers to "never back down" in dangerous situations.

HEGEMONIC MASCULINITY AND POLICING AS A GENDERED ENTERPRISE

Masculinity exists in contrast with femininity. One cannot exist without the other. All societies represent cultural constructions of gender, but not all have the concept of "masculinity" (Connell, 2005). In Europe, before the eighteenth century, women were seen as inferior or incomplete in comparison to males. But, the idea of women being qualitatively different in character became part of the bourgeois ideology of the equal but separate model in the nineteenth century (Connell, 2005). But gender is not fixed or universal; it is fluid and situational. The different meanings attached, for instance, to "women," "men," "masculinity," and "femininity" reflect the ways in which people's bodies and behavior are categorized. In the United States "masculine" characteristics are overwhelmingly attached to "being male" and "feminine" traits are largely attached to "being female." Therefore, performing in masculine and feminine ways in relation to one's sex or the sex one chooses to appear to represent from a biological point of view means "doing gender" according to normative expectations.

Masculinity is conceptualized as a necessary construct in the successful function of institutions such as the police. The structure and culture of policing celebrate masculinity. For instance, warlike rhetoric and training, competition, aggressive crime-control tactics, narrow definitions of physical strength, a sense of entitlement over others, and male bravado help reinforce male comradeship. Policing becomes an important cultural and social resource for many male officers, and few careers today continue to overwhelmingly represent males as does the policing field. With the slow but gradual increase of female police officers over the last four decades, organizational and cultural efforts to preserve masculinity as the norm become even more necessary to maintain dominant images of police bodies and behavior and to preserve police solidarity.

Hegemonic masculinity embodies dominant accepted practices within policing. Here lies one of the challenges for women who have been subjected to patriarchal definitions of femininity. Being "feminine" is constructed to mean being soft, passive, vulnerable, fragile, sensitive, nurturing, respectful, and peaceful. Masculinity is constructed to be the opposite of femininity. And masculine characteristics are used to claim and/or assert masculinity in police group dynamics. Indeed, compromises are made by men as women join the occupational culture of policing, but, regardless, most men (and women) rarely challenge the dominant scripts. For example, even female officers may voice sexist comments. According to Huisman et al. (2005), many of the female police officers present during a domestic violence training session for police officers chose to remain silent. But when some did speak, they voiced sexist attitudes alongside male officers. The trainers were confronted with a barrage of attacks from the male officers who questioned their expertise in the area, labeled them as man-hating lesbians, and argued that a high percentage of domestic violence complaints were not legitimate.

People's social commitments and conscious awareness of the "nature of things" is limited and/or undermined by the aesthetic of different categories of bodies. Foucault (1979) refers to the body as the "docile body" regulated by the norms of cultural life. For Connell (2005:233) masculinity "is simultaneously a place in gender relations, the practices through which men and women engage that place in gender, and the effects of these practices in bodily experience, personality and culture." Indeed, there are multiple masculinities, and "hegemonic masculinity" is not a fixed entity. Rather, as Connell (2005) notes, masculinity occupies the hegemonic position in particular gender relations: "Recognizing multiple masculinities, especially in an individualist culture such as the United States, risks taking them for alternative lifestyles, a matter of consumer choice. A relational approach makes it easier to recognize the hard compulsions under which gender configurations are formed, the bitterness as well as the pleasure in gendered experience" (ibid., 236).

Identity categories such as "woman" and "man" are often understood in fixed terms where different particular behaviors and bodily aesthetics are assumed for each. But these categories must be made permeable, and assumptions regarding masculine and feminine traits as innately attached to a specific sex must cease. As Butler reminds us, the definition of "woman" must be constantly scrutinized because the articulation of specificity "invariably produces factionalizations and exclusions" (1993:15). For Brownmiller (1985), femininity is at its core a "tradition of imposed limitations." In policing, officers learn normative behavior through bodily discourse; that is, through actions and images that promote particular policing "skills," body "types," and behavior. In our visually oriented culture, the image of policing is inseparable from often exaggerated masculine traits; that is, "hypermasculinity." Officers are expected to be aggressive, determined, always in control, and emotionally disciplined in order to control particular emotions in given situations. Bodies are a site of struggle. Indeed, people resist dominant gender constructions in different ways, but the vast majority accept these hegemonic constructions as "common sense" and "natural."

Policing continues to be actively produced as "masculine" and "male." Hegemonic masculinity as central to the police function and overall image sustains positions of dominance and subordination in a particular domain. Few women consider careers in policing. Women account for approximately 13 percent of all officers (U.S. Department of Labor, 2008; National Center for Women and Policing, 2003). The National Center of Women and Policing (2003) reports that women comprised 14.3 percent of all sworn police officers in 1999, but by 2000 the percentage dropped to 13 percent, and then to 12.7 percent in 2001. At the federal level for the same year, women constituted 14.4 percent of all federal agents (Hickman and Reaves, 2001). The number of women in both middle- and upper-management positions is significantly smaller, with the least representation in the latter. The number of women in top command positions remains very small. Even if the number has hypothetically tripled today to approximately six hundred from Schulz's (2004) recorded number of two hundred in 2000, that would mean that just over 3 percent of chiefs and sheriffs in the country are women. There continues to be a gender configuring of recruitment and promotion, internal police policies, and in the division of labor. These processes serve to preserve policing as a gendered enterprise where officers "see" the "value" in a largely masculine identity. These experiences "naturalize" officers' responses to police corruption in ways that create a culture of tolerance for it.

Gender Configuring of Recruitment and Promotion

Title VII of the Civil Rights Act in 1964 prohibited the discrimination in employment on the basis of race, color, religion, national origin, and sex. Therefore, women in the 1960s could apply for uniform patrol positions rather than the traditional "policewoman" positions. In 1968, two women representing the Indianapolis Police Department, Betty Blankenship and Elizabeth Coffal, became the first women to be hired to carry out regular police patrol duties as their male counterparts, which included carrying a firearm, wearing a uniform, driving a marked police car, and answering all police-related calls (National Center for Women and Policing, 2005a; Lord, 1995). But during this time, police organizations began to introduce physical agility tests for police applicants with an overemphasis on upper body strength, and it introduced policies requiring officers to be a certain height and weight. Some departments went so far as to require officers to be five feet ten inches tall as a minimum (Fyfe et al., 1997).

Also, since the Civil Rights Act did not apply to municipal governments, many local laws and ordinances continued to prohibit the hiring of women for patrol work. This changed in 1972 when Title VII was amended to apply to state and municipal governments enabling women to pursue careers in law enforcement at all levels of government. But despite changes in legislation, recruitment focused on attracting "bodies" that were taller, muscular, and male and who could demonstrate physical strength in very particular ways (for example, being able to bench press two hundred pounds or do twenty chin ups). In most organizations, police policies relating to physical agility tests for applicants were designed to attract particular people (Langworthy and Travis, 2003); women were certainly not their target group. By the early 1970s, women comprised less than 1 percent of all police officers. The average age for female officers was thirty-five, most had university or college training, and their roles continued to be limited to social-service type work with women and children and in support roles such as clerical work (Martin, 1980; Perlstein, 1971, 1972). As a result, women began to file lawsuits for gender discrimination. Height, weight, and physical fitness standards that disproportionately discriminated against women violated Title VII because they did not meet "the test of Griggs."

In 1971, in *Griggs v. Duke Power Company* (401 U.S. 424 [1971]), the U.S. Supreme Court ruled that a policy or practice may be discriminatory if it has a disproportionate effect upon a particular group of people and is not job related or justified by job necessity. This meant that police departments had to show that a certain height or weight on the part of applicants was required for the job of police officer. Over time, police departments began to eliminate their height and weight restrictions and made some changes to their physical tests. But despite these, many police agencies in the United States today continue to require applicants to take tests that emphasize upper body strength. Others have set different testing standards for women and men. For example, in Michigan the MCOLES (Michigan Commission on Law Enforcement Standards) require male applicants who are between the ages of thirty to thirty-nine to complete a minimum of thirty push-ups, thirty sit-ups, and complete the one-half mile shuttle run in at least four minutes and thirty-eight seconds; whereas female applicants in the same age group are required to complete a minimum of seven push-ups, nineteen sit-ups, and complete the shuttle run in at least five minutes and fifty-nine seconds (Michigan.gov/ mcoles). This gendered configuration of bodies in relation to sex and patriarchal measurements of "physical strength" create the perception that women who want to be police officers are "less qualified" and exceptions must be made to "accommodate" women rather than to question the validity of these tests to begin with. There is no evidence to suggest that officers who can do more push-ups or sit-ups or bench press more weight are more effective or competent officers. These tests serve as good illustrations of how police organizations operationalize "effectiveness" and/or "competency" that are tied to narrow definitions of physical strength assumed to be central to the police identity as "crime fighters" (Corsianos, 2009).

Even with the Civil Rights Act of 1991, which was passed in response to a number of U.S. Supreme Court decisions that had limited the rights of employees who sued their employers for discrimination (e.g., *Wards Cove Packing Co. v. Antonio*, 490 U.S. 642 [1989]), courts have continued to rule in favor of police policies relating to physical testing standards for applicants. The Civil Rights Act of 1991 expressly recognizes that Title VII prohibits "disparate impact discrimination." Employees can prove discrimination by showing that an individual practice or group of practices resulted in a "disparate impact on the basis of race, color, religion, sex, or national origin, and the respondent fails to demonstrate that such practice is required by business necessity." But in 2002 the U.S. Court of Appeals for the Third Circuit ruled in favor of the Southeastern Pennsylvania Transit Authority's (SEPTA, the law-enforcement agency that patrols the subway system in Philadelphia) requirement that applicants run 1.5 miles in twelve minutes. The Court of Appeals upheld the district court's conclusion that applicants who fail the fitness test would be less likely to "successfully execute critical policing tasks" (*Lanning v. SEPTA*, 308F. 3d 286 [3rd Cir. 2002]). Ironically, SEPTA's "requirement" was not used to disqualify existing transit officers who could not pass the test, and already employed officers were given incentives to improve their physical state and pass the test, but there were no consequences for failing. Also, the ones who failed were not shown to be less able in carrying out their day-to-day duties (Grossman, 2002).

Title VII lawsuits against police agencies during the 1970s often resulted in court orders or consent decrees requiring police organizations to hire and/ or promote women through the use of quotas and timetables. Female officers described experiencing resistance by male colleagues that was at times life threatening (Hunt, 1984; Martin, 1980; Bloch and Anderson, 1974) and were subjected to overenforcement of rules and negative performance evaluations affecting promotion opportunities (Martin and Jurik, 2007). According to the National Center for Women and Policing (2003), by 1987 more than 50 percent of police agencies serving populations larger than fifty thousand had established affirmative action programs that had a direct impact in the increases in women throughout the 1980s and 1990s. But in recent years many of these consent decrees have expired and are not being renewed. The effect of these has been a drop in the number of female police officers in some organizations. For instance, the number of sworn female officers in the Pittsburgh Police Department in 1975 was only 1 percent. That same year a court-ordered consent decree established an affirmative action program for the department. And by 1991, the number of women increased to 27.2 percent, which was the highest in the country at the time. However, failure to renew the court order since 1990 led to the hiring of only 8.5 percent of women versus the 50 percent rate mandated earlier. Thus, by 2001, the total number of women dropped to 22 percent (National Center for Women and Policing, 2003).

Gendered differences are further seen in hiring, promotions, and performance evaluations. For instance, in many police departments, oral interview boards that evaluate candidates applying for promotion consist mainly of current male officers who must determine which applicants possess the "necessary" skills and are "deserving" of promotion. Given their backgrounds and personal biases, it is not uncommon to value candidates who have experience in the military or security services. As a result, it is not uncommon for women to receive lower scores since their work experiences, which may include social services, education, and child care, are not equally valued (Corsianos, 2004, 2009; Harrington and Lonsway, 2004; Martin, 1990).

Also, socializing is a form of networking and is important for promotion. But women with child care responsibilities are often disadvantaged since they cannot regularly socialize with other officers after work. Therefore, even though on the surface many promotional processes may appear to be objective, in practice, they tend to be subjective; that is, decisions relating to who is promoted are based on discriminatory practices and are often made before the formal interview process begins (Corsianos, 2009; Martin and Jurik, 2007; Harrington and Lonsway, 2004).

Similarly, performance evaluation criteria may appear to be gender neutral but may end up being based on men's performance standards. Harrington and Lonsway (2004) found that women's accomplishments in areas such as proactive policing, work with specific communities, and victims of crime were not valued as much as the types of activities that produced arrests, putting them at a disadvantage during evaluations. And Martin (1990) found that performance evaluation criteria used in assessing "quantity of work" in the Chicago Police Department only included number of arrests, court attendance, traffic enforcement, and award history.

Gender Configuring of Policies and Practices

The gendering configuration of policies and practices in police organizations remains clearly evident when looking at the category of people who are used as "the norm." In the United States, police policies and practices have overwhelmingly been established with larger, taller, male bodies in mind. Little if any attention is given to how a particular policy or practice will negatively impact a category of people. For instance, most police organizations fail to consider how rotating shift work and the lack of on-site day care facilities disproportionately discriminate against women. Similarly, other agencies have ordered police uniforms, weapons, and equipment to typically accommodate a physically larger body, and/or a "male body" specifically. There have been reports of female officers given "male bulletproof vests," making it very uncomfortable for women with larger breasts; guns with wider gun grips that put a disproportionate number of female officers at a disadvantage when firing their weapons (since many have smaller hands); permanently fixed front-load holsters that disadvantage shorter officers with shorter torsos (mostly women), especially as they sit; police latex gloves in "large" sizes, placing officers with smaller hands at risk of possible blood contamination as the gloves can slip off. Also, pregnant officers are often without police maternity uniforms and equipment that can accommodate their changing body (Corsianos, 2009).

Furthermore, discrimination against pregnant officers has taken many forms. Some departments have discriminated against pregnant officers by requiring them to qualify on the range every six months. As a result, some pregnant officers have been fired or forced to take unpaid disability leave because they refused to get requalified because of possible harms to the fetus from the high noise levels on the gun range and lead pollution. Also, some departments have unlawfully removed pregnant officers from their police assignments or have refused to provide them with nonpatrol assignments, forcing the officers to take unpaid leave until the child is born, or have required the officers to report their pregnancies even if not making a request for a nonpatrol assignment (Harrington and Lonsway, 2004).

But the image of the "feminine," nurturing, pregnant female officer runs counter to the dominant "hypermasculine" police image; that is, the physically strong, "straight" male officer who courageously fights crime and protects citizens. Resistance toward pregnant officers is undeniable. Management cannot require a pregnant officer to take disability or sick leave when she is physically fit to work, nor can they make the decision to change her assignment without her request because of her pregnancy. The U.S. Supreme Court in *UAW v. Johnson Controls* (499 U.S. 187 [1991]) ruled that employers were prohibited from implementing any policies that prohibited women of child-bearing age from hazardous jobs. The *Johnson* decision prevents police departments from forcing pregnant officers, who are physically fit to work, to take leave. At the same time, they cannot refuse a request for transfer to a nonpatrol assignment (see Corsianos, 2009). Police organizations must make alternate positions available for pregnant officers if they are also available for officers who have been injured either on or off the job. The federal Pregnancy Discrimination Act (PDA) "requires that pregnant women and women disabled by childbirth or related medical conditions be treated at least as well as employees who are not pregnant but who are similar in their ability or inability to work" (National Center for Women and Policing, 2005). And yet many police departments continue to be unaware of the laws relating to pregnancy and employment. Some agencies have unlawfully removed pregnant officers from their policing positions after they reported their pregnancy to management. Some have refused to provide pregnant officers with any light-duty assignments, instead forcing them to take unpaid leave until their child is born. And others have required women to report their pregnancies and then have removed them from their current positions for the "safety of the fetus" (Corsianos, 2009; Harrington and Lonsway, 2004).

Gender Configuring in the Division of Labor

As mentioned earlier, a disproportionate number of female police officers work in the more "feminized" units, including domestic violence, sexual assault, juvenile, community policing, education, and court services (Corsianos, 2009; Martin and Jurik, 2007). These units typically do not produce the number of arrests or "high profile" cases as do the drug, antigang, and homicide units; the perceived prestigious units. Research has shown that experience in these "feminized" areas can put many female officers at a disadvantage when trying to get promoted or to gain access to specialized units such as permanent detective positions, since experience in the more valued assignments often leads to more opportunities for high-profile arrests and awards, more recognition from management, and more credibility within policing circles. In some agencies, officers are secretly chosen for the prestigious permanent detective positions based on their previous crime-control experiences, their reputation as "team players," and their ability to socialize with other officers after work at popular police settings (Corsianos, 2009). The gendered division of labor preserves the continuation of gendered experiences by police officers that result in social as well as economic consequences. For instance, Corsianos (2009) found that even though detective positions were lateral entries, they were considered prestigious and were perceived by officers as a sort of promotion given their pay increase, clothing allowance, and ability to earn more money in court time and overtime. The gender configuring within policing serves to demonstrate that "women" as a category are to be understood as "feminine" and/or "not masculine," or, in significantly fewer instances (for instance, out lesbian officers who choose to perform in more masculine ways), as "not masculine enough" because ultimately they are still "seen" as "women." In the process, hegemonic masculinity is promoted and a culture of tolerance for police corruption is maintained.

Chapter Five

Media Constructions of Police Corruption

As discussed in chapter 3, females commit less crimes in comparison to males, and despite early "liberation" theorists, the rate of women's criminal offending is significantly lower in comparison to males, and the actual criminal behaviors reveal gendered patterns (Flavin, 2001; Naffine, 1996, 1987; Chesney-Lind and Shelden, 1992; Morris, 1987; Smart, 1982). But despite this information, the mainstream media chooses to sensationalize particular crimes involving female suspects, particularly when the crimes are excessively violent and provide "sensational" appeal (Belknap, 2006). The constant reporting of these incidents creates a "moral panic"; that is, it creates the illusion that violent criminal offending by women is rampant and has become an "epidemic" of sorts. On the other hand, with regard to police corruption, here too the media will choose to sensationalize particular cases that are deemed "newsworthy." But since police corruption remains a gendered enterprise, particular cases that are prioritized and sensationalized by the media typically do not involve female suspects. What contributes to their "newsworthiness," among other factors discussed below, is that the suspects are police officers mandated to enforce laws and not act outside them. And some critics have negatively evaluated the media's tendency to "overstate" the frequency of police corruption and have referred to their reaction as one of "moral panic" (Lawrence, 1997). This is similar to feminist and critical criminologists' criticism of the mainstream media for creating the public perception that female criminal activity has become an epidemic (Belknap, 2006; Chesney-Lind, 1997). But in the case of police corruption, to characterize it as being exaggerated is not only naive, but it is also dangerous, as seen in earlier chapters. Interestingly, the ones that are prioritized by the media often involve particular violent acts. Indeed, in the pursuit to attract a larger audience, the media capitalizes on cases with sensational appeal that can cater to incomplete or inaccurate reporting in order to "get the scoop" and "grab attention" without being careful about the details (Kurtz, 1994). But to evaluate the frequency of police criminality as being blown out of proportion does a disservice to society and disrupts any possibility for creating a "policing by consent." It also ensures limited public surveillance of policing. The purpose of this chapter is to examine the types of police corruption cases that are deemed "newsworthy" by the mainstream media and their role in how the misconduct is reported, as well as to critically evaluate the argument that police criminality is grossly exaggerated and overstated by the media. Also, examples of mainstream news articles on police corruption cases are provided in the second half of the chapter to highlight the kinds of behavior that are perceived to "be" corruption as well as newsworthy and to provide evidence of hegemonic masculinity; for instance, in how particular forms of violence are "naturalized" and the sense of entitlement, "brotherhood," secrecy, and autonomy that exist within policing.

Mainstream crime news focuses on the sensational and the unusual, often reinforcing biases and stereotypes (McCormick, 1995; Mills, 1990; Faith, 1987). But police corruption appears to be far more common than members of the public representing middle and upper socioeconomic backgrounds recognize, and the public only "learns" about the few that are typically uncovered by the investigative work of journalists following a "tip" and which produce "good" evidence against the suspected officer(s) and often involve a "legitimate" victim(s). Crime news stories are typically not educational; they do not inform the public about the various serious implications of police criminality, nor, for instance, about the role of the police culture, police discretionary powers, and the organizational structure that make misconduct possible. For Kurtz (1994) and McCormick (1995), features of mainstream crime news reporting include sensationalism and "entertainment." This way the probability of capturing the attention of the public is increased by strategically providing all the lurid details with the traditional voyeurism of crime news reporting. And, as Barak (2003:194) notes, "The emergence of 'infotainment,' or the triumph of entertainment over *pure news* as exemplified by such television news shows as ABC's *20/20*, CBS's *60 Minutes*, and NBC's *Dateline*, tend to reproduce a homogenization of images, texts, and narratives that shape and influence our collective dreams and nightmares."

Typically, the reports of the volume of specific types of violent crimes by the mainstream news media seem to overstate the frequency of these crimes in relation to the numbers reported by the crime statistics (for example, Uniform Crime Reporting, National Crime Victimization Survey), which indicate that the most common crimes are nonviolent. The media reports, however, suggest that traditionally defined violent crimes such as murder, stranger assault, and robbery are the most frequent types of crimes committed (Belknap, 2006; Barak, 2003; Chesney-Lind, 1997). When looking at police corruption specifically, selective instances of misconduct are made available for public consumption, particularly ones related to violent crimes. The emerging "moral panic" over sensationalized cases of police corruption has been challenged by some who assert that police criminality today, including use of force, is not a common occurrence but rather appears to be less frequent and/or has declined overall (International Association of Chiefs of Police, 2011; Walker, 2005; Garner et al., 2002).

Given the variety of powers provided to the police and the evidence of abuse of powers, the public cannot afford to not pay attention (Burris and Whitney, 2000; Nelson, 2000; Geller and Toch, 1996; Kappeler, Sluder, and Alpert, 1994; McAlary, 1994; Skolnick and Fyfe, 1993). But instead, when particular cases are "discovered" by the media, they focus on the ones that have dramatic, sensational, and "entertainment" appeal. The fact that the suspected offender is a police officer increases the dramatic potential, but this alone is not enough to generate media interest. The misconduct must be perceived as "serious" and atypical in comparison to the vast array of publicly recognized forms of police corruption. And the focus is usually on the individual officer(s) involved; that is, the "bad apple(s)," leaving little room for alternative interpretations in explaining police misconduct beyond the individual(s). For instance, in one article (included below) published by the *Washington Post/Associated Press* (February 25, 2011), thirty-one police officers were suspended as the Baltimore Police Department "faces the city's largest alleged police corruption scheme in decades." The president of the police union was quick to point out that these officers are the *isolated few* from the 2,800-member force. He added that "officers who work the street feel very strongly about their oath" and "a good cop is not going to tolerate a bad cop." In another recent case reported by the *Anchorage Daily News* (February 24, 2011), an Anchorage police officer who sexually assaulted women inside the police station and in his patrol car was convicted of twenty criminal counts, including first- and second-degree sexual assault, official misconduct, and illegal use of a computer. Prior to the original sexual assault allegation, Officer Anthony Rollins had been investigated for having sex while in uniform and on the job. Investigators found "no evidence of criminal wrongdoing," but he apparently "was punished severely" for having sex while on duty. Interestingly, "Detectives found five more victims after the initial report." The chief of police admitted that other officers have also been caught in the past for having sex on duty, but that "none of them were found to have committed crimes," he said. But despite the lesson "learned" from the convicted officer's history and sequence of events, the chief was quick to point out that the guilty officer "was an anomaly in the department."

The police and news organizations maintain a working relationship. Police agencies are the primary suppliers of crime stories in general, and, over time, the police as a "credible" source have become conventional wisdom (Ericson, 1989; Fishman, 1981). The relationship can be described as one of "give and take." Police have access to a "crime story" that they make available to the media, but at the same time they control how the incident is framed. For Sacco (1995:172), the crime story "must be viewed as serious enough and as visual enough to be chosen over competing issues." For instance, he provides an example from Best's work (1989) on child victimization, where the stories used in the news reports included frightening examples to typify the experiences of child victims. According to Sacco (1995:174), "News stories about random crimes have great dramatic value, as the media frenzies that surround serial murders illustrate. Moreover, the advocates to whom news workers have access during the early stages of problem development often stress the random nature of a particular form of victimization since problems must be seen as more urgent when everyone is threatened." These arguments are relevant to police corruption cases that are publicized by the media. As mentioned earlier, the police misconduct must be viewed as "serious," have sensational appeal, and is preferred if it can be presented as random in nature, where members of the public are convinced it can happen to anyone.

Also, the heightened use of camcorders, digital cameras, and smartphones has meant that it is no longer uncommon to have video and audio recordings of crimes, and these can then be broadcast to the world via the Internet. The increasing accessibility and sophistication of recording devices have made capturing a crime on video more probable; this further increases the desire to focus on a case that has "visual evidence," as seen in some of the news articles further down. This dramatic "value" of a crime serves to transform members of the public into voyeurs who passively watch images on a screen.

U.S. laws are so pervasive that it is not difficult to engage in behavior that violates some type of law. But the current system of selective law enforcement reflects the classist, racist, and sexist ideologies with regard to the types of behavior deemed to be "criminal" and more "serious" (Reiman and Leighton, 2010; Barak, Flavin, and Leighton, 2001). Additionally, selective law enforcement is typically applied to individuals, which reflects the dominant ideology that individuals rather than institutions are responsible for particular social problems. As Gordon (2002:117) noted, "Individuals are criminally prosecuted for motor accidents because of negligent or drunken driving, for instance, but auto manufacturers are never criminally prosecuted for the negligent construction of unsafe cars or for their roles in increasing the likelihood of death through air pollution. Individual citizens are often prosecuted and punished for violence and for resisting arrest, equally, but those agents of institutions, like police and prison guards, or institutions themselves, like

Dow Chemical, are never prosecuted for inflicting unwarranted violence on others." Similarly, in publicized police corruption cases, responsibility for the misconduct is overwhelmingly placed on the suspected officer by the media, the public, and, at times, by the police organization when the "evidence" against the officer makes it difficult for upper management to deny. And it is only few cases of police corruption that the media can gain access to and are deemed "newsworthy," as discussed earlier; most types of misconduct on the part of the police are ignored, hidden, and/or not recognized as wrong within policing circles (Corsianos, 2004).

Given police organization's growing "legitimacy" over the years on the part of many representing the middle and upper socioeconomic classes, wrongdoing on the part of the police becomes less visible or less offensive when police misconduct is alleged against economically and/or socially marginalized populations. Gordon (2002:114) asserts that the United States has a "dual system of justice" in which the police, courts, and prisons pay particular attention to only a few crimes that are committed largely by poorer people (Reiman and Leighton, 2010; Barak, 2003; Barak, Flavin, and Leighton, 2001). On the other hand, crimes committed by the police are of particular interest to the media given the suspects are police officers themselves who are expected to enforce the laws and not violate them and where the public can be convinced that these acts are "random in nature," putting everyone at "risk." But, as mentioned earlier, the priority for the mainstream media is to dramatize rather than educate and raise consciousness. The media often aims to create the impression that it can happen to anyone. In doing this, more members of the public will pay attention during this limited period of reporting as it now concerns their own safety and that of their family.

Police corruption refers to many different forms of police abuses of power (see chapter 2). But the inability to provide an accurate measurement of corruption presents challenges to their effective management (Moran, 2002) and also to supporters of police reform who are without more inclusive statistics that can serve to shock and inform the public. But even current statistical data that is introduced as fact by self-identified "value-free" researchers do not speak for themselves; they must be, as Curran and Renzetti (2001) note, "interpreted." For Ivkovic (2003:593), "The degree of success of a reform is often determined on the basis of its political appeal and the absence of subsequent scandals, rather than on the true impact the reform has had on the actual corruption in the agency."

Attempts to measure misconduct have come from the following: the media; formal inquiries (for example, the Knapp Commission); citizen action groups (for instance, Human Rights Watch); citizen complaints and officer discipline data; surveys and interviews (see Barker, 1978, 2006; Corsianos, 2003); litigation cases (for example, cases that are won or settled can provide evidence of police misconduct); police incident data that indicate officers' use of force, including the discharge of a firearm (Williams and Hester, 2003; White, 2002; Crawford and Burns, 1998; Garner et al., 1995); and system audits (for instance, auditing the receipt and storage of police evidence or tapes of interviews with suspects). But despite the various means available, one cannot fully know the extent of police corruption within an organization. In other words, the type and frequency as well as the details of police misconduct cannot be authoritatively known given the current police culture and policing as an "institution." But its existence as a common occurrence, on the other hand, cannot be denied given the possibilities for misconduct that are made available and the reluctance of police organizations to "see" the different types of behaviors that "are" indeed corruption.

For Tiffen (2004:1175):

> Police corruption to greatly varying degrees seems to be a feature of most large societies. Its sources lie in the nature of police work. The scope for secrecy and relatively unaccountable power is always conducive to corruption. In addition, the inherent difficulties of policing, including the need in both intelligence and enforcement to be regularly dealing with a range of characters . . ., presents more opportunities and temptation than the rest of the population is normally subjected to.

The term *moral panic* is often used to describe social reactions to deviant or collective behavior, and it has been used in a variety of capacities (Goode and Ben-Yehuda, 1994). The concept of moral panic carries a negative evaluation of the media and public reaction. And, as more and more attention is given to the problem, then people begin to perceive it as an "epidemic." Tiffen (2004) identifies a number of features that might be included in a "moral panic." They include: "volatility of reaction," in which public concerns about the problem surface quickly, and "moral absoluteness," in which the ambiguous tenets of the problem are not considered, rendering it entirely negative. For Tiffen (2004:1185), "Newsworthiness and moral simplicity tend to go together." Another feature could be "causality in terms of sinister agents," where the cause is linked to some anonymous, evil agent rather than institutional or environmental sources. Other features of moral panic include: "disproportion in projecting prevalence," in which people begin to perceive it as an epidemic as more and more attention is given to it; "alarmist predictions," in which "the more frightening the forecast, the more newsworthy it is"; and "the recital of urban myths" and "a self-propelling relationship between newsworthiness and vocal reaction," in which authority figures and interest groups continue to make public statements and use the media coverage to promote their views and ensure the issues remain newsworthy (ibid.).

Many of these features can be applied to the mainstream news reporting of police corruption cases. For instance, oftentimes a particular incident is presented in "moral absolute" terms, leaving little or no room for critical evaluation. Also, the focus tends to be on the individual "evil agent" or "bad apple(s)," once again leaving no room to examine important components such as the police culture, police discretionary powers, and the police as an "institution." And, yes, the public will often perceive the case as "serious" if it is presented as random in nature, as discussed earlier; this can serve as an example of what Tiffen calls a "frightening forecast" because it affects the public at large. But, on the other hand, rarely do members of the middle and upper socioeconomic classes view these instances as an "epidemic." They are often interested in and/or concerned with what is happening, but as the media spotlight on the incident fades so does the public interest; many don't ask the necessary questions relating to how the abuses of power are made possible. In fact, public surveillance of the police remains minimal (Kappeler, Sluder, and Alpert, 1994). News reports on violent acts are often the result of "procedures not to know" (Kasinsky, 1994). By relying almost exclusively on "official" sources, the news media promotes and reproduces the dominant views of what qualify and are "understood" to be "serious" crimes (Barak, 1994; Ericson, Baranek, and Chan, 1987).

Therefore, to criticize the media for "overstating" the frequency of police corruption or to make the argument that the media convinces the public that police corruption is an epidemic is problematic. Most often the mainstream media will focus on an individual corruption case. And, less frequently, they will connect the incident with other earlier cases of police misconduct within the department. It is in these fewer instances where the argument of "an epidemic" emerges. But an "epidemic" has been defined as the "rapid development, spread, or growth of something unpleasant" (dictionary.com). An epidemic leads the masses to be fearful and to respond to the event quickly and often irrationally. This is not the case in reported police corruption cases. It is in the interest of the mainstream news media to focus on the crimes of individuals rather than institutions. In an age of global capitalism, the media's primary connection is with the development of advanced capitalism (Barak, 2003), and not the destruction or delegitimization of the police as a central institution in the preservation of capitalism and dominant ideologies. For Tiffen (2004:1186), the term *moral panic* "will always be contentious because it seems to undermine the seriousness of a problem. It is used most comfortably to describe social reactions the analyst sees as irrational." In other words, the "problem" is more imaginary than real based on perceived fears.

As stated earlier, constructing police corruption as a moral panic that is intended to undermine the seriousness and frequency of police criminality is naive. To do so is to fail to recognize the wide range of possibilities for police criminality and the power and authority given to individual officers over citizens. Based on police accounts of corruption (Corsianos, 2009, 2004; Barker, 2006, 1978; Nelson, 2000; Burris and Whitney, 2000; Websdale, 1999), it appears that police abuse of powers for personal and/or organizational gain is not uncommon. Police misconduct easily takes place when the public does not pay attention. As Tiffen notes (2004:1191), "Corruption thrives best away from the public surveillance, when external attention is minimal." The incidents that are "discovered" and reported by the mainstream media typically involve police abuse of power that is deemed "serious" by the public, include "good" evidence against the suspected officer (e.g., video tape, audio recording, etc.) that the organization cannot entirely deny, and often involve a victim(s) that is/are viewed to be credible and legitimate. For Dean, Bell, and Lauchs (2010), police corruption is typically identified by investigative journalists who are able to uncover particular cases of police misconduct. But this is often after first receiving a tip from a source believed to be credible. Therefore, paying close attention to what the police do is rational and necessary. The closer the public scrutiny of the police is then the greater becomes the ability to "see" the types and frequency of police corruption.

THE MAINSTREAM MEDIA AND GENDERED OFFENDING

Violent criminal behavior that is particularly heinous seems to be often sensationalized when the suspect is a female. Despite the differences in the types and rate of criminal offending between women and men, particularly violent, heinous crimes believed to be committed by women seem to generate further publicity (Belknap, 2006; Chesney-Lind, 1997). Some examples here would include the media circus surrounding Aileen Wuornos, who was dubbed "the first female serial killer" in the United States. The public support for sentencing her to death was overwhelming. The mainstream media portrayed her as a "monster" who worked as a prostitute exploiting "vulnerable men" and who ultimately committed a series of murders against "innocent victims." This was a woman who was tried and convicted by the public from the beginning of her trial as a result of the unfavorable media reports about her history and "lifestyle." News stories focused on her apparent sexual fantasies and kinky fetishes (*Aileen: Life and Death of a Serial Killer* documentary, 2003) with all the lurid details and traditional voyeurism of crime news reporting (McCormick, 1995).

More recently, many in the public had tried and convicted Casey Anthony for the murder of her daughter, Caylee. Casey was portrayed as a "party girl" who no longer wanted to be a mother and chose to kill her daughter to free herself from this responsibility. Here, too, the public had tried and convicted her before the trial even started. The public response to the "not guilty" verdict was deafening. The death threats, the tears, and anger on the part of outraged members of the public have been overwhelming. In the former instance, Aileen was constructed by the mainstream media as an "immoral woman" who worked as a prostitute for most of her life and never had any type of "legitimate" employment as well as an "unnatural woman"; a woman who was not particularly "feminine," not conventionally "pretty," and who committed a series of excessively violent crimes. In the latter example, Casey, too, was constructed as an "unnatural woman," but in different ways. Unlike Aileen, Casey was conventionally "pretty" and "feminine" but was also portrayed as "unnatural" for killing the child she gave birth to. She was portrayed as a "party girl" and a "slut" who was more interested in sex and hanging out at parties than being home with her daughter and who ultimately chose to kill her child because she was interfering with her "lifestyle."

In fact, women are more likely to be victims of violent crimes rather than criminal offenders, but the media creates the "knowledge" that the growing number of violent female offenders is "the problem" (Brownstein, 2000). Women's and men's criminal offending is highly interconnected to their gender identity (see chapter 3), as seen in Miller's study (1998) in the differences between female and male robbers. Also, Faith (1993) points out that shoplifting serves as one example where gendered patterns in offending are maintained. Females stole household items, clothing, groceries, and "feminine" items such as makeup, whereas males stole electronic equipment, tools, and other items of significantly higher value. For the most part, females stole items whose value was under $1,000, whereas males were significantly more likely to commit thefts that exceeded this amount.

Women's experiences contradict the idea propagated by the media that the increase in women's criminal offending is the result of women's newfound freedoms to commit crimes equally to men. The "tidal wave" of female criminal offending was falsely perceived to be the result of the second "wave" in the women's movement (see chapter 3). Soon the mainstream media had contributed to the "common knowledge" that female offending was really no different than male offending, and this became the conventional wisdom of the popular culture. Chesney-Lind discussed the "female crime wave" of the 1990s and the preoccupation with "girl gangs." Criticizing the "moral panic" on the part of the media, she pointed out that "there is little evidence to support the notion of a new, violent female offender" (Chesney-Lind and Shelden, 1992:29). As Faith (1993:70) points out, "Females are commonly subject to many more private forms of social control than are males, and the female 'deviant' is deemed more deviant than her male equivalent. She suffers greater social stigmatization when she breaches idealized gender standards." This contributes to the reasons for why female officers are less likely to be involved in police corruption, as discussed in earlier chapters. But in terms of news media accounts of female officers involved in police corruption cases, there are few recent reports. Admittedly, it will be interesting to see how the mainstream media will portray the next "sensational" police corruption case whose leading suspect(s) is/are female officer(s).

RECENT PUBLICIZED CASES OF POLICE CORRUPTION

An Internet search of recent police corruption cases in the mainstream news media in the United States led to several examples involving male officers but difficulty in locating cases that involved only female officers, or female and male officers participating together. The examples below involved mostly male officers, with the exception of the last three that included misconduct on the part of female officers. These articles highlight the kinds of acts perceived to "be" corruption as well as newsworthy, and they provide evidence of hegemonic masculinity as a central tenet of police identity; for instance, in how particular forms of violence are "naturalized" and in "the brotherhood," secrecy, autonomy, authority, and sense of entitlement over "civilians" that exist within policing. They also serve to highlight some of the differences in the types of misconduct and/or level of involvement between male and female police officers as seen in chapter 3.

FATAL ASSAULT
According to CNN (April 13, 2011):
Two New Orleans police officers were convicted Wednesday in federal court in a 2005 beating death and cover-up after initially telling investigators the victim was suffering from a drug overdose. Several neighbors of the man who was killed testified they saw Officer Melvin Williams approach Raymond Robair on the street in Robair's neighborhood and kick him in the side and beat him repeatedly with a baton, according to the Justice Department. Officials said after the beating, Williams—along with a second officer, Matthew Dean Moore—placed an unconscious Robair into their police car and drove him to Charity Hospital. According to a Justice Department release, witnesses at the trial said the two police officers falsely informed the hospital staff they found Robair under a bridge and all they knew was that Robair was a drug user. Based upon that information, the hospital treated Robair for a drug overdose rather than blunt force trauma. Robair suffered fractured ribs and a ruptured spleen as a result of the beating. He was pronounced dead within a few hours. The Justice Department said Williams and Moore were convicted of obstructing justice by writing and submitting a false and inaccurate incident report. Moore was also convicted of one additional felony count for making false statements to FBI agents in March 2010. Williams faces a possible maximum sentence of life in prison. Moore faces a possible maximum sentence of 25 years in prison.

In this article the readers are told that the officers "were convicted" in the "beating death" of a man, and that they tried to cover it up by telling investigators that "the victim was suffering from a drug overdose." Several crimes are identified, and lurid details about the assault are provided. We are told that the officer kicked Robair and "beat him repeatedly with a baton," and that the "unconscious Robair" was then driven to the hospital by the officers. We are led to believe that his death could have possibly been prevented had the officers revealed to the hospital staff that Robair had suffered "blunt force trauma." But, instead, the officers informed the hospital that Robair was a "drug user," which resulted in them treating him for a drug overdose. Robair had "suffered fractured ribs and a ruptured spleen as a result of the beating" and "was pronounced dead within a few hours." From reading other articles (e.g., www.nola.com; April 13, 2011) the deceased is identified as a "Treme resident," where the median household income is below the poverty line. In this case, the victim was poor and could have been easily "overlooked" by the criminal justice system. However, here the victim died after being in contact with the police, and there were "several" neighbors who witnessed the beating and were willing to come forward. These witnesses reported that it happened in "Robair's neighborhood," contradicting the officers' story that "they found Robair under a bridge." This case provides both shocking and dramatic details. The readers learn about the scandalous actions of the officers relating to both the beating and cover-up, the lurid details of the assault, and the ultimate death of a human being. The article concludes by telling the readers that one officer "faces a possible maximum sentence of life in prison" and the other "faces a possible maximum sentence of 25 years." But, as is typical in the news media reporting of police corruption, the focus is on the individual officers and not on how this tragedy happened. No information is provided, for instance, on the wide range of police discretionary powers given to officers; the lack of supervisory oversight; the overemphasis on aggressive crime-control tactics; the centrality of masculinity or "hypermasculinity" within policing; the "us versus them" mentality; and/or the history of excessive use of force and fatal assaults in the department.

RAPE:
New York Post (February 20, 2011), reported the following:
An NYPD patrolman accused of raping a drunken woman in her apartment made a chilling confession, apologizing to the victim for "getting really crazy" the night of the alleged 2008 attack, a former Manhattan prosecutor says. A few days after she was allegedly assaulted, the victim secretly recorded East Village cop Kenneth Moreno in a face-to-face encounter on the street in front of the 9th Precinct station house where Moreno worked, the source said. "He tries to deny they had sex, but eventually he admits to it," said the ex-prosecutor, referring to the meeting orchestrated by the Manhattan District Attorney's Office. "He says, 'It wasn't done intentionally. I didn't mean to hurt you. I just

got caught up. I'm sorry.'" The tape will play a key role in the case against Moreno, 43, and his partner, Franklin Mata, 28, who go on trial next week for rape, burglary and official misconduct and face up to 25 years in prison. While Mata sat nearby, Moreno allegedly forced himself on the passed-out fashion executive, whom the two officers helped up to her apartment on East 13th Street after she got blitzed partying with pals in December 2008. The victim called the Manhattan DA's sex-crimes office, which launched an investigation in conjunction with the NYPD's Internal Affairs Bureau. She wore a wire and confronted Moreno about what he did. She told him she recalled waking up on her bathroom floor, then being in her bed as the cop stripped off her clothes and had his way with her. His explanation: "It turned from us trying to help you to getting really crazy." But after Moreno says he's sorry, he offers to date her. "If you stop drinking, I'll be your boyfriend," he says. Sources familiar with the charges say the trial could last several weeks and involve a slew of witnesses—people who saw the cops and the victim that night and forensic experts expected to testify about the effects of intoxication as a drunk person can't legally consent to sex. The defense is expected to argue that the sex was consensual and will likely attack the credibility of the cops' accuser, a stunning brunette and successful fashion designer who had recently moved from San Francisco. Moreno and Mata met her about 1 a.m. on Dec. 7, 2008, when a cabdriver called 911 and said his passenger was drunk, had vomited in his taxi and needed help getting into her East 13th Street apartment.

Moreno, then a 17-year veteran, and Mata, with three years on the force, arrived and assisted the woman into the building and up the stairs of the five-story walk-up. The three walked in at 1:10 a.m., according to videotape from a ground-floor bar, Heathers, two doors down, and spent seven minutes inside, during which she continued to vomit. They left, promising to return later to check on her condition. They returned at 1:56 a.m. and were let in by another resident, whom they told they were investigating a noise complaint. They stayed for 17 minutes before being forced to leave to handle a traffic accident at 13th Street and First Avenue. After dealing with the crash, one of them allegedly used a pay phone at the scene to make a 911 call, claiming to be "John Edward." The caller said a homeless man was lurking at an East 13th Street building close to the woman's. A police dispatcher sent them to that location. The two entered the woman's building at 2:59 a.m., using her key, which they'd taken from her earlier, and stayed until 3:33 a.m., according to the bar's video. The footage shows them shielding their faces from a camera they spotted during the second trip. They didn't realize a second camera captured the effort to conceal their identities. Once inside the apartment, Moreno removed the woman's clothing, including her boots and tights, as she floated in and out of consciousness, sources said. Prosecutors say Moreno put on a condom and had sex with the woman as she lay face-down on her bed while Mata sat on a couch in the living room. Later that morning, the victim reached out to friends in the building and to Heather Millstone, who owns the bar that captured video of the officers. "I've been raped," she told her, according to Millstone. "It was the police." The friends convinced her to seek treatment at Beth Israel Hospital and to contact the Manhattan DA's Office. Investigators uncovered incriminating evidence, including a red Bic lighter that the victim found under her bed and didn't recognize. A search of Moreno's police locker turned up three of the same lighters. Investigators suspect the Bic fell from his pocket when he was assaulting the victim.

This article has many "appealing" features for the mainstream news media. Readers are told that a police officer is "accused of raping a drunken woman in her apartment." We are told the "alleged victim" is a "stunning brunette and successful fashion designer." There are several "visual" elements in the form of video and audio recordings. For one, we are told that "a few days after she was allegedly assaulted, the victim secretly recorded" the police officer "in a face-to-face encounter" in front of the precinct station, where "he tries to deny they had sex, but eventually he admits to it" and apologizes to the victim for "getting really crazy." There's also a "videotape from a ground-floor bar" that captures the officers assisting the woman into the building. The video shows them returning about forty minutes later and being let in by another resident who was told "they were investigating a noise complaint." And that "they stayed for 17 minutes before being forced to leave to handle a traffic accident." But, after the accident, one of them alleg-edly makes a fake 911 call claiming to be *John Edward* to report a *homeless man lurking at an East 13th Street building close to the woman's.*" This 911 call has since been made available online (www.nypost.com—"DA: 911 Farce by Cop," April 12, 2011); the person who made the call appears to be attempting to disguise his New York accent, but it becomes evident with particular words. He also at one point uses "police lingo" to refer to the homeless man as "male white" but then quickly corrects himself by saying "a white guy." And when the dispatcher asks him for a contact phone number, he says that he's visiting from Canada and doesn't have one. Interestingly, the same two officers arrive at that location and are then captured by the video entering the woman's building. We are told that the officers entered her building "using her key which they'd taken from her earlier" and that they stayed for thirty-four minutes "according to the bar's video." "The footage shows them shielding their faces from a camera they spotted during the second trip," but "they didn't realize a second camera captured the effort to conceal their identities."

Additionally, several lurid details of the sexual assault are provided, such as "the cop stripped off her clothes and had his way with her"; "Moreno removed the woman's clothing, including her boots and tights"; and that "Moreno put on a condom and had sex with the woman as she lay face-down on her bed." Another central feature to this article is the level of "victim blaming," as seen in many sexual assault cases. One of the common rape myths is that victims are somehow responsible for their sexual victimization (Harmed, 2005; Lee et al., 2005; Benedict, 1992; Scully, 1990; Glavin, 1986; Russell, 1984); for instance, they are blamed for what they were wearing when they were assaulted, for being at "inappropriate" places or for being at places at "inappropriate" times, and for consuming alcohol and/or being intoxicated. In several instances in the article, the reader is given information about the victim's drinking; for instance, in the first sentence we are told that an "NYPD patrolman" is "accused of raping a drunken woman"; that "Moreno allegedly forced himself on the passed-out fashion executive"; that "she got blitzed partying with pals"; that forensic experts are "expected to testify about the effects of intoxication as a drunk person can't legally consent to sex"; that "the defense" "will likely attack the credibility of the cop's accuser" because of her drinking that night; that the "passenger was drunk, and vomited in his taxi"; that at her apartment "she continued to vomit"; and as Moreno removed her clothes "she floated in and out of consciousness." The reporting of sexual assault in this manner distorts the actual crime (DeKeseredy and Schwartz, 1998; Koss, 1996; Fairstein, 1993; Koss and Oros, 1982). It supports the common rape myth that "the alcohol" caused the sexual assault; that is, ultimately, the victim who drinks and/or is intoxicated is responsible for what happens to "her" (Belknap, 2006; Harned, 2005).

Also, the emphasis on stranger sexual assaults by the mainstream media creates the perception that these types of assaults are most common, reinforcing another rape myth; that is, that sexual assaults are committed by strangers. In actuality, most sexual assaults are committed by acquaintances (Benedict, 1992; Boyle, 1991; DeKeseredy and Hinch, 1991; Russell, 1984). The readers are not provided anything educational about sexual assaults including, for instance, the gendered nature of sexual assaults, the frequency of this crime, and the dominant rape myths that often serve as barriers to obtaining convictions. To the contrary, this article reproduces some of the common rape myths. It also provides no information on the power disparity between men and women and the sense of entitlement some men feel they have over women's bodies (Belknap, 2006; Benedict, 1998; Sanday, 1996, 1990; Russell, 1990; Spencer, 1987; Malamuth, 1981). Nor is there any information on the relationship between patriarchal ideologies, violence against women, and the police culture.

But despite what appears as solid evidence against the officers, three months after the above article was published, jurors acquitted both officers of the rape charges but convicted them of three counts of official misconduct for entering the woman's apartment. And both have been fired from the police department. Interestingly, one of the jurors, Richard Schimenti, was quoted in a CBS New York story (May 26, 2011), saying: "I did think that they might have had sex, but that doesn't mean that they did have sex. There's no DNA."

One of the few "unfavorable" reports of the officers posttrial was featured in an article titled "Too Drunk to Remember, Not Too Drunk to Be Raped?" by Andy Ostroy (Huffingtonpost.com, June 1, 2011), where it describes Moreno as the one

> who admittedly picked up the very drunk woman, took her to her apartment and then over the course of several hours re-entered her apartment three times, using her keys. He "flirted" with her, "snuggled" beside her in bed while she wore only a bra, kissed her head, and sang to her. What's more, there is a recording of a fake 911 call they made to justify returning to the apartment, and the victim had later confronted Moreno outside his precinct while wearing a recording device. After insisting that nothing had happened, he then admitted that they "had sex" and that he had used a condom. . . . At the core of the defense was its claim that she was too drunk to be a credible witness, but it is precisely that state of debilitating intoxication that served as the very invitation for the officers to make their highly inappropriate and illegal entry into her apartment where she was supposedly just "comforted" as opposed to raped. Furthermore, there was no DNA. . . . Are we as an intelligent society really expected to believe that Moreno simply lay aside her in her bed, innocently caressing her as he sang Bon Jovi's "Living on a Prayer" gently in her ear? It's pretty safe and fair to assume that the officers' behavior was anything but altruistic given the highly unethical nature of their presence in her apartment in the first place. And given the suspicious backdrop, it's easy to accept the accuser's accounts as the truth. Don't tell me a red-blooded adult male who makes repeated trips into a drunken young woman's apartment does this with the sole intent of taking care of her.

But even in this "unfavorable" account of the officers, although the reader is told that "it's easy to accept the accuser's accounts as the truth," the journalistic pattern of "victim-blaming" is still evident. In the line that reads "don't tell me a red-blooded adult male who makes repeated trips into a drunken young woman's apartment does this with the sole intent of taking care of her," the message given is that ultimately "women" must avoid "putting themselves in these situations" because any "red-blooded adult male" will not be able to help himself when confronted with a "drunken young woman." This is a typical cultural construction of sexual assault where the woman is held responsible for the "uncontrollable" sexuality of "red-blooded" males (Belknap, 2006; Harned, 2005; Glavin, 1986). As in the earlier article, nothing is said about the gendered nature and frequency of sexual assaults, nor about the common rape myths that make it difficult to obtain convictions (as was seen in this case). The "red-blooded male" here is a police officer expected to "serve and protect." No information is given about the level of discretionary powers and lack of police oversight that enabled these officers to return to the victim's apartment three times after the initial contact. Nor is any information provided on other sexual assault complaints and convictions against officers. Relevant tenets of the police culture are not presented; for instance, how this very police culture can "enable" one officer to sit on the couch in the victim's living room while leaving his partner in the bedroom with the woman for about thirty minutes. There is no discussion of the sense of "brotherhood" (Corsianos, 2009; Martin and Jurik, 2007; Farkas and Manning, 1997; Van Maanen, 1973) within policing or sense of "entitlement" that some men feel they have over women's bodies, where they feel that they can have forced or coerced sex whenever they want and with whomever they want (Belknap, 2006; Benedict, 1998; Sanday, 1996, 1990; Russell, 1990; Spencer, 1987; Malamuth, 1981). Clearly, there was no "hint" to the possibility of how policing as an "institution" and hegemonic masculinity, as a central tenet of police identity, create, encourage, and/or condone these crimes.

FATAL ASSAULT AND OTHER ABUSES:
According to the *Huffington Post* (May 12, 2011):
Newark resident Rasheed Moore was driving toward the intersection of 18th Avenue and S. 13th Street in January 2005, when his vehicle collided with an on-duty police car containing Newark police officers Matthew Ruane and Pasquale Popolizio. Thirteen gunshots later—all fired by Officer Ruane against the unarmed driver—Moore was dead. Five years later, in December 2009, the municipality shelled out $1 million to Moore's family in a settlement after a jury concluded that the officers had used excessive force against Moore. Hundreds of similar allegations and stories over the past several years have prompted the Justice Department to launch a federal investigation of the Newark Police Department, digging into claims that the force has treated Newark's citizens discriminatorily, brutally, and illegally. Assistant Attorney General Thomas Perez announced the investigation on Monday in a joint press conference with Newark mayor Cory Booker and U.S. attorney Paul Fishman. "[The] investigation will examine allegations of excessive force, unconstitutional stops, searches and seizures, discriminatory policing on the basis of race, ethnicity, national origin, sexual orientation or gender identity, whether detainees confined to holding cells are subjected to unreasonable risk of harm, and whether officers retaliate against citizens who legally attempt to observe or record police activity," said Perez in a statement on Monday.

This case has all the desired features for the mainstream news media. For one, it is viewed as "serious." The reader is told that a vehicle collided with an on-duty police car and that "thirteen gunshots later—all fired by Officer Ruane against the unarmed driver," the motorist is dead. We are also told that the "municipality shelled out $1 million" to the deceased's family in a settlement after "a jury concluded that the officers had used excessive force." This event is constructed as being "random in nature," and therefore the message given is that it can happen to anyone. We learn that there have been "hundreds of similar allegations and stories over the past several years." Therefore, there are potentially many more "legitimate" victims beyond the deceased. All these serve as "good" evidence of police misconduct contributing to its "newsworthiness." And, finally, these events have "prompted the Justice Department to launch a federal investigation of the Newark Police Department, digging into claims that the force has treated Newark's citizens discriminatorily, brutally, and illegally." The report further provides "shocking" and dramatic appeal by listing all the different allegations of police misconduct that will become subject to the investigation, such as "excessive force, unconstitutional stops, searches and seizures, discriminatory policing." Once again, there is no discussion on the possibilities for corruption risks that are made possible internally and how violent acts against "civilians" become justified and condoned by police.

ROBBERY AND ATTEMPTED MURDER:
According to the *Chicago Tribune* (April 19, 2011):
A former Chicago police officer pleaded guilty Tuesday to federal felony charges stemming from one of the worst misconduct scandals in the department's history. Keith Herrera, 33, admitted taking part in three robberies in which he and other officers with the elite Special Operations Section stole hundreds of thousands of dollars in cash from suspected drug dealers and other citizens after making illegal traffic stops or searches of their homes. Herrera, who remains free on bond until his scheduled sentencing on July 14, faces up to 13 years in prison, but prosecutors said in a plea agreement that if Herrera continues to cooperate, they will recommend a reduced prison sentence. Herrera pleaded guilty to civil rights and tax-related charges and admitted he pocketed about $40,000 from the robberies in 2005. He admitted he never reported the money as income on his federal tax return for that year. Herrera later secretly wore a wire recording then-Officer Jerome Finnegan, identified by authorities as the scheme's ringleader, allegedly plotting the murder of a Special Operations Section officer whom he suspected of cooperating with authorities. Herrera, Finnegan, former Officer Stephen Del Bosque and current Officer Eric J. Olsen were charged in federal court this month in connection with the case. Del Bosque pleaded guilty Monday to a misdemeanor civil rights charge. He faces up to 12 months in prison. The U.S. attorney's office has said that Finnegan and Olsen also have agreed to plead guilty. Since the scandal broke five years ago, seven additional officers have pleaded guilty to wrongdoing in Cook County court. Most of them received reduced sentences in exchange for their cooperation in the federal probe. The Special Operations Section was disbanded in 2007 because of the scandal.

In this article we learn that the police officer "pleaded guilty" "to federal charges stemming from one of the worst misconduct scandals in the department's history." One of the officers "admitted" to "taking part in three robberies in which he and other officers with the elite Special Operations Section stole hundreds of thousands of dollars in cash . . .," and he also "pleaded guilty to civil rights and tax-related charges." But, in furthering the "shock

value," the readers are told about the "audio evidence" when the guilty officer agreed to wear a "wire" during his conversation with "Officer Jerome
Finnegan, identified by authorities as the scheme's ringleader," which recorded Finnegan "allegedly plotting the murder of a Special Operations Section officer whom he suspected of cooperating with authorities." Therefore,
in addition to the robberies that led to the accumulation of "hundreds of
thousands of dollars" and civil rights and tax-related charges, this case includes a plot to murder another officer. And, multiple officers are involved; a
total of eleven officers have been linked to this "scheme."

Since "drug dealers" are traditionally not viewed as "legitimate" victims
by many members of the public, the article points out that the money was
taken "from suspected drug dealers and other citizens." The words "and other
citizens" help to create the image that some police actions were "random in
nature," since "other citizens" were also subject to police abuse of powers
and not just the "suspected drug dealers." And, as in the previous articles, the
focus is on members of this "elite team" that was disbanded "because of the
scandal." No information is provided about the level of discretionary powers
given to police officers, the lack of supervisory oversight over officers in
general and this unit in particular, or about the "nature" of police culture or
organization that allows for these kinds of abuses.

EXCESSIVE FORCE:
According to WKMG Orlando (May 19, 2011):
A veteran Orlando police officer is under investigation after Local 6 News
started asking questions about surveillance video that shows the officer using
an "arm bar" technique on a 100-pound woman whose teeth were broken after
she landed face-first on the ground. The video, captured by a city camera and
obtained by investigative reporter Mike Holfeld, shows Officer Livio Beccaccio taking 20-year-old Lisa Wareham by the left arm before she hits the pavement. Wareham was initially charged with battery on a law enforcement officer and resisting arrest, but Local 6 learned Friday the state attorney's office
dropped all the charges against her. Her attorney, Andrew Zelman, said they
plan to file a lawsuit on Monday against the officer and the Orlando Police
Department. The incident . . . was caught on video by an Innovate Response to
Improve Safety (I.R.I.S.) camera mounted at Magnolia Avenue and Central
Boulevard. The incident broke Wareham's front teeth. "It happened so fast. I
was so scared. There is no way to describe it," she said. "I went to sit up and I
felt something in my mouth. I spit (my teeth) out. I didn't even know what to
think," she said. Wareham said there was a disturbance nearby and a man was
shoved into her. She said as she was questioning the man as to why he bumped
into her, Beccaccio led her away and hurled her to the ground. Beccaccio's
police report said, "Wareham, with her right hand, reached across her body
and smacked me several times in my right hand and arm." Video shows an
Orlando police officer taking a woman down to the ground. The video shows
Beccaccio holding Wareham by her left arm, and she ends up on the pavement
in less than 10 seconds. Wareham never appears to resist or try to strike

Beccaccio, the video shows. In the official report, Beccaccio writes, "Wareham stumbled forward and fell to the pavement." Beccaccio was there responding to the disturbance, but the video shows the scene to be calm when Beccaccio and other OPD officers arrived. Zelman said OPD has had the video since at least March. According to Zelman, nothing was being done about the case until Holfeld's investigation into alleged excessive force cases involving the Orlando Police Department aired Monday night on Local 6. OPD Lt. Barbara Jones sent an email to Holfeld on Wednesday confirming that the incident "is being reviewed and under official investigation."

This story has both visual and dramatic appeal. The "surveillance video" "shows the officer using an *arm bar* technique on a 100-pound woman whose teeth were broken after she landed face-first on the ground." We learn that the woman was initially charged with "battery on a law enforcement officer and resisting arrest," but later, "the state attorney's office dropped all the charges against her." This constructs the victim as "legitimate" because readers are left to conclude that the police allegations against her were false. The officer's report said that Wareham "smacked" the officer "several times" in his "right hand and arm" and that "Wareham stumbled forward and fell to the pavement." But, the city video, from the Innovative Response to Improve Safety (I.R.I.S.) camera, shows the officer holding "Wareham by her left arm, and she ends up on the pavement in less than 10 seconds. Wareham never appears to resist or try to strike Beccaccio." The woman is described as weighing one hundred pounds and being twenty years old, whereas Beccaccio is described as being "a veteran Orlando police officer," suggesting that he is older with more life experience or someone who should have "known better." Wareham described being "so scared." "There is no way to describe it, she said. I went to sit up and I felt something in my mouth. I spit (my teeth) out. I didn't even know what to think." Further "shocking" details are provided when we are told that the police had the video for at least two months, but "nothing was being done about the case" until a reporter's investigation on alleged excessive force cases involving the Orlando Police Department aired on local news. Following this, an OPD lieutenant emailed the reporter to confirm that the case "is being reviewed and under official investigation." The *frightening forecast*, to use Tiffen's (2004) term, is that the public would probably not have known about this incident had it not been for the work of the investigative journalist who uncovered the videotape; and therefore, the public is left wondering how many more of them are there. And what remains absent in the article are demands for answers from the police as to why they had this information and did not act until the airing of the investigative report; the lack of police accountability and lack of transparency is not the focus. No information is given about the use of excessive force by officers and falsely charging citizens or what police organizations can do to decrease these incidents. And no connection is made between the police culture and police behavior.

TAKING KICKBACKS:
According to the *Washington Post/Associated Press* (February 25, 2011):
With 31 officers suspended, Baltimore police are facing the city's largest alleged police corruption scheme in decades. The 17 officers charged are accused of taking kickbacks for diverting drivers at accident scenes to an unauthorized towing company and repair shop. . . . The criminal complaint filed Wednesday charges the officers and the owners of Majestic Auto Repair Shop in Rosedale with conspiracy to commit extortion in the course of their official duties. Officers are supposed to allow the owner to arrange for a tow, or if the owner declines, to use police communication channels to contact only an authorized towing company. But the complaint alleges owners of Majestic, which wasn't a city-authorized shop, paid officers to arrange for their company to tow vehicles from accident scenes. Officers received $300 for each vehicle they steered to Majestic, and one officer received more than $14,400 over two years, according to the complaint. The officers would tell owners that Majestic could help with the insurance claim and waive the deductible, advising them not to call the insurance company before talking with the repair shop owner, according to the complaint. Police union president Detective Bob Cherry . . . said that this was the largest number of officers charged in one scheme that they could remember. The allegations could hurt the public's trust, but Cherry hopes people realize these officers are just a small segment (of the) 2,800-member force. "Officers who work the street feel very strongly about their oath," Cherry said. "If these allegations are proven, we don't want them on the street, either. A good cop is not going to tolerate a bad cop." . . . Officials declined to discuss how investigators learned of the alleged scheme, but one of the incidents that internal affairs investigators looked at was the arrest of Paula Protani of Frankford Towing, Guglielmi said. Protani, who is also a spokeswoman for the group of city authorized towers, had made several complaints about Majestic, so when she spotted a Majestic truck at a crash in 2009, she went over to take a picture. She told the officer on the scene that Majestic was not allowed to be there and he told her to leave, then arrested her, she said. After spending hours at Central Booking, Protani filed a complaint with the department.

We are told that "31 officers have been suspended" and that seventeen of the officers charged "are accused of taking kickbacks for diverting drivers at accident scenes to an unauthorized towing company and repair shop" in what is described as "the city's largest alleged police corruption scheme in decades." The officers are charged "with conspiracy to commit extortion in the course of their official duties." We are further told that officers received "$300 for each vehicle" that they "steered" to the unauthorized towing company, and that "one officer received more than $14,400 over two years." "The officers would tell owners that Majestic could help with the insurance claim and waive the deductible, advising them not to call the insurance company before talking with the repair shop owner." The assumed "legitimate victims" here are the motorists who were subject to police extortion as well as the city-authorized towing companies who lost business as a result of this scheme. Paula Protani, of Frankford Towing, is also individually identified as a "legitimate victim," as she is described as the "spokeswoman for the group of city authorized towers" and was arrested by police after she took a picture of a Majestic truck at a "crash" and told the officer that Majestic was not allowed to be there. Readers are told that "officials declined to discuss how investigators learned of the alleged scheme," but "one of the incidents that internal affairs investigators looked at was the arrest of Paula Protani." "Serious crimes" are alleged, "legitimate victims" are identified, and "sensationalist" images are provided of an "innocent woman" arrested for simply taking a picture and informing police about their duties. This article creates the perception that all motorists in need of towing or repair service are "at risk" at the hands of "corrupt cops." The article does not consider that the problem, for instance, could be "systemic" and the result of a "secretive culture" that condones police misconduct, but rather the focus is on the individual officers. Attention is given to the police union president, who "hopes" that "people realize these officers are just a small segment (of the) 2,800-member force," creating the perception that these officers, if found guilty, are simply the "bad apples."

EMBEZZLEMENT:
According to the *New Times* (February 25, 2011):
NEW BERN, NC—Frank Galizia, a former chief deputy of the County Sheriff's Department, will have to serve 18 months in federal prison for his role in an embezzlement scheme involving four other members of the department. In addition, Mr. Galizia will have to serve three months supervised probation and pay a portion of $84,000. Judge Louise Flanagan sentenced him today. He reports to prison after June 7. Mr. Galizia is the last of the defendants to be sentenced in the scheme, which involved the stealing of federal funds given to the county specifically to be used in covert drug operations. He pleaded guilty in July to aiding and abetting the embezzlement of funds while serving in the sheriff's department under former sheriff Ralph L. Thomas Jr. Mr. Thomas, who was sentenced in October, is serving a 14-month prison sentence for his part in the scheme.

Here we learn that a member of upper management, the "former chief deputy," "will have to serve 18 months in federal prison" for his part in an "embezzlement scheme." Five officers are identified as taking part in this "scheme," including the sheriff, who was sentenced to a fourteen-month prison sentence. The "scheme" involved the stealing of federal funds given to the county specifically to be used in covert drug operations. The assumed victims are the "law-abiding citizens" who pay their taxes and expect federal money given to police departments to be spent lawfully and "responsibly" to fight the drug "war" and to "protect" them. In this article we don't know how the officers were able to access the money, how long the scheme lasted, and how they were discovered. Once again, the public is not given any information about the possibilities for police corruption or what steps the organization can take to try to prevent it from happening again in the future. As in previous news articles, the attention remains on the individual officers involved.

Also, the *New Orleans Times Picayune* (April 5, 2011) reported another kickback scandal:

> New Orleans Police Capt. Michael Roussel testified in federal court last week that he didn't know he was involved in an illegal kickback scheme—he was just a consultant. New Orleans Police Department Capt. Michael Roussel was convicted of corruption charges. The veteran officer, who arranged meetings last June between the owner of a private security firm and Entergy's head of corporate security, painted himself as a disinterested—and naive—bystander. "It was between them," he said of the deal to inflate a contract for security services in case of a hurricane. "If I thought a crime was being committed there, I would have been the first one out the door," he said. The jury didn't buy that story and found Capt. Roussel guilty of one count of conspiracy and two counts of wire fraud. A police officer couldn't possibly fail to understand that a deal to inflate a contract and pay kickbacks was illegal. Louis Dabdoub, a former NOPD captain who now heads corporate security for Entergy, didn't have any trouble recognizing fraud when Capt. Roussel reached out to him last year and urged him to make a deal with Joseph Branch, owner of a Texas-based security company. Mr. Dabdoub went to Superintendent Ronal Serpas, who contacted the FBI, and Mr. Dabdoub agreed to go undercover. Mr. Branch pleaded guilty last month to one count of conspiracy to defraud Entergy Services Inc. His testimony and that of Mr. Dabdoub show that Capt. Roussel was a key player. Videotapes of their meetings recorded conversations about the likelihood of a hurricane hitting the city and their hopes of getting rich from such an event.

Although the details of the crimes are less clear in this article, we are told that a "veteran" "police captain" was found guilty of "one count of conspiracy and two counts of wire fraud." The captain "arranged meetings" "between the owner of a private security firm and Entergy's head of corporate security." But the head of corporate security for Entergy, Louis Dabdoub, "recognized" the proposed scheme to commit fraud and contacted the police superintendent, who then contacted the FBI. Dabdoub "agreed to go undercover," which produced "videotapes" of his meetings and conversations with the police captain and the owner of the Texas-based security company. We are told that the videotapes "show that Captain Roussel was a key player" and included conversations "about the likelihood of a hurricane hitting the city and their hopes of getting rich from such an event." The reference to another hurricane "hitting the city" brings to mind the devastation of Hurricane Katrina, the lives that were lost and the thousands who were displaced. But here the officer and the owner of the private security firm are recorded talking about the real possibility of another hurricane and their hope to carry through with their criminal plans "from such an event." This incident is alarming in that a "police captain," someone who is higher up in the "chain of command," is "hoping" for a hurricane to fully execute his plan against "innocent victims." The description of the video recordings provides both the "visual" and "dramatic" appeal to readers as well as the evidence of the officer's guilt and creates the perception that anyone can be at "risk."

Below are three news stories on police corruption that involved female officers specifically, or both female and male officers together.

OFFICIAL MISCONDUCT AND ASSAULT:
According to NY1 (April 29, 2011):
A partial mistrial was declared Friday in the case of two off-duty police officers accused of beating up a man in 2008. The judge declared a mistrial on felony assault charges against officers Koleen Robinson and Michelle Anglin. It came on the 11th day of deliberations, when a juror called in Friday to tell the court he was injured. When the defense objected to an alternate juror stepping in, the judge declared a mistrial. Notes from the jury this week has shown it was already having difficulty coming to a decision on the assault charges. The transit officers were accused of beating Marlon Smith and another man after getting into an argument over an open car door in the Bronx. Smith needed 25 staples to close a gash in his head. The defense says Smith started the fight, and they're ready if the Bronx distinct attorney retries the case. "You would expect based upon the zealousness of how they approached this particular case that they're probably gonna move forward to retry the assault counts," said Anglin's attorney, Neville Mitchell. "It's very hard to know that you were injured by someone who tried to hurt you, then they flip the script to say you were the one who hurt them. It was clear to see that they were the ones that hurt me," Smith said. During the trial, the defense maintained that the officers were only protecting themselves against Smith. They said he went so wild he even tore the shirt off one of them. When asked by NY1 if he beat up the officers, Smith said: "Not at all. I was on the way to get my kid." Only one day before the mistrial was declared on the assault charges, the jury did reach a guilty verdict against the officers on a misdemeanor charge of official misconduct. Their lawyers are trying to get that conviction tossed out. They say that the NYPD will hold a hearing on that matter, and it shouldn't have been a part of the court case.

We learn that two identified off-duty officers, who were accused of "beating up a man," were convicted of official misconduct, but that "the judge declared a mistrial" on the "felony assault charges." The two women identified as "transit officers" were "accused of beating" Smith "and another man" that resulted in Smith needing "25 staples to close a gash in his head." The defense expects that the DA will retry this case given the "zealousness of how they approached" this case, he said. The readers are led to believe that perhaps the officers should never have been charged and that they perhaps are the ones who are the "legitimate" victims. We're told that the DA was "zealous" in how he approached the case; the jury was "having difficulty coming to a decision on the assault charges" and that "the lawyers are trying to get the conviction" of official misconduct "tossed out" since "it shouldn't have been a part of the court case." Even though Smith needed staples, "the defense maintained that the officers were only protecting themselves against Smith." They said, "He went so wild he even tore the shirt off one of them." The article has sensational appeal in that two female officers were accused of "beating up a man"; this plays to both the attractions and fears of an audience consumed with gendered "understandings" of interpersonal forms of violence in which women are accused of being the physical aggressors toward men. As in the articles above, the media perpetuate ideological constructions of criminality on the part of individuals, and the concern is never about the police institutional and structural forms of violence.

According to *Chicago Sun-Times* (April 8, 2011):
Former Chicago Police Officer Jerome Finnigan and another member of the now-disbanded Special Operations Section were charged Thursday in federal court with stealing hundreds of thousands of dollars from drug suspects, while two other officers were charged with lying in court. Finnigan, 48, was previously charged in 2007 with plotting to kill a fellow officer who he believed was cooperating with investigators. He's been in a federal lockup ever since. Lawyers who have sued Finnigan have been frustrated their cases were put on hold as they waited for the feds to complete their criminal investigation. "Why did it take four years to come out with the same charges that were in state court?" said attorney Louis Meyer, whose firm has four pending lawsuits involving Finnigan. Former Chicago Police Officer Keith Herrera, who wore the wire that captured Finnigan's alleged murder-for-hire scheme, also was charged Thursday in federal court with Officer Eric Olsen, 37, who's been on desk duty, and former Officer Stephen DelBosque, 35. All four intend to plead guilty, prosecutors said. Finnigan and Herrera, 33, face separate charges in state court for participating with a ring of Special Operations Section officers that allegedly kidnapped and robbed drug suspects. Those charges will be dismissed under the deal. The Special Operations Section was disbanded in 2007 after the allegations came to light. Seven other officers have pleaded guilty to wrongdoing in state court. Finnigan was the alleged mastermind of the shakedown operation, which stole about $600,000 from drug suspects in 2004 and 2005 in five separate incidents, federal prosecutors said. Finnigan's cut was $200,000 and Herrera's was about $40,000, authorities said. In one of the five incidents, Finnigan, Herrera and other officers illegally searched a home in the 2000 block of North Keeler on Aug. 15, 2005, prosecutors said.

The officers allegedly ransacked an upstairs apartment of a drug suspect, stealing about $86,000 while turning in the drugs they found. The officers also allegedly broke into a downstairs apartment of a family unrelated to the drug suspects and handcuffed 13-year-old Jose Fematt, who was babysitting his sister. A female officer drove the boy around the neighborhood in a squad car, asking about his upstairs neighbor and about drugs, according to a lawsuit filed last month by Fematt. "My client's never been arrested," said Fematt's lawyer, Torri Hamilton. "He graduated from high school and works full-time now. It's a really backward world where in neighborhoods like this the drug dealers may be nicer to you than police officers who are breaking down the doors, putting handcuffs on you, driving you around and threatening you. Certainly in this case, they were not role models." Finnigan and Herrera were each charged with one felony count of civil-rights conspiracy and one count of filing a false income-tax return. DelBosque and Olsen face misdemeanor civil-rights charges for allegedly giving false testimony about drug arrests.

This case involving police corruption on the part of the Special Operations Section in the Chicago Police Department was discussed earlier in another article. But in the article above the involvement of a female police officer is made known. Here, too, we learn about the hundreds of thousands of dollars that were stolen, the plot to kill another fellow officer, and the "four pending lawsuits involving Finnigan." Four male officers are named, and we are told that "all four intend to plead guilty" and that they "face separate charges in state court for participating with a ring . . . that allegedly kidnapped and robbed drug suspects," but that these particular charges will be dismissed under some type of deal that was made. In addition to the identified four main officers, we are told that "seven other officers have pleaded guilty to wrongdoing in state court." As in the earlier article, Finnigan is identified as "the alleged mastermind of the . . . operation" that included "five separate incidents" where officers "stole about $600,000" with Finnigan taking a $200,000 "cut." In one of the incidents, "Finnigan, Herrera, and other officers illegally searched a home. . . . The officers allegedly ransacked an upstairs apartment of a drug suspect stealing about $86,000 while turning in the drugs they found." But, we also learn that other "legitimate" victims were involved. "The officers also allegedly broke into a downstairs apartment of a family unrelated to the drug suspects and handcuffed 13-year-old Jose Fematt, who was babysitting his sister." At this point we learn that "a female officer drove the boy around the neighborhood in a squad car, asking about his upstairs neighbor and about drugs." The female officer is never identified, but readers are left to assume that she is one of the "seven other officers" who have "pleaded guilty to wrongdoing." This information stems from a lawsuit filed by Fematt who has since graduated from high school and "works full time." Clearly, the female officer is not at the center of the "scheme" as are the four male officers identified. But the extent of the female officer's involvement is unclear. No information is provided to the reader about the role of "the brotherhood" in police culture; women's involvement, or lack thereof, in police misconduct; the powers of the police over members of the public; and/or the lack of police accountability.

TICKET FIXING:
HuffingtonPost.com (June 6, 2011) reported:
Long the bane of the NYPD, a Bronx jury spoke last week, raising the bourgeoning Ticketgate police scandal to a new level. The jury acquitted Bronx attorney Stephen LoPresti of drunken-driving charges—a guy with three prior drunk-driving convictions—because jurors did not believe the two arresting officers, who admitted fixing tickets in unrelated cases. Officer Harrington Marshal testified that he had asked a police union official to make two tickets of family members vanish. Officer Julissa Goris testified that she had asked her police union delegate to kill a ticket issued to her boyfriend's cousin. Also, when her mother received a ticket, Goris accompanied her to court, spoke to a sergeant, and her mother did not have to pay the fine. "The message is clear," said Adam D. Perlmutter, one of LoPresti's defense lawyers. "Corruption won't be tolerated in the Bronx or anywhere." A defense attorney's natural bombast notwithstanding, in this instance Perlmutter seems to have gotten it right—at least when it comes to fixing tickets. News reports say that up to 300 cops may be involved, including Patrolmen's Benevolent Association delegates and a trustee acting as middlemen. In addition, the president of the Sergeants Benevolent Association says fixing tickets is a wide-ranging and long-standing police courtesy and unstated job benefit. Nobody—not Mayor Bloomberg who has called the scandal a "black eye" for the police department; not Police Commissioner Ray Kelly, who has said virtually nothing; maybe not even Bronx District Attorney Robert Johnson, whose grand jury reportedly has been hearing testimony about ticket fixing for more than a year—know where this is going and what will come out. Some have even suggested, perhaps over-dramatically, that Ticketgate approaches pre-Knapp-Commission-era corruption and may warrant an independent commission. Ticketgates' main stage is the Bronx, where more than in any other borough, juries don't trust cops. And cops don't trust Bronx juries. For years, PBA attorneys have opted to have their cases heard by Bronx judges instead of Bronx juries. Most of these judges have been older white men, more sympathetic to cops than most Bronx citizens. Just such a judge acquitted police officer Stephen Sullivan for fatally shooting Eleanor Bumpers during an eviction in 1984. Such a judge acquitted off-duty officer Michael Meyer for fatally shooting an unarmed squeegee man who was soaping up his windshield in 1998. Such a judge acquitted Francis X. Livoti, accused of using a department-banned choke hold that led to the death of asthmatic Anthony Baez in 1994. Then there was the infamous shooting of unarmed Amadou Diallo, killed in a hail of 41 bullets, fired by four officers in 1999. The PBA was so fearful that these four officers would be tried by a Bronx jury (or nearly as bad, by a younger black, female judge, who was supposedly selected at random) that the union pulled off a remarkable piece of legal legerdemain. First, they arranged to move the trial to Albany. Then, the court's chief administrator, Jonathan Lippman—now the state's chief judge—handpicked a cop-friendly jurist to preside

over the case. The officers were all acquitted. In her salad days, the *New York Times* columnist Gail Collins coined the phrase, "The Bronx curse," meaning that when something bad happens, it's always worse in the Bronx. Maybe that explains the phenomenon of Larry Davis. In 1986, the drug-dealing, 20-year-old Davis shot six cops, who police said had come to his sister's apartment to question him about the killing of four drug dealers. Davis escaped and led police on a 17-day manhunt. When he gave himself up after cops had cornered him in a Bronx housing project, crowds applauded him. When he pleaded self-defense, a Bronx jury acquitted him. District Attorney Johnson, too, is something of a uniquely Bronx product. Elected in 1988, he is currently the state's only African-American district attorney. Like many of his constituents, he has had issues with the police. Because he opposes the death penalty, some in law enforcement circles have viewed him as anti-cop. After the fatal shooting of Bronx Street Crime cop Kevin Gillespie in 1996, Gov. George Pataki took the extraordinary step of removing the case from Johnson's jurisdiction and appointing a special prosecutor. (Although former Manhattan District Attorney Robert Morgenthau also opposes the death penalty, Pataki never took a case from him.) The issue became moot when Gillespie's alleged killer hanged himself in prison. Two years later, Police Commissioner Howard Safir told the *New York Times* that he has "no respect" for Johnson. "No. Not at all," he said to the writer, Jeffrey Goldberg. Safir later said that he was misquoted. More recently, to the horror of many in the department, Johnson prosecuted veteran detective Christopher Perino for perjury after a secretly recorded audio-tape caught him in a lie. A Bronx jury convicted him in 2009 and he was sentenced to four months in prison. All but forgotten is that after Bronx juries acquitted Larry Davis both of shooting the six cops and of killing the four drug dealers, Johnson continued to pursue him. In 1991, his office convicted Davis, who had changed his name to Adam Abdul Hakeem, of murdering another drug dealer, Ramon Vizcaino. The guilty verdict, said Johnson, "means that a very dangerous individual is going to be made to pay for his wanton acts."

This article reports ticket fixing among the NYPD, where "up to 300 cops" are believed to be involved. But it also focuses on the racial tensions that have existed between Bronx residents and police officers, as seen in the case where the lawyer was acquitted on the "drunken-driving charges" despite three prior drunk-driving convictions. The jurors did not believe the officers who had "admitted to fixing tickets in unrelated cases." The male officer "testified that he had asked a police union official to make two tickets of family members vanish." The story involves a female officer: "Officer Julissa Goris testified that she had asked her police union delegate to kill a ticket issued to her boyfriend's cousin. Also, when her mother received a ticket, Goris accompanied her to court, spoke to a sergeant, and her mother did not have to pay the fine." But what provides "dramatic appeal" here is the number of officers allegedly involved in the ticket fixing, the support for it by the Sergeants Benevolent Association president, and the contentious history and mistrust between the police and Bronx residents. The article points out that according to "new reports," "up to 300 cops may be involved including Patrolmen's Benevolent Association delegates and a trustee acting as middlemen." Readers are also told that "some have even suggested, perhaps overdramatically, that Ticketgate approaches pre-Knapp Commission-era corruption and may warrant an independent commission." The words *perhaps overdramatically* suggest that this scandal may be "overly exaggerated" and does not perhaps "deserve" to be compared to the pre-Knapp Commission-era. The mayor, however, is quoted as referring to this scandal as a "black eye" for the police department, but the article tells readers that no one knows "where this is going and what will come out," as a grand jury has been hearing ongoing testimony about ticket-fixing instances. Another "shocking" feature to this article is the president of the Sergeants Benevolent Association, who stated that "fixing tickets is a wide-ranging and long-standing police courtesy and unstated job benefit." The president openly admits that it does happen and that police officers are entitled to this "courtesy," placing the police "above the law."

But, unlike most others, this news article is the exception in that an attempt is made to contextualize the "police scandal" by providing a brief history of the racial tensions between the police and the Bronx community. We are reminded that the "Ticketgate scandal" is taking place in the Bronx, "where more than in any other borough, juries don't trust cops. And cops don't trust Bronx juries." Detailed information is given about how Bronx judges, who are mostly "older white men," have acquitted police officers who have fatally shot civilians or who have used excessive force against them, leading to death. On the other hand, we are told about "the drug-dealing, 20-year-old Davis" who shot six cops, pleaded self-defense, and "a Bronx jury acquitted him." And, to the "horror of many in the department," Johnson, the state's only African American district attorney, prosecuted a veteran detective for perjury with the use of a "secretly recorded audio-tape" that "caught him in a lie"; the officer was subsequently convicted and "sentenced to four months in prison."

Chapter Six

Increasing Police Accountability through Community Policing

This chapter considers the possibilities for the Community Policing (CP) model in redefining popular constructions of the police, which in turn can serve to resocialize officers in their perceptions of police behavior as they relate to the abuse of power. The discussion on CP is important in any evaluation of police corruption, particularly since the majority of police departments continue to present themselves as operating on some level from a CP model and have embraced various tenets of CP (Greene, 2004; Roth, Roehl, and Johnson, 2004; Skogan, 1996, 1990). However, despite these alternative representations, police organizations overall continue to overwhelmingly reflect the traditional crime-control approach (Corsianos, 2009; Greene, 2004; National Research Council, 2004; Skogan, 2004; Zhao, He, and Lovrich, 2003) and create corruption risks. But the CP model, theoretically, has the potential to minimize police corruption by evening the power relations within police organizations ideologically and structurally. This chapter will consider the possibilities for CP to challenge the centrality of hegemonic masculinity and patriarchal ideologies in policing and decrease police corruption risks. At the same time, however, an analysis of the challenges to integrating CP in meaningful ways will be presented.

Large police departments across the country began to promote CP in the early 1990s as their new, innovative approach to policing. There was increasing pressure placed on police organizations to redefine their strategies, given their inability to reduce crime rates and improve safety (Skogan, 2004, 1996; Dietz, 1997; Trojanowicz and Bucqueroux, 1990; Rosenbaum, 1986). Since the introduction of police patrol vehicles as well as random patrols with an emphasis on reactive policing (see chapter 1), police officers became undeniably less visible. The increased "invisibility" instilled in officers the "us versus them" attitude, where the public became the "opposing team" in the quest to control crime and maintain order (Kappeler, Sluder, and Alpert, 1994). With the beginning of the movement to "professionalize" the police (see chapter 1), police organizations have adopted a reactive crime-control mission (Walker and Katz, 2008).

By the 1990s, however, the CP model promised to promote proactive policing approaches to improve police-community relations. An early example of a more structured and organized CP initiative was seen in the Kansas City Preventive Patrol Experiment (Bureau of Justice Statistics, 1994). This field experiment found that randomized patrol work had a limited impact on crime rates and citizens' attitudes toward the police, which led police leaders to consider alternative patrol strategies such as proactive policing. Today, most police departments promote CP as an important part of their operations (Greene, 2004; Roth, Roehl, and Johnson, 2004; Skogan, 1996, 1990). According to Skogan (2004), it is hard to find a police chief that does not claim to have adopted particular "community-friendly programs." But, despite the implementation of some CP programs and/or the rhetoric of CP, police organizations continue to maintain and promote traditional dominant ideologies and the paramilitaristic power structure (Corsianos, 2009; National Research Council, 2004; Skogan, 2004; Zhao, He, and Lovrich, 2003; Ericson and Haggerty, 1997; Manning, 1997). Hegemonic masculinity and patriarchal ideologies remain central to the police identity. As Greene (2004:48) notes:

> The best that can be said to date is that many police departments . . . have adopted a framework for response that includes elements of problem solving. . . . But . . . it is clear that the police imagination remains captured by nineteenth-century ideas about crime and police response, most particularly as zero-tolerance policing has gained popularity among the police and politicians in recent years.

For McLaughlin (2007), creating more patrols, faster response times, and increasing police visibility will not reduce the number of crimes committed. And despite the resources for CP initiatives given to police departments from all levels of government, police officers continue to work in a traditional, hierarchical, paramilitaristic police structure that promotes aggressive crime control, reactive policing, secrecy, a "brotherhood" among officers as well as a sense of entitlement over "civilians." Thus, the police culture and policing methods have largely remained the same as in previous decades (Corsianos, 2009, 2001; Greene, 2004; National Research Council, 2004; Roth, Roehl, and Johnson, 2004; Skogan, 2004; Zhao, He, and Lovrich, 2003; Neugebauer, 1999; Ericson and Haggerty, 1997; Manning, 1997; Ericson, 1994). Also, even though most police departments claim to "do" CP, there is no consensus as to the definition of what CP is or what changes, if any, have been accomplished as a result of it. For McLaughlin (2007), CP in practice seems less about specific programs and practices than "a set of aspirations wrapped in slogans."

WHAT IS COMMUNITY POLICING, AND HOW CAN IT REDUCE POLICE CORRUPTION?

The CP model has been described as follows (Corsianos, 2009:118–19):

1) Police-community relations should be improved by lessening the distance between the police and the public. This could be accomplished by more interaction and exchange of ideas. For instance, officers should meet citizens who live and work in the neighborhoods they serve in order to begin to "build bridges" between the police and the various communities. They should visit places such as community centers, schools, businesses, places of worship, and others to introduce themselves, discuss CP goals, and work together with the public to identify and offer solutions to specific problems.

2) More foot patrol units and bicycle units should be introduced in order to help make the police more visible and approachable to members of the public.

3) Proactive policing should be emphasized over reactive policing. In an era of problem solving, the police should not rely only on reacting to crimes and problems after they have occurred but also should take it upon themselves to identify crimes by doing undercover work and by talking to citizens. Also, the emphasis should be on crime prevention through police efforts to improve social conditions. The police should identify "social problems" (for example, homelessness, runaways, traffic congestion, noise levels, street litter, etc.) with community members and work together to secure specific services such as employment, housing, sanitation, and health care.

4) Officers should be committed to making members of the public feel safer in the communities in which they work and live. This will encourage law-abiding citizens to become more involved in their communities, which will in turn promote safety.

5) The police should not be viewed as the sole experts in reducing and preventing crime, but, rather, crime control should be a collective effort between the police and the public.

6) Officers should be encouraged to live in the area they police. This will make officers experience a heightened level of accountability and responsibility to the community they serve since they will have a personal interest in the area (for example, they own a home in the area, pay property taxes, their children attend school in the area, etc.).

7) Smaller police substations should be created and more officers should be hired to police smaller patrol districts. The parameters of patrol districts in many cities are often too wide, making it very difficult, if not impossible, for officers to get to know people in the areas they police. The presence of more officers patrolling smaller patrol districts would increase the probability of officers and citizens becoming acquainted and working toward "building bridges" together.

8) Police departments should move toward a flatter organizational power structure. By moving away from the traditional paramilitaristic hierarchical structure that demands respect and obedience to the chain of command, every officer would be given an equal voice in the success of CP initiatives. The front-line/patrol officers are the ones who are expected to play the largest role in the success of CP, but, under the current structure, they are also the least likely to challenge the orders given by their immediate "superiors/supervisors." Under the paramilitaristic hierarchical structure, they must respect the chain of command and share their opinions and criticisms only with their immediate supervisors. On the other hand, under the flatter organizational power structure, ranks could be maintained, given the different responsibilities associated with each position, but they would all be viewed as equal partners in the policing system. All officers would play an equal role in voicing their suggestions. This would empower the front-line/patrol officers to share their concerns and suggestions (along with the concerns and suggestions from community members) with "higher" ranking officers (members of the brass and other levels of management). This would be more effective than hearing only from members of management, who tend to be too removed from "the streets" given the administrative nature of their roles.

The CP philosophy has the potential to promote a cooperative, collective relationship between the police and communities that can raise accountability on the part of the police toward citizens and ultimately decrease police misconduct. For Saunders (1999), "Community policing is a form of policing centered on the principles of partnership, prevention, and problem solving and that incorporates the latest information technologies into daily police practice." The CP approach is transformational and demands an ideological shift in the way policing is viewed, performed, and discussed. The move from traditional, reactive approaches to preventative, socially integrated, and cooperative modes of policing is not an easy task given the structure and culture of policing. Community policing is often characterized as bridging the divide that has alienated police from their communities. Instead of the traditional, hierarchical forms of policing, CP is more decentralized, which is intended to give front-line officers the flexibility and autonomy necessary to develop more intimate ties with their community (Marks and Sun, 2007).

It has been articulated as the necessary "means" required to transform policing by moving its strategies away from the traditional mechanistic model of policing that focuses on law enforcement and aggressive crime control, limited public interaction, motorized random patrol, reactive policing, and a centralized dispatching of radio calls and one that can empower the front-line officers who are essentially key players in building bridges with communities (Corsianos, 2011). CP approaches remain committed to "crime control" but are organized beyond reactive law enforcement and include crime prevention, proactive policing, community problem solving, improvement of police-community relations by reducing the social distance between the police and the public through increased police accountability and improved service to the public, and a flatter organizational power structure that promotes team work and a collectivist spirit among all officers (Morash and Robinson, 2001; Zdanowicz, 2001; Jolin and Moose, 1997; Cordner, 1994; Goldstein, 1990; Trojanowicz and Bucqueroux, 1990; Bayley, 1988; Wilson and Kelling, 1982).

One central tenet to CP is the emphasis on "service" to communities. It is often viewed as an integral part in countering the image of the police as a "force" consisting of "macho, aggressive crime fighters" who are "above the law." The image of the CP officer does not connote the kinds of traits associated with "hypermasculined superheroes" who protect and help only select "legitimate" citizens and "put away the bad guys." Slogans such as "to serve and protect," "to protect with courage, to serve with compassion," "community owned and operated" are good illustrations of this rhetorical movement. It has also been argued that CP calls for more "feminine" characteristics on the part of officers including, but not limited to, being able to deescalate potentially violent situations, being effective communicators, expressing empathy for victims of crime, being good listeners when dealing with citizens' complaints and/or concerns, and working collectively with citizens to identify problems in particular neighborhoods as well as to come up with solutions (Corsianos, 2009; Martin and Jurik, 2007).

CP approaches are described as having the potential to remove the police from the position of "authority figures" who "oversee" the public and can encourage constant interaction and cooperation between all officers and communities, rather than just having specialized community policing units and serving privileged citizens. In other words, all officers should become "community policing" officers in their understanding of their roles and in their commitment to working collectively within the organization and with the public. For instance, in Miller's (1999) study of a Midwestern police department, officers were either patrol officers or Neighborhood Policing officers (NPOs). Miller reported that this particular organization had CP units for a decade, and ten years after its inception the program had expanded from the original six to twelve neighborhoods, but there was still tension between patrol and neighborhood officers. She described the tension to be the result of at least two reasons: one being confusion and misunderstanding of the work of NPOs, and the second was the tendency to see these positions as "stepping stones" to getting promoted. Also, many of the NPOs felt the pressure to gain more respect from the patrol officers, and one of the strategies used was to increase their law enforcement visibility and to be seen less as social workers. This divided police officers as one group worked to gain acceptance and legitimacy by the other who was perceived as doing more normative police work. To begin to commit to more equitable service to communities, the CP model must be implemented throughout the entire organization in all aspects of police operations rather than through the superficial "implementation" of particular CP programs or units.

Claims of success in various CP initiatives have been reported, even though the primary operations of police organizations as a whole have remained the same (Corsianos, 2009; Greene, 2004; National Research Council, 2004; Skogan, 2004; Zhao, He, and Lovrich, 2003; Manning, 1997). For instance, in Chicago, CAPS (Chicago Alternative Policing Strategy) was intended to have annual citywide neighborhood meetings where police and citizens would work together to determine both the problems and possible solutions. Overall, "an evaluation of CAPS found that it did result in greater citizen involvement with the police, improved cooperation between the police and other governmental agencies (e.g., sanitation), a decline in neighborhood problems and improving public perception of the police departments" (Walker and Katz, 2008). Success was also reported by Lurigio and Rosenbaum in their evaluation of twelve cities. Lurigio and Rosenbaum found that involvement in community policing had a somewhat positive effect on officer attitudes and on the public's perceptions of the police. More involvement within the community created more job satisfaction for officers and improved morale. Hickman and Reaves (2001) reported that between 1997 and 1999, the percentage of local police departments using routine bicycle patrol increased from 28 percent to 34 percent, and routine foot patrol increased from 50 percent to 53 percent.

CP initiatives have been presented as having the potential to produce information sharing, which can increase the likelihood of arrest but also call on the police to work with citizens to address violations of the "social order"—the idea being that if "visible signs of disorder" (for example, abandoned buildings and cars, garbage on the streets) are reduced, so too are crimes and the fear of crime (Bayley, 1996, 1988; Goldstein, 1990, 1977;

Trojanowicz and Bucqueroux, 1990; Spelman and Eck, 1987; Trojanowicz, 1983; Wilson and Kelling, 1982). More indirect approaches to social control may be deemed more appropriate at times rather than a constant overreliance on law enforcement and arrests, and, in some cases, the number of arrests made may be limited based on neighborhood needs. The CP model can allow for variation in policing priorities, recognizing that not all communities may be the same (even within the patrol parameters of a particular precinct) and that all officers must respond to the different public safety needs identified by different groups (Thacher, 2001). As mentioned earlier, "crime control" remains an important part of the CP philosophy but is viewed as the product of the combined efforts of both the police and the public and more "feminine" traits become central in accomplishing the goals of the organization, whereas the traditional, hierarchical, mechanistic police model emphasizes crime control through aggressive law enforcement and promotes hypermasculinity (Martin and Jurik, 2007). CP can encourage information exchange and support from the public and quick police response to the public's concerns (Morash and Robinson, 2001; Zdanowicz, 2001; Jolin and Moose, 1997; Eck, 1990; Eck and Spelman, 1987) by moving away from the paramilitaristic, authoritarian model to one that promotes open communication between the police and the public.

A flatter power structure within the organization has the potential to increase police accountability by giving a voice to all officers, making them important players in accomplishing specific goals and improving morale. The downward shift of the command structure can empower officers by encouraging them to engage in critical thinking and problem solving. This organizational structure is described as being more fluidic, where every member of the organization is seen as a team player and possesses some knowledge of the organization as a whole. Every individual has *some knowledge* rather than the hierarchical model where only the people at the top of the pyramid have access to information about the entire organization. Emphasis is placed on shared responsibility, where every police officer is expected to contribute to organizational problems (Greene, 2004; Goetz and Mitchell, 2003; MacDonald, 2002; Manning, 1997; Skogan, 1996, 1990; Cordner, 1994; Guarino-Ghezzi, 1994; Chalom, 1993; Stenson, 1993; Trojanowicz and Bucqueroux, 1990; Goldstein, 1990; Bayley, 1988). A flatter power structure can promote equitable practices by creating systems that allow for information sharing among all officers; in turn, they are given a voice and viewed as equal partners.

Efforts can be concentrated on officers accomplishing specific goals because every member is seen as a competent professional who should be trusted to make sound decisions in specific situations. Restrictions on officers' discretionary powers are expected to be at a minimum given their roles as partners with communities and providers of service to the public. This requires trust on the part of the officers to ensure that they do not abuse their powers and are committed to serving citizens equitably and respectfully. The potential for abuse can be minimized if officers are conditioned in a culture that views policing as a "service" to the public and is committed to providing "quality" service to neighborhoods and citizens more fairly.

Under this new working environment, a collectivist relationship between all officers at all ranks can be established. Rather than "obeying" the "chain of command" and taking orders from "superiors" (reflective of the paramilitaristic, hierarchical police structure), the CP model promotes continuous interaction among all officers; that is, more collectivist-oriented relationships where people receive "advice" rather than "orders" and where officers work together to achieve particular goals. These are intended to promote teamwork, open communication, transparency, accountability, and even out the power relations between officers regardless of rank (Corsianos, 2009; Morash and Robinson, 2001; Thacher, 2001; Zdanowicz, 2001; Wyrick, 2000; Miller, 1999; Manning, 1997; Goldstein, 1990; Trojanowicz and Bucqueroux, 1990; Bayley, 1988; Spelman and Eck, 1987). This can promote equity between officers regardless of gender, race, sexual orientation, and other identity categories by giving a voice to all more equally, and ultimately minimize police corruption by making police more accountable to the public. But, first, evening out the internal power dynamics and changing the ideologies that currently maintain heterosexual male privilege are required (Corsianos, 2011).

Also, it has been suggested that officers be trained in problem identification, analysis, and solutions and have good interpersonal skills (Jurik and Martin, 2001). This can increase accountability and limit police corruption by promoting traits that are disproportionately associated with female officers (they are less likely to use excessive force, less likely to be involved in other forms of police corruption, receive fewer citizen complaints, are better able to deescalate potentially violent situations, and communicate effectively) (Martin and Jurik, 2007; McElvain and Kposowa, 2004; Bureau of Justice Assistance, 2001; Lersch, 1998; Carter, Sapp, and Stephens, 1988).

However, as discussed in chapter 3, police organizations continue to emphasize a rather narrow definition of physical strength, as seen in the physical tests and/or exercises used for hiring, training, and in the overall crime-control police image that remains popular in both the police and public imagination. Police training parallels the military, particularly as it relates to following orders and respecting the chain of command and the use of brute strength to carry out specific activities (Corsianos, 2009; Martin and Jurik, 2007; Prokos and Padavic, 2002; Gerber, 2001; Miller, 1999; Heidensohn, 1992; Martin, 1990; Morash and Greene, 1986; Bell, 1982; Charles, 1981). But the idea of police work being primarily based on "physical strength" and aggression is misleading. On any given shift, front-line officers spend most of their time patrolling the streets, communicating with people, "running license plates," making notes in their memo books, and filing reports (Garcia, 2003; Manning, 1997). In fact, law enforcement comprises only a small part of everyday police work (Walker and Katz, 2005; Martin, 1999). But the dominant beliefs that the police "physically protect" citizens and "fight crime" fuel the image of the police as "physically strong crime fighters and protectors." The Vancouver Police department in Canada has been a strong supporter of the CP model for over two decades. In the 1990s, it began to challenge their crime-control image and emphasis on brawn. Rather than giving points to applicants for having military and security experience, they identified four preferred qualifications for police officers. These included a university degree or college diploma, a second language or culture, voluntary experience, particularly in the area of criminal justice, and employment experience that reflected individual strengths such as interpersonal skills (Eng, 1997). There was a push to hire officers with more diverse skills and a university education and to move away from relying on physical testing for hiring that largely emphasized upper body strength and did not reflect the day-to-day job of "community-friendly" officers. This was an important step in challenging traditional understandings of the police and encouraging applicants who earlier may never had considered themselves possible police candidates. In working to redefine the police image, organizations must be willing to continuously examine, as Henry and Milovanovic (1999) noted, the conditional "truths" that people rely on to actively build their social world.

The CP model has the potential to make the connection between "identity categories" such as gender, race and sexual orientation, and the differences they create in people's experiences, and can promote more equitable policing practices within the organization and in the services provided to the public. This would require police departments to commit to an equity analysis of all police policies and practices to ensure that no category of officers (e.g., women) is disproportionately discriminated against. Police organizations must respond by implementing policies and practices that benefit all diverse groups. For instance, as discussed in chapter 3, policies that require officers to work rotating shifts end up disproportionately discriminating against female officers. The primary reason for this is that despite some changes in traditional "female" and "male" roles, mothers in opposite-sex relationships continue to take on a larger portion of the child-caring responsibilities (Benokraitis and Feagin, 1995; Stapinski, 1998; England, 2001). Rotating shifts present many challenges to these women who are not able to pick up their children from school, spend time studying with them, take them to their after-school activities, read with them, put them to bed, and more. Similarly, the lack of policies in some areas can disproportionately discriminate against groups of people such as women. For instance, some U.S. police departments do not provide maternity uniforms or equipment for pregnant officers or have discriminated against pregnant officers by not placing them in a nonpatrol assignment after a request was made (Corsianos, 2009; National Center for Women and Policing, 2005).

Also, performance evaluations that are included in officers' personnel files document their work activities and are also used in evaluations for promotion. But these evaluations often lack procedures that recognize and reward officers' work outside of law enforcement/crime control roles. For instance, CP initiatives are not recognized and valued as are traditional policing roles that produce a high number of arrests (Miller and Hodge, 2004).

As discussed earlier, police organizations currently promote hegemonic masculinity and patriarchal ideologies. These are not conducive to building bridges, creating transparency, and ultimately limiting police corruption. Evening power relations within means identifying and removing the various instances of discriminatory police rhetoric, images, and police practices. This would require not only ideological changes relating to the purposes for formal policing and what police officers "do" and how they should "look" but also organizational changes to end the current discrimination experienced disproportionately by categories of people as seen in hiring, promotions, performance evaluations, position assignments, police equipment, work schedules, parental leave, and sexual harassment (Corsianos, 2009; Martin and Jurik, 2007; Harrington and Lonsway, 2004; Garcia, 2003; Prokos and Padavic, 2002; Gerber, 2001; Lonsway, 2000; Martin, 1999; Orban, 1998; Jackson, 1997; McLean, 1997; Belknap and Shelley, 1993; Morash and Greene, 1986). The current organizational power structure that produces and promotes difference in outcome of welfare among its officers undermines the potential for the successful implementation of the CP philosophy, which in turn undermines the ability to effectively respond to the uneven power relations between the police and communities.

A flatter power structure that has been proposed in some of the CP literature can enable officers to work in different units and recognize officers' "good service" through awards, appreciation ceremonies, and internal newsletter announcements. This could include the contributions of officers in decreasing particular crimes as a result of the successful implementation of CP initiatives or victim-offender mediation. But this philosophy would have to be integrated in all aspects of police operations. This is necessary in order to move away from the traditional prioritization of arrest rates used to determine positive police performance and change the current marginalization of certain types of police activities. The front-line/patrol officers are critical players in the CP model since they are the ones who are in constant contact with communities. Through continuous police-public interaction, officers can gain a better understanding of the needs and concerns of particular neighborhoods, which they can then share with management to gain support for resources for planning and implementation (Gaines, 1997; Lord, 1996). Interpersonal skills are needed to work with individuals and groups and to collectively identify problems and solutions that can create transparency in police operations, increased accountability, and decrease the likelihood in the abuse of police powers for personal and/or organizational gain. This is very different from the traditional police structure that requires front-line officers to bring information to their immediate "superiors" and not "break rank" by going to persons above them and the support for secrecy and protection of officers regardless of inappropriate and/or illegal conduct.

Peak, Stitt, and Glensor (1998) assert that ethical dilemmas are prevalent in policing ranging from varying concepts of duty to ethical relativism and situational ethics where one "justifies" one's "immoral" actions by viewing them as necessary or acceptable in particular instances. Without sufficient training and guidance, ethical dilemmas can potentially lead officers to make "unethical" decisions that may have severe consequences for those involved. The most important aspect of CP for Peak et al. (1998) appears to be providing adequate training and guidelines for officers as it relates to decision making. But how can these be provided when the "traditional police supervisor is largely unprepared by training and experience for the requirements of COPPS strategy," and "most officers . . . do not see their supervisors as sources of ethical and practical guidance and direction, but rather as authority figures" (ibid.:25). Even though some assert that "ethics" cannot be taught but rather "learned" over time during one's formative years, it is also argued that police do learn proper and improper behaviors through job experience as well as formal training (Sherman, 1982). For Peak et al. (1998:27), "Training will have an even stronger impact if it is clear . . . that the training has the unequivocal support of the chief executive officer and is reinforced by managers and supervisors."

The continuous promotion of equitable politics is necessary in order to encourage equitable praxis and transform popular constructions of the police. According to Marks and Sun (2007), transformational change requires structural and institutional arrangements of an organization's culture, strategies, mission, leadership, and overall appearance. A commitment to the CP model, structurally and ideologically, can begin to redefine policing as an "institution" and ultimately reduce corruption risks.

THE CHALLENGES TO INTEGRATING THE CP PHILOSOPHY

There are several challenges to moving away from the current, dominant constructions of the police that overwhelmingly support and promote the image of the police as "crime fighters" and maintain hegemonic masculinity

(Connell, 1995; Messerschmidt, 1993). For instance, as discussed in chapter 3, the continued marginalization and discrimination of female officers are well documented and have included discriminatory policies, intimidation, sexist comments relating to physical strength and ability to protect themselves and other officers, retaliation, and discrimination in promotions and position assignments (Corsianos, 2009, 2004; Martin and Jurik, 2007; Harrington and Lonsway, 2004; Gerber, 2001; Heidensohn and Brown, 2000; Van Wormer and Bartollas, 2000; Martin, 1999, 1994, 1980; Miller, 1999; Nichols, 1995; Fielding, 1994; Robinson, 1993; Belknap, 1991; Feinman, 1986; Morash and Greene, 1986; Homant and Kennedy, 1985; Kennedy and Homant, 1985; Price, 1974). Police organizations produce and reproduce discriminatory experiences on the part of officers based on identity categories that privilege some over others. How then can the police be expected to be accountable to communities and be willing to equitably serve citizens when they do not promote nondiscriminatory practices and ideologies within the organization?

Police Perceptions of "Worthy" Individuals and Its Relation to Police Service

Another challenge to the CP model is the current police attitudes in viewing some people as "less worthy" and certain areas as "more dangerous," which leads to differences in the level and quality of police service. Police do not serve "society" or "the people" but rather "some" parts of society and "some people" at the expense of others (McLaughlin, 2007; Black, 1990). Policing translates, as Ericson (1982) noted, to "patrolling the petty." Police largely view "crimes" as those that are committed "on the streets" (e.g., drug use, assaults, prostitution, theft, etc.). And, therefore, the image of "the criminal" is largely tied to class and 'race' identities given the types of crimes that are disproportionately committed by poorer people and racial minorities and disproportionately policed. "Street crimes," also referred to as "blue-collar crimes," are often visible and the police can intervene to make arrests. But white-collar or corporate crimes that affect everyone on some level are rarely identified as crimes and policed. These crimes include the criminal actions of corporations and financial institutions that resulted in billions of dollars in "bail out" money given to them at the cost of American citizens, even though millions of homeowners did not receive any type of help that would have prevented them from foreclosing on their homes. Other examples include dangerous products sold to consumers; insider trading and stock market manipulations; unnecessary surgeries or prescriptions; denial of health-related services by insurance companies; price fixing; false advertising; unsafe products sold to consumers; fraud; embezzlement; and computer crimes. At times both the police and the public may be focused on publicized cases of police corruption but remain largely unaware of the level of corporate corruption that has a direct impact on the lives of people. Many erroneously assume that there are strict regulations and oversight of the financial market and view the police as an entity that protects the public and maintains peace. While police "patrol the petty" and chase "the bad guys" (i.e., mostly street-level criminal offenders), the white-collar crimes go largely unrecognized.

In addition to failing to recognize many of the above examples as "crimes," police typically lack the resources, training, and knowledge to police some of the fewer ones that may be considered criminal (fraud, embezzlement, computer crimes). The police overwhelmingly protect those in privileged positions (Neugebauer, 1999, 1996; Gordon, 1987) and apply selective law enforcement to those who are economically and socially marginalized (Reiman and Leighton, 2010; Gordon, 1987; Ericson, 1982). Community policing initiatives to date have frequently been used to police the most marginalized populations, including panhandlers, the homeless, and street youth. And since the 1990s laws have been passed to regulate youth deviance, and zero-tolerance policies have become the norm for dealing with minor transgressions and incivilities in schools (DeKeseredy, 2007; Currie, 2004). The "zero tolerance" approach to "community policing" in New York City that was put into practice by New York City police commissioner William Bratton led to the arrest of tens of thousands of people for "minor" offenses (Skogan, 2006).

"Knowledge" of policing reflects a systematized knowledge that has considerable influence in the discursive practices of policing. For officers, the state of knowing what crime is and what their roles are reflects a systematized knowledge of a policing "science" based on evidence of how policing has been done and what 'works' in policing as well as the use of policing rhetoric. This knowledge translates to particular police practices and ideologies that, in turn, maintain and promote this very "knowledge." Widely accepted knowledge of policing represents a set of sociopolitical forces that secure particular "truths," including "the police fight crimes," "police protect society and citizens," and "police serve communities." This is contrary to the positivists' argument that knowledge is objective and can be achieved through the administration of value-free methodological approaches. But unlike the laws of the physical world, a fixed set of laws relating to the social world does not exist. Human behavior is complex and the result of a multitude of social, economic, political, and psychological factors, and what is constructed as "knowledge" is political. What is "true" today may not necessarily be true tomorrow, and new interpretations of today's "truths" reveal the power dynamics in the construction of what ultimately is accepted as "knowledge."

The Ethos of Individualism

The ethos of individualism does not encourage partnerships between parties that may have different agendas, and, more importantly, do not share the same "risks" when policing functions are not met or lead to problems and/or failures. The ethos of individualism permeates every aspect of American life. Americans largely view successes, whether they are financial, personal, familial, and/or organizational, as being largely the result of individuals' merits (Macionis, 2005; Ehrenreich, 2001). Many accept dominant constructions of these "successes," such as economic success, for example, as representing self-discipline, hard work, and commitment rather than the result of a number of factors such as the relationship between one's type of work to the larger economic state; family inheritance/socioeconomic status; family connections; one's 'race', ethnicity, and/or gender; luck/coincidence; and/or inherited traits; or view organizational successes as being solely the result of talented individuals within the organization without considering the wider political and economic "demands." Oftentimes, Americans think in terms of "what's in it for me" rather than "what's in it for us as a society." These types of ideologies make many critical of universal programs such as subsidized health care or education or an alternative style of policing, such as CP for all, regardless of income. There is often opposition from members of the middle and upper socioeconomic classes in allocating public funds to provide health care or education to those who are economically disadvantaged (Logan, Oakley, and Stowell, 2008; Kozol, 1992). Similar arguments have been made about the police. In wealthier areas, the public police have more resources, are more accountable to the community, and are more likely to provide better police service, whereas in poorer areas police 'service' often takes a different form, as discussed earlier.

The current economic state has led to significant cuts in police budgets across the country; and poorer, urban areas have been hit hard. Police agencies have had to put a "freeze" on hiring and/or lay off police officers (Wiseman, 2011). Also, in recent decades, as noted by Fischer and Poland (1998), wealthier folks are increasingly policed by the "private police" to protect their properties, businesses, and privately owned "public spaces" that are accessed daily by the public. And police organizations operate with the same sense of "individualism" by promoting their successes as the result of the good work of officers from within and are reluctant to accept a change in policing that would require them to publicly "share" these successes with members of the public.

Also, police and community members frequently subscribe to different concepts of public safety. Police often rely on a "professionalized definition of 'public safety' centered on serious crime as defined by criminal law," while some communities "tend to care more about less-serious safety problems . . . variously called 'soft crime' or 'disorder'" (Thacher, 2001:776). Even though finding workable solutions to this difference in priorities could result in a weakening of the policing of certain "hard crimes," Thacher cited multiple situations in which policing institutions were able to avoid downsizing the policing of particular "hard crimes" while responding to the needs of communities. For instance, some police agencies expanded their workforce to create special units for handling "soft crime," and in others they were able to expand the ideological frameworks used by their officers as a means of encouraging them to take "soft crime" more seriously.

Additionally, police and community members may have different understandings of how and to what degree officers may exercise authority over individuals and at what point their actions may be viewed as harassment. This issue may be further exacerbated by the police who increase their proximity to communities (e.g., by placing more officers on foot patrol) as a way to build bridges with the community, while community members may view this as increased harassment.

But, as discussed in chapter 2, the public appearance of the police accomplishing identified organizational goals must be maintained. Organizations may want to "appear" as if they are involving the public, but this is an unlikely enterprise given the "risks" to the maintenance and survival of the organization. Police departments operate "individualistically" in the construction of a "knowledge of insecurities," which enables processes of exclusion as they become hidden within desirable rhetoric, such as "creating safe neighborhoods," "improving police-community partnerships," and "citizen empowerment." As Fischer and Poland (1998) note, the processes of exclusion are emerging as crucial aspects of social control and governance in late modern societies. Public spaces become subject to surveillance and control by the public police, and particular police initiatives such as CP are used to empower officers not to serve everyone equally but rather to ban "problem" people from particular spaces. The concern is not with fairness and social justice but with the purification of public space (Sibley, 1988). As Ericson (1994) has noted, surveillance and the management of risk factors are critical to the development of specialized knowledge, which is required to "engineer" community "safety." Emphasis is placed on the control and management of behavior and the mobility and whereabouts of "risky" individuals or populations. The exclusions of "risky behaviors or individuals" has become central to the operation of governance (Fischer and Poland, 1998). These do not reflect a collectivist spirit on the part of police working with all groups of people, providing quality service, and building communities that improve the lives of people. Rather, these reflect the ethos of working to maintain and preserve dominant individual and organizational interests at the expense of disempowered others and providing a policing function that provides service to privileged members of society who are viewed as "deserving." Additionally, these have created mistrust toward the police by some communities, which further challenge any meaningful movement toward CP.

Mistrust of Police by Some Communities

Mistrust of police have been reported by different minority ethnic and racial communities but has been most evident among African and Hispanic American communities (Lundman and Kaufman, 2003; Fridell et al., 2001; Withrow and Jackson, 2002; Powers, 1986) and more recently, post-911 Arabs and Muslims (AIUSA, 2004; Heumann and Cassak, 2003; Harris, 2002). Minorities have disproportionately experienced racial profiling, excessive use of force, deadly force, and selective law enforcement by police officers. Many African Americans describe instances of being unfairly questioned by the police because they were "profiled"; that is, were suspected of having committed some type of crime because of their physical appearance.

A national telephone poll of 2006 individuals conducted in 1999 by the Gallup Organization found that 77 percent of blacks and 56 percent of whites believe racial profiling was a widespread practice in the United States. Also, Amnesty International USA (2004) found that 42 percent of blacks, almost 75 percent of young black males, and 6 percent of whites surveyed report that they are victims of racial profiling. Minorities believe that their encounters with the police are more punitive than encounters involving nonminorities (Lundman and Kaufman, 2003). Also, minorities appear more willing to interpret negative aspects of traffic stops (e.g., officer rudeness) as racially motivated (Withrow and Jackson, 2002; Fridell et al., 2001).

Racial profiling refers to the use of race as the primary factor in police decisions to stop and question citizens. But clearly there has been a disconnect between police perceptions of abuse of powers and members of minority groups. For instance, a survey of 1,087 police chiefs found that 60 percent believed that racial profiling was not a problem in their jurisdictions, and 29 percent said it was only a minor problem. And many police officers appear to be in support of the use of 'race' based on the differential arrest and victimization rates between racial groups. According to Donzinger (1996), African Americans are arrested at significantly higher rates than whites (five to one for misdemeanors and three to one for violent crimes), and African American males have higher victimization rates (e.g., victims of homicide).

Some studies show that officers believe that minorities are more likely to commit crimes (mostly drug crimes), and thus police feel "justified" in focusing enforcement efforts on minorities (Heumann and Cassak, 2003; Cleary, 2000) and view racial profiling as an acceptable method (Barlow and Barlow, 2002). This ties in to earlier discussions of officers' perceptions of what criminals "look like" and what actions are deemed "crimes." Officers do not seem to be aware of the relevance of selective law enforcement and the relationship between categories of people and "access" to particular crimes (e.g., white-collar versus street crimes). For instance, with respect to the former, the National Household Survey of Substance and Drug Abuse found that 13 percent of whites and 12 percent of African Americans said they used illegal substances. And 71 percent of crack cocaine users are white, 17 percent are African American, and almost 8 percent are Hispanic. But according to the U.S. Sentencing Commission (2000), arrestees for crack cocaine are approximately 6 percent white, 84 percent African American, and 9 percent Hispanic. The National Household Survey of Substance Abuse found that 81 percent of powder cocaine users were white, approximately 8 percent are African American, and 8.5 percent are Hispanic. But according to the U.S. Sentencing Commission, arrestees for powder cocaine are 18 percent white, 30 percent African American, and 50 percent Hispanic.

One reason that more African Americans are arrested is that more are being searched (Ramirez, McDevitt, and Farrell, 2000). Some recent research shows that minorities (especially African Americans) are slightly more likely to be stopped for traffic violations and are much more likely to be searched and arrested (Gaines, 2006; Engel, and Calnon, 2004; Novak, 2004; Rojek, Rosenfeld, and Decker, 2004). And police have the authority to stop motorists without probable cause or reasonable suspicion that a crime has taken place. They can use traffic violations as a pretext for stopping motorists suspected of criminal activity (*Whren v. United States*, 1996; see chapter 2).

The Court's decision in *Whren* did not create the practice of pretextual stops. Rather, it validated this long-standing police practice. Some have claimed that it gave the police virtually unlimited authority to stop anyone for any reason if a traffic violation has been observed. And all evidence gathered from the stop is admissible, regardless of whether or not it relates to the stated reason for the stop (assuming there are no constitutional violations); officers can conduct warrantless searches using dogs or use the plain-view exception. But what is overlooked is that certain forms of police corruption are disproportionately committed against minorities (Burris and Whitney, 2000). Deadly force by police results in an average of 373 civilian deaths each year; the majority are young and male, and a disproportionate number is African American (Brown and Langan, 2001).

Research has found that young black males, who are perceived by police as uncooperative and/or disrespectful, experience the most police physical abuse (Lersch and Mieczkowski, 2005). However, as discussed by Walker and Katz (1992), studies have not looked at how the behavior and demeanor of suspects may be the result of behavior on the part of the officer. In other words, is it the behavior of the citizen or the officer that leads to a violent confrontation? Fridell and Pate (1997) examined the possibility of violent episodes in situations when an officer expects hostility when dealing with certain groups, and, in effect, can create a negative response from a civilian.

Also, officers as well as members of the middle and upper socioeconomic classes view arrest and conviction rates as measures of criminal behavior rather than measures of police behavior, which shape public perceptions of "problem people" and "dangerous behavior." Critics of the Uniform Crime Reports argue that these crime statistics tell us more about police behavior rather than the actual crimes taking place in society. Before one can accept these reported crimes as representative of actual crime in the country, one must first invest time in understanding how police culture shapes and influences police discretionary powers that can lead to selective law enforcement against particular groups of people. Additionally, one must understand how the political climate directly influences the crimes that are disproportionately policed and the individuals that become constructed as "problem people" (Fischer and Poland, 1998). For instance, in the early 1900s, the majority of arrests made by police were for public drunkenness. But today, public drunkenness is not treated as a priority, whereas the enforcement of drug laws has become a central component to policing. Following the government's declaration of the "war on drugs," incarceration rates for drug users have skyrocketed since the 1980s. The emphasis on drug laws reflects the current political climate that constructs illicit drugs as "dangerous," particularly when used by the poorest members in society (Reiman and Leighton, 2010; Barak, 2003).

The crime statistics are affected by particular police strategies, such as the level of proactive versus reactive policing, and the police budget determines the level of resources made available to engage in proactive work that can lead to significant increases in arrests. But the "official" crime statistics largely shape people's perceptions of crime. Officers assume that arrest and conviction rates are valid measures of criminal behavior, and the public generally accepts the UCR as an accurate account of the type and frequency of crimes in society. These represent challenges in the quest to achieve an equitable and transparent policing system; that is, a policing by consent.

Public trust in police is crucial to building healthy relationships between communities and police. When communities trust in police, it enhances the legitimacy of police actions and police effectiveness through increased citizen cooperation (Goldsmith, 2005). However, as Goldsmith asserts, trust is rather fragile and often lacking in community-police relationships. By focusing on low-trust situations, Goldsmith attempts to explain the variables that undermine public trust in police and suggests possibilities to cultivate and maintain trust. They include: structural location and historical functions (for example, groups' relation to police and society at large); commitment to uphold particular laws and regimes (i.e., the enforcement of laws that lack public support); impunity (i.e., failing to hold police legally accountable in the same way as average citizens); "reason to suspect" or the suspicious nature of police and the "us versus them" attitudes on the part of police; and performance-related issues including neglect, indifference, incompetence, venality, extortion, discrimination, inconsistency, intimidation, excessive force, and brutality. Building or rebuilding community trust in the police is a rather formidable task, requiring extensive retooling of policing as an "institution," and it is dependent upon a balance of community and police participation in the process. For Goldsmith (2005), communities need to feel that the police are working with them and not against them. He further adds that police must act "fairly, transparently, and respectfully" with citizens, and that middle and upper management must embrace these values and serve as models for lower-ranking officers. Moreover, limiting the use of force by officers is equally important. He asserts that police violence "confirms a lack of public influence and control over police," and that in order to build trust, communities must feel they have influence over the police (ibid.:459).

In working to maintain their appearance as being in control and effective, some police agencies have created ethics training programs. But we should be critical and cautious of ethics programs as demonstrated by the recurring corruption scandals throughout police agencies with ethics training (e.g., NYPD and LAPD). Ethics training should serve as an "adjunct" rather than a central tenet of any anticorruption approach (Moran, 2005). But, ultimately, the police "believe" in what they do; that is, that they are a needed service in society that can control crime and maintain order. Therefore, the "incentive" for change is tied into organizational survival rather than to a genuine commitment to create a policing by consent.

The Post-911 Climate and the "War on Terror"

As noted by Thomas (1966:301; orig. 1931), "Situations that are defined as real are real in their consequences." The attacks on September 11, 2001, galvanized Americans and led to increased public support for more resources in the area of securities. Terrorists hijacked American Airlines Flight 11 and United Airlines Flight 175 and intentionally crashed the planes into the World Trade Center in New York City; one plane targeted for each tower. American Airlines Flight 77 was also hijacked and crashed into the Pentagon in Arlington, Virginia. The final attack may have been impeded as a result of the flight crew intervening, which resulted in United Airlines Flight 93 crashing into a field near the town of Shanksville in rural Somerset County, Pennsylvania. Some 2,977 people died in these attacks (http://en.wikipedia.org/wiki/Casualties_of_the_September_11_attacks).

What followed was a growing culture of fear and support for the increased militarization of public spaces. The expanding influence of the military presence is evident as the United States has more police, weapons, soldiers, and prisons today than at any other time in its history. There has been a reallocation of domestic resources and government funding from various social programs into military security measures both domestically and internationally (Giroux, 2004). As Giroux (2004:214) notes, "The traditional distinctions between military, police and criminal justice are blurring; the police now work in close collaboration with the military. This takes the form of receiving surplus weapons, technology/information transfers, the introduction of SWAT teams modeled after the NAVY Seals, which are experiencing a steep growth in police departments throughout the U.S. and a growing reliance on military models of crime control." Discussions on Community Policing, even though still presented by chiefs of police as significant, continue to largely serve as rhetoric as many police organizations have become more preoccupied with discussions on protections against terrorism and counterterrorism measures. The recent killing of the country's "number one terrorist," Osama bin Laden, appears to have created a sense of confidence for some in counterterrorist strategies, including the use of torture methods by the military such as "water-boarding"—which was reported as directly contributing to the finding of bin Laden (Harden, 2011).

After 9/11, the FBI was mandated to prevent and protect the United States from terrorist attacks (Council of State Governments; Eastern Kentucky University, 2006). The Department of Defense defines terrorism as "the calculated use of violence or the threat of violence to inculcate fear; intended to coerce or to intimidate governments or societies in the pursuit of goals that are generally political, religious, or ideological" (Department of the Army, 2003:3-07). The "war on terrorism" was authorized by the U.S. Congress under the Authorization for Use of Military Force against Terrorists passed on September 18, 2001. And law enforcement agencies have assumed some of the responsibility in this "war"; however, there is confusion as to what precisely are the "new roles" of police officers. Some agencies have claimed to have taken measures to prevent "terrorism," but little data has been collected on the details of their strategies, which agencies have been the most "productive" in this area, how these have "changed" police agencies, and how other departments can redirect their activities (Pelfrey, 2007). According to Eastern Kentucky Council of State Governments (2006),

> New terrorism-related demands and resources are now competing with other national public safety priorities, placing a strain on local law enforcement agencies. Local officials cite drug enforcement and community policing initiatives as two local priorities that are being affected by shifting federal programs. For example, drastic cuts have been made to the Edward Byrne Memorial State and Local Law Enforcement Assistance Grant and Community Oriented Policing Services programs, which once provided critical support to local and state community policing initiatives and drug enforcement and treatment efforts.

Moreover, federal funding for terrorism-related research has been substantial in relation to other areas such as CP (Zahn and Strom, 2003). Nearly $49 billion was funded for "combating terrorism" in 2003, and nearly $53 billion was requested for 2004. The 2004 budget request was 83 percent higher than the amount funded prior to 9/11 (Zahn and Strom, 2003).

According to Murray (2005), support for CP will continue to be challenged, and some will entirely dismiss it as being too "soft" in the "war against terror." Although the term *war against terror* is not officially used by the administration of President Obama (preferring to use the term *Overseas Contingency Operation*), it is still commonly used by politicians, the media, and the public at large. Murray contends that some organizations will continue to rely on various tenets of CP, but others will favor the traditional model that reflects varying degrees of paramilitarism.

But aggressive crime-control approaches that include police surveillance on particular groups will remain the priority. Targeted groups by police have included the poor and racial and ethnic minorities such as African and Hispanic Americans, but since 9/11 police interests have also included Arabs and Muslims (AIUSA, 2004; Heumann and Cassak, 2003; Harris, 2002). This has been done, in part, to show the public that something is being done to "fight terrorism" (Marks and Sun, 2007).

Since 9/11 police powers have been expanded, and police can more easily conceal their operations, including abuses, from public scrutiny. Shortly after 9/11, Congress introduced the USA PATRIOT Act (Uniting and Strengthening America by Providing Appropriate Tools Required to Intercept and Obstruct Terrorism). The PATRIOT Act is a federal bill used to expand police powers and jurisdiction in the "fight against terrorism." And

> on May 26, 2011, President Barack Obama signed a four-year extension of three key provisions in the USA PATRIOT Act: roving wiretaps, searches of business records (the "library records provision"), and conducting surveillance of "lone wolves"—individuals suspected of terrorist-related activities not linked to terrorist groups. (http://en.wikipedia.org/wiki/Patriot_Act)

The hegemonizing procedures of domination are operationalized through language. Words such as *terrorists, threat, risk*, and *war* are powerful "tools" in securing public support for the expansion of police powers regardless of the potential for abuses. Language is a powerful social resource that is often used by those in positions of power to secure particular outcomes. For instance, language has been strategically used by members of government to create a culture of fear that leads to public support for increased resources to hire more police officers and implement aggressive crime-control tactics regardless of the range of police abuse of powers that are made possible. Theoretically, the CP model has the potential to develop police-community partnerships and increase transparency and accountability on the part of the police. Responding to the uneven power relations between officers is an important component to ultimately addressing the uneven power relations that exist between communities, categories of people, and the police. Indeed, the CP model presents possibilities for the transformation of the policing system, but currently there exist overwhelming challenges to securing its implementation in any meaningful way and decreasing corruption risks.

Chapter Seven

Concluding Remarks

As noted by Kappeler, Sluder, and Alpert (1998), police have engaged in corruption since the creation of formal police organizations. Police corruption can take many forms, and it refers to officers' abuse of police powers for personal and/or organizational gain; the advantage can be material/financial, social, and psychological and/or emotional. Police corruption occurs in police organizations in which officers participate in corrupt practices either on their own or with their partner, but do so independently from others, and in agencies, where in addition to these, corruption can be organized and shared among many of the members within the organization or within a particular unit (Barker, 2006; Withrow, 2006; Walker, 2005, 1977; Corsianos, 2003; Burris and Whitney, 2000; Crank and Caldero, 2000; Nelson, 2000; Lynch, 1999; Delattre, 1996; Geller and Toch, 1996; Kappeler, Sluder, and Alpert, 1994; Skolnick and Fyfe, 1993). But many forms of corruption are not recognized as such or are overwhelmingly ignored internally by police organizations. Policing as an "institution" is informed by hegemonic masculinity and patriarchal ideologies that contribute to the creation and preservation of a culture of tolerance for police corruption.

The most common statement issued by police administrators after an incident of police corruption is reported by the media is one that refers to the officer(s) involved as a "bad/rotten apple(s)." This is not surprising, nor is it beyond the normative response by any police organization. The goal of any public institution such as the police is to ensure organizational survival (Manning, 1997), but the three goals that are promoted externally by police organizations and largely recognized by the public are law enforcement, order maintenance, and community service. The police must maintain a minimum level of these three (Simon, 1964) in order to create the appearance of being in control and being effective.

There may be differences in organizational priorities between police agencies (Maguire, 2001, 1997; Zhao, 1996; Crank and Wells, 1991; Crank, 1990; Sanders, 1977; Mohr, 1973; Wilson, 1968), and organizational priorities may change within particular agencies (Wilson, 1968; Simon, 1964; Manning, 1997), however, most of the time it appears that police organizations promote "law enforcement" as a central goal. There is no denying the overwhelming emphasis placed on arrests, as seen in the ways officers talk about and socially construct "the good pinch" and in managements' response to officers' "good" work when making arrests (McLaughlin, 2007).

Additionally, the promotion of a "knowledge of insecurities" by police is prioritized in the public imagination and overshadows any knowledge of dangerous and/or illegal behavior on the part of the police. The construction of a knowledge of insecurities is an ongoing exercise on the part of organizations in ensuring the public's commitment to the quest for security, and this simultaneously becomes the "tool" of choice for organizations in "constructing" and responding to corrupt officers. Moreover, popular cultural constructions of the police become a site of contestation for organizations attempting to respond to publicized cases of police corruption. The dominant images of the police continue to include the police as "crime fighter" and "enforcer of laws" (Corsianos, 2009; Martin and Jurik, 2007; Neugebauer, 1999, 1996; Stenson, 1993; Ericson, 1982, 1981). These are further strengthened by the publicly accepted police organizational goals and the wider cultural constructions of living in a "risk society" and the need for collective efforts toward achieving security. But, the police as partners in the quest for security cannot also be part of a system that enables and condones "risky" and "dangerous" behavior among its officers. Thus, as discussed by Walker (2005), the "rotten apple" theory has powerful emotional and political appeal. But it also allows members of the public to "see" that this is the act of a particular person(s). This enables the public to understand corruption as something that is done by one or a few "rogue officers" while maintaining confidence in the behavior of the majority.

While police may have different understandings of what constitutes police corruption, they are aware of the importance of promoting and maintaining an overall positive image of the police to the public, and herein exists a conflict of identity that forces police officers to constantly engage in identity protection. Officers protect their individual identity through "reframing— where the meaning attached to a specific occupation is transformed; recalibrating—where the tasks that constitute the role are re-categorized so as to emphasize the more acceptable or palatable tasks; and refocusing—where an attempt is made to shift attention to non-stigmatized aspects of the role" (Dick, 2005:1369). Police officers have the power to redefine and contest the meaning of their behavior despite dominant external constructions such as those by the media. Thus, following publicized cases of police corruption officers often absolve themselves of any wrongdoing by framing their own actions, or those of other officers, within discourses of "danger" and "risk." Policing as an "institution" and various tenets of the police culture that include, for instance, secrecy, an "us versus them" mentality, loyalty to "the brotherhood," and violence as a justified "tool" to responding to "civilians" create corruption risks; that is, opportunities for misconduct are made possible.

However, perceptions of risk are gendered and, therefore, opportunities for misconduct vary along gender lines. Female officers use less force in arrest situations with members of the public than male officers (Schuck and Rabe-Hemp, 2005; Garner and Maxwell, 2002), overall use policing approaches that rely less on physical force (Bureau of Justice Assistance, 2001), and appear to better manage their anger and avoid the use of force (Abernethy and Cox, 1994). Also, the average male officer in a large police department will cost taxpayers significantly more than the average female officer with regard to force liability lawsuit payouts (National Center for Women and Policing, 2002).

Differences in socialization between the sexes are central to our understanding of why women continue to commit fewer crimes. Gender roles are learned through socialization from infancy. The beliefs that many people have about people appearing to belong to a particular sex are the result of dominant historical, socioeconomic, and political forces. Women ·overall have been largely socialized to be nurturers, caretakers, emotional providers for their children, more passive and dependent, and to conform to the normative standards set by society and take less risks. Differences in socialization also contribute to explaining female officers' greater support and commitment to Community Policing (CP) (Corsianos, 2009; Miller and Hodge, 2004; Miller, 1999), which provide further insight into why fewer women are involved in police corruption since support for CP initiatives suggests a commitment to improving police-community relationships and responding to the internal police operations and power dynamics in more equitable ways.

Women also have more to lose socially and financially if labeled a "criminal," which contributes to our understanding of why fewer women and girls commit crime (Belknap, 2006; Faith, 1993; Morris, 1987). In relation to men, economic opportunities for women are disproportionately fewer, as seen in the "feminization of poverty" (U.S. Census Bureau, 2008), but they become significantly more scarce, almost nonexistent, for women with criminal records. Similarly, women in policing have more to lose if labeled "corrupt" and/or associated with particular instances of police misconduct as a result of their gender status. As noted by Faith (1993:70), "Females are commonly subject to many more private forms of social control than are males, and the female *deviant* is deemed more deviant than her male equivalent. She suffers greater social stigmatization when she breaches idealized gender standards."

Indeed, female officers on one level challenge the gender normative standards by seeking a career that continues to be male dominated and "hypermasculinized." But, on the other hand, a disproportionate number of female officers are represented in gender-specific units that can be perceived as more "feminized." So even though they become part of a patriarchal, masculinist work environment, differences in socialization lead officers to "choose" or be given assignments that are more gender specific. They are less likely to take on "risks" that could "label" them "corrupt" or "deviant" within police circles.

Women officers are less likely to assume the types of risk associated with the various forms of police corruption given the occupational and organizational challenges they have had to overcome to become officers and the challenges they confront as police officers (Harrington and Lonsway, 2004; Harrington, 1999; Martin, 1994, 1980). Also, the "risk" of "being made an example of" by the organization may mean termination or even criminal charges, depending on the type of act committed. This risk may be too great for particular officers who do not have "full membership" given the continued existence of gendered experiences within the culture. The seriousness of these risks may be further exacerbated by external realities that can include, for instance, officers who are single mothers raising young, dependent children and where policing provides some level of financial security in the form of pay and benefits. In assessing gendered risk, the level of trust one has in relationships with colleagues is also relevant. Since women often see themselves as the "outsiders within the station" (Martin, 1994), and given the gendered challenges experienced within the culture, they may be less likely to trust male peers and may perceive them to be more likely to protect each other while leaving female colleagues exposed.

The structure and culture of policing celebrate "masculinity." For instance, warlike rhetoric and training, competition, aggressive crime-control tactics such as excessive use of force, narrow definitions of physical strength, a sense of entitlement over others, and male bravado help reinforce male comradeship. Policing becomes an important cultural and social resource for many male officers, and few careers today continue to overwhelmingly represent males as does the policing field. With the slow but gradual increase of female police officers over the last four decades, organizational and cultural efforts to preserve masculinity as the norm become even more necessary to maintain dominant images of police bodies and behavior and preserve police solidarity. The gender configuring within policing as seen in recruitment and promotions, internal police policies, and in the division of labor serves to demonstrate that "women" as a category are to be understood as feminine and/or "not masculine," or in significantly fewer instances, as "not masculine enough," because ultimately they are still "seen" as "women." In the process, hegemonic masculinity and patriarchal ideologies are promoted and a culture of tolerance for police corruption is maintained.

Masculine characteristics are accepted as "common sense" and are "naturalized." Physical force is expected, condoned, preferred, and even celebrated. These particular masculine-constructed performances are deemed necessary to "fight criminals" and create "community safety." They are also promoted as "heroic" given dominant societal constructions of "danger," the use of violence as a means to accomplish identified goals, and the role of police in perceived dangerous situations that are avoided by others in society. Since "crime fighting" is seen as being entirely done by police officers, police organizations actively construct the heroic identity in the public imagination with strategic rhetoric, such as the police are the "thin blue line" between a state of peace and order and one of anarchy and chaos; "the police protect the public"; "the police control crime"; "police put away the *bad guys*"; and "the police are always available to assist in times of need." In addition to using these forms of rhetoric for organizational maintenance and survival, they are also used by the police to remind the public of what the police "do." These popular manifestations of the police are further used by individual officers to remind themselves of their value in society and to excuse police behavior that is believed to be in compliance with these popular constructions of the police, despite "questionable" tactics used. By critically evaluating the media and public accounts of the incident, a culture of tolerance for police corruption is maintained by officers despite variations in their individual perceptions.

Also, officers consider the possibilities of misuse and abuse of police powers as inevitable given the complexity of tasks police officers perform on a daily basis. Seasoned officers "know" that policing translates to a "high risk" profession given all the possibilities for mistakes, opportunities for abuse of powers, and the diverse interpretations of police actions by different groups. The socialization process conditions officers to view policing as "risky" and "dangerous." Police begin to understand the complexities of their work from training within and through exposure to the unique demands of their profession (Skolnick, 1994). Also, police instructors who are responsible for disseminating "police knowledge" to new recruits at police academies often present material that reinforces dominant masculinist police ideologies, including perceptions of dangers on the job (Murphy and Caplan, 1993; Cohen and Feldberg, 1991). Most police training overemphasizes the potential for death and injury, and instructors spend a great deal of time teaching "officer survival" skills (Kappeler et al., 1996). Skolnick (1994) notes that danger is one of the most important facets in the development of a police working personality. And the police learn the potential for danger through "war stories" and field training by seasoned officers after the police academy (Kraska and Paulsen, 1997). Therefore, despite the increase in diversity among officers in some larger police agencies in recent years, evidence of assimilation to the dominant police culture has been well documented (Martin and Jurik, 2007; Harrington and Lonsway, 2004; National Research Council, 2004), as officers largely reenact police culture even though they simultaneously renew it in less meaningful ways; that is, in ways that do not pose a serious threat to the dominant culture.

Furthermore, the news media are important players in personalizing police corruption cases, albeit for different reasons than the police, but some critics have negatively evaluated the media's tendency to "overstate" the frequency of police corruption and have referred to their reaction as one of "moral panic" (Lawrence, 1997). Indeed, in the pursuit to attract a larger audience, the media capitalizes on cases with sensational appeal that can cater to incomplete or inaccurate reporting in order to "get the scoop" and "grab attention" without being careful about the details (Kurtz, 1994). But to evaluate the frequency of police criminality as being blown out of proportion does a disservice to society and disrupts any possibility for creating a "policing by consent."

Mainstream crime news focuses on the sensational and the unusual, often reinforcing biases and stereotypes (McCormick, 1995; Mills, 1990; Faith, 1987). But police corruption is far more prevalent than members of the public representing middle and upper socioeconomic backgrounds recognize, and the public only "learns" about the few that are typically uncovered by the investigative work of journalists following a "tip" and that produces "good" evidence against the suspected officer(s), and often involves a "legitimate" victim(s).

Given the variety of powers provided to the police, the evidence of abuse of powers, and the different types of police corruption that are largely not recognized by police organizations, the public cannot afford to not pay attention. When particular cases are "discovered" by the media, attention is given to the ones that have dramatic, sensational, and "entertainment" appeal. The fact that the suspected offender is a police officer increases the dramatic potential, but in addition to this, the misconduct must be perceived as "serious" and atypical in comparison to the vast array of forms of police corruption. The focus is usually on the individual officer(s) involved—that is, the "bad apple(s)"—leaving little room for alternative interpretations in explaining police misconduct beyond the individual(s).

Moreover, given police organizations' growing legitimacy over the years for many representing the middle and upper socioeconomic classes, wrongdoing on the part of the police becomes less visible and/or less offensive when police misconduct is alleged against economically and/or socially marginalized populations. On the other hand, crimes committed by the police are of particular interest to the media given the suspects are police officers themselves expected to enforce the laws and not violate them and in instances where the public can be convinced that these acts are "random in nature," putting everyone at "risk." But the priority for the mainstream media is to dramatize rather than educate and raise consciousness. The media often aims to create the impression that it can happen to anyone. In doing this, more members of the public will pay attention during this limited period of reporting as it now concerns their own safety and that of their family. Also, it is in the interest of the mainstream news media to focus on the crimes of individuals rather than institutions. In an age of global capitalism, the media's primary connection is with the development of advanced capitalism (Barak, 2003), and not the delegitimization of the police as a central institution in the preservation of the socioeconomic order.

Furthermore, for officers, the state of "knowing" what crime "is" and what their roles "are" reflects a systematized knowledge of a policing "science" based on "evidence" of how policing has been done and what 'works' in policing as well as on the use of policing rhetoric. This "knowledge" translates to particular police practices and ideologies that, in turn, maintain and promote this very "knowledge." Any widely accepted knowledge such as the current policing system represents a set of sociopolitical forces that secure particular "truths," including "the police fight crimes" and "the police protect society and citizens." Moreover, the current ethos of individualism does not encourage partnerships between parties that may have different agendas, and, more importantly, do not share the same "risks" when goals are not met and/or problems emerge. Police organizations operate with this sense of "individualism" and promote their "successes" as the result of the "good work" of officers from within, and they are reluctant to accept a change in policing that would require them to publicly "share" these "successes" with "civilians."

Organizations may want to appear as if they are involving the public, but this is an unlikely enterprise given the risks to the maintenance and survival of the organization. Police departments operate individualistically in the construction of a knowledge of insecurities, which enables processes of exclusion as they become hidden within desirable rhetoric such as "community policing" and "citizen empowerment." As Ericson (1994) has noted, surveillance and the management of risk factors are critical to the development of specialized knowledge, which is required to "engineer" community "safety." Emphasis is placed on the control and management of behavior and the mobility and whereabouts of "risky" individuals or populations. The exclusion of "risky behaviors or individuals" has become central to the operation of governance (Fischer and Poland, 1998). These do not reflect a collectivist spirit on the part of police working with all groups of people, providing quality service, and building communities that improve the lives of people. Rather, these reflect the ethos of working to maintain and preserve dominant individual and organizational interests at the expense of disempowered others and providing a policing function that caters to privileged members of society who are viewed as "deserving." Additionally, these fuel the mistrust toward the police by some communities, which further challenge any meaningful movement toward the creation of a policing by consent where police corruption is minimized and police accountability and transparency become "the norm."

Bibliography

Abernethy, A., and C. Cox. 1994. "Anger Management Training for Law Enforcement Personnel." *Journal of Criminal Justice* 22(5): 459–66.

ACLU (American Civil Liberties Union). 2009 (March). "Reclaiming Patriotism: A Call to Reconsider the Patriot Act." New York.

———. 1997. "Fighting Police Abuse: A Community Action Manual." New York. http://www.aclu.org/racial-justice_prisoners-rights_drug-law-reform_immigrants-rights/fighting-police-abuse-community-ac

Adler, F. 1975. *Sisters in Crime: The Rise of the New Female Criminal.* New York: McGraw-Hill.

Aileen: Life and Death of a Serial Killer. 2003. Documentary. Directed by Nick Broomfield and Joan Churchill. Lafayette Films.

Alain, M., and M. Grégoire. 2008 (June). "Can Ethics Survive the Shock of the Job? Quebec's Police Recruits Confront Reality." *Policing & Society* 18(2): 169–89.

Alpert, G. P. 1989. "Police Use of Deadly Force: The Miami Experience." In R. Dunham and G. Alpert (Eds.), *Critical Issues in Policing: Contemporary Readings.* Prospect Heights, IL: Waveland Press, 480–95.

Amnesty International USA (AIUSA). 2004. *Threat and Humiliation: Racial Profiling, Domestic Security and Human Rights in the United States.* New York: Amnesty International USA.

Ashforth, Blake E., and G. E. Kreiner. 1999. "'How Can You Do It?': Dirty Work and the Challenge of Constructing a Positive Identity." *Academy of Management Review* 24(3): 413–34.

Bailey, W. G. (Ed.). 1995. *The Encyclopedia of Police Science,* 2nd ed. New York: Garland Publishing.

Balfour, G., and E. Comack (Eds.). 2006. *Criminalizing Women: Gender and (In)Justice in Neo-Liberal Times.* Halifax, NS: Fernwood Publishing.

Baltzell, E. Digby. 1964. *The Protestant Establishment: Aristocracy & Caste in America.* New York: Vintage Books.

Barak, Gregg. 2003. *Violence and Nonviolence: Pathways to Understanding.* Thousand Oaks, CA: Sage Publications.

——— (Ed.). 1994. *Media, Process, and the Social Construction of Crime: Studies in Newsmaking Criminology.* New York: Garland.

Barak, Gregg, J. M. Flavin, and P. S. Leighton. 2001. *Class, Race, Gender, and Crime: Social Realities of Justice in America.* Los Angeles: Roxbury Publishing Company.

Barker, Tom. 2006. *Police Ethics: Crisis in Law Enforcement,* 2nd ed. Springfield, IL: Charles C. Thomas.

————. 1983. "Rookie Police Officers' Perceptions of Police Occupational Deviance." *Police Studies* 6(2): 30–38.

————. 1978. "An Empirical Study of Police Deviance Other Than Corruption." *Journal of Police Science and Administration* 6(3): 264–72.

Barker, Tom, and D. L. Carter. 1986. *Police Deviance*. Cincinnati, OH: Anderson Publishing Company.

Barker, Tom, and J. Roebuck. 1973. *An Empirical Typology of Police Corruption: A Study in Organization Deviance.* Springfield, IL: Charles C. Thomas.

Barlow, D. E., and M. H. Barlow. 2002 (September). "Racial Profiling: A Survey of African American Police Officers." *Police Quarterly* 5(3): 334–58.

Barnett, Jim. 2011 (April 13). "2 New Orleans Police Officers Convicted in 2005 Beating Death." CNN. http://articles.cnn.com/2011-04-13/justice/louisiana.police.convictions_1_police-officers-drug-overdose-second-officer?_s=PM:CRIME

Batton, C., and C. Kadleck. 2004 (March). "Theoretical and Methodological Issues in Racial Profiling Research." *Police Quarterly* 7(1): 30–64.

Bayley, D. H. 1996. *Police for the Future*. New York: Oxford University Press.

————. 1988. "Community Policing: A Report from the Devil's Advocate." In J. R. Greene and S. D. Mastrofski (Eds.), *Community Policing: Rhetoric or Reality?* New York: Praeger, 225–38.

BBC News. (2006, April 7). "NY Police Guilty of Mafia Murders." http://news.bbc.co.uk/2/hi/americas/4885674.stm

Becker, H. S. 1966. *Outsiders: Studies in the Sociology of Deviance*. New York: Glencoe Press.

Begley, Sharon. 1995 (March 26). "Gray Matters." *Newsweek Magazine*: 48–54.

Belknap, Joanne. 2006. *The Invisible Woman: Gender, Crime and Justice*, 3rd ed. Belmont, CA: Thomson Wadsworth.

————. 1995. *The Invisible Woman: Gender, Crime, and Justice*, 1st ed. Belmont, CA: Wadsworth Publishing Company.

————. 1991. "Women in Conflict: An Analysis of Women Correctional Officers." *Women & Criminal Justice* 2: 89–115.

Belknap, Joanne and J. K. Shelley. 1993. "The New Lone Ranger: Policewomen on Patrol." *American Journal of Police* 12(2): 47–75.

Bell, D. J. 1982. "Policewomen: Myths and Realities." *Journal of Police Science and Administration* 10(1): 112–20.

Benedict, Helen. 1992. *Virgin or Vamp: How the Press Covers Sex Crimes*. New York: Oxford University Press.

Benedict, Jeffrey R. 1998. *Athletes and Acquaintance Rape*. Thousand Oaks, CA: Sage.

Benokraitis, Nijole, and Joe R. Feagin. 1995. *Modern Sexism: Blatant, Subtle, and Covert Discrimination*. Englewood Cliffs, NJ: Prentice Hall.

Bergen, R. K., J. L. Edleson, and C. M. Renzetti (Eds.). 2005. "Violence against Women: Classic Papers." Boston, MA: Pearson Education.

Bertrand, M. A. 1969 (January). "Self-Image and Delinquency: A Contribution to the Study of Female Criminality and Woman's Image." *Acta Criminologica* 2(1): 71–144.

Best, Connie L. 1989 (Spring). "Criminal Victimization: Recent Research Findings." *Navy Clinical Psychology Newsletter*.

Birzer, M., and R. Tannehill. 2001. "A More Effective Training Approach for Contemporary Policing." *Police Quarterly* 4(2): 233–52.

Bittner, E. 1970. *The Functions of Police in Modern Society: A Review of Background Factors, Current Practices, and Possible Role Models*. Rockville: National Institute of Mental Health.

Black, D. 1990. "The Elementary Forms of Conflict Management." In School of Justice Studies, Arizona State University, *New Direction in the Study of Justice, Law, and Social Control*. New York: Plenum Press.

Bloch, P., and D. Anderson. 1974. "Policewomen on Patrol: Final Report." Washington, DC: Urban Institute and Police Foundation.

Blumenson, E., and E. Nilsen. 1998. "Policing for Profit: The Drug War's Hidden Economic Agenda." *University of Chicago Law Review* 65: 76–84.

Board of Inquiry. 2000. "Board of Inquiry into the Rampart Corruption Incident: Final Report." Los Angeles: Los Angeles Police Department.

Board of Inquiry. 2000 (March). "Rampart Area Corruption Incident." Los Angeles: Los Angeles Police Department Public Report.

Bobb, Merrick. 1998. "Special Counsel, 9th Semiannual Report." Los Angles: Los Angeles Sheriff's Department.

Boham, R. M., and K. N. Haley. 2005. *Introduction to Criminal Justice*, 4th ed. New York: McGraw-Hill Companies.

Boni, N. 1998. "Deployment of Women in Policing." Payneham, South Australia: National Police Research Unit.

Boyle, Christine. 1991. "Sexual Assault: A Case Study of Legal Policy Options." In Margaret A. Jackson and Curt T. Griffiths (Eds.), *Canadian Criminology: Perspectives on Crime and Criminality*. Toronto: Harcourt Brace Jovanovich.

Bradley, R. 1998. "Public Expectations and Perceptions of Policing." Public Research Series Paper 96. A Publication of the Policing and Reducing Crime Unit. London: Home Office Research.

Brandl, S. G. 1996. "In the Line of Duty: A Descriptive Analysis of Police Assaults and Accidents." *Journal of Criminal Justice* 24(3): 255–64.

Breci, M. G. 1997. "Female Officers on Patrol: Public Perceptions in the 1990s." *Journal of Crime and Justice* 20(2): 153–65.

Breines, W., and L. Gordon. 1983. "The New Scholarship on Family Violence." *Signs: Journal of Women in Culture and Society* 8(3): 490–531.

Brenzel, Barbara M. 1983. *Daughter of the State: A Social Portrait of the First Reform School for Girls in North America, 1856–1905*. Cambridge, MA: MIC Press.

Brown, J. M., and P. A. Langan. 2001. *1976–1998: Justifiable Homicide by Police Officers Murdered by Felons*. Washington, DC: U.S. Department of Justice.

Brown, M. F. 1983. "Shooting Policies: What Patrolmen Think." *Police Chief* 50(5): 35–37.

Brownmiller, Susan. 1985. *Femininity*. New York: Ballantine Books.

Brownstein, Henry H. 2000. *The Social Reality of Violence and Violent Crime.* Boston: Allyn and Bacon.

Bruno v. Codd, 396 N.Y.S. 2d 974 (Sup. Ct. Special Term 1977).

Buchbinder, H., V. Burstyn, D. Forbes, and M. Steedman (Eds.). 1987. *Who's on Top: the Politics of Heterosexuality*. Toronto: Garamond Press.

Bureau of Justice Assistance. 2001. *Recruiting and Retaining Women: A Self-assessment Guide for Law Enforcement*. Washington, DC: Bureau of Justice Assistance, 1–7.

Burris, J. L., and C. Whitney. 2000. *Blue vs. Black: Let's End the Conflict between Cops and Minorities*. New York: St. Martin's Griffin.

Butler, J. 1993. *Bodies That Matter: On the Discursive Limits of Sex*. New York: Routledge.

———. 1989. *Gender Trouble: Feminism and the Subversion of Identity*. New York: Routledge.

Buzawa, E., and C. Buzawa. 1996. *Domestic Violence: The Criminal Justice Response.* Thousand Oaks, CA: Sage Publications.

Cao, L., X. Deng, and S. Barton. 2000. "A Test of Lundman's Organizational Product Thesis with Data on Citizen Complaints." *Policing: An International Journal of Police Strategies & Management* 23(3): 356–73.

Cao, L., J. Frank, and F. T. Cullen. 1996. "Race, Community Context, and Confidence in Police." *American Journal of Police* 15(1): 3–22.

Carte, Gene E. 1986. "August Vollmer and the Origin of Police Professionalism." In M. Pogrebin and R. Regoli (Eds.), *Police Administrative Issues: Techniques and Functions*. Millwood, NY: Associated Faculty Press, 3–9.

Carte, Gene E., and Elaine Carte. 1975. *Police Reform in the United States: The Era of August Vollmer, 1905–1932*. Berkeley, CA: University of California Press.

Carter, D. L. 2002. *The Police and the Community*, 7th ed. Englewood Cliffs, NJ: Prentice Hall.

———. 1990. "Drug Related Corruption of Police Officers: A Typology." *Journal of Criminal Justice* 18(2): 85–89.

Carter, D. L., and A. J. Katz-Bannister. 2004. "Racial Profiling: Issues and Implications for Police Policy." In Q.C. Thurman and J. Zhao (Eds.), *Contemporary Policing: Controversies, Challenges, and Solutions*. Los Angeles: Roxbury, 235–47.

Carter, D. L., A. D. Sapp, and D. W. Stephens. 1989. "The State of Police Education: Policy Direction for the 21st Century." Washington, DC: Police Executive Research Forum.

Cerulo, Karen A. 1997. "Identity Construction: New Issues, New Directions." *Annual Review of Sociology* 23: 385–409.

Chalom, M. Autumn. 1993. "Community Policing: Toward a New Paradigm of Prevention?" *International Review of Community Development* 30: 70: 155–61.

Champion, Dean J. 2001. *Police Misconduct in America*. Santa Barbara, CA: ABC-CLIO.

Chappell, Allison T., and L. Lanza-Kaduce. 2009 (December 29). "Police Academy Socialization: Understanding the Lessons Learned in a Paramilitary-Bureaucratic Organization." *Journal of Contemporary Ethnography*. Sage Publications. http://jce.sagepub.com/cgi/content/abstract/0891241609342230v1

Chappell, Allison T., and Alex R. Piquero. 2004. "Applying Social Learning Theory to Police Misconduct." *Deviant Behavior* 25(2): 89–108.

Charles, M. T. 1981. "The Performance and Socialization of Female Recruits in the Michigan State Police Training Academy." *Journal of Police Science and Administration* 9(2): 209–23.

Chemerinsky, Erwin. 2001. "An Independent Analysis of the Los Angeles Police Department's Board of Inquiry Report on the Rampart Scandal." Los Angeles: Police Protective League.

Chesney-Lind, Meda. 1997. *The Female Offender: Girls, Women, and Crime*. Thousand Oaks, CA: Sage Publications.

———. 1995. "Girls, Delinquency, and Juvenile Justice: Toward a Feminist Theory of Young Women's Crime." In Barbara Raffel Price and Natalie J. Sokoloff (Eds.), *The Criminal Justice System and Women: Offenders, Prisoners, Victims, and Workers*. New York: McGraw Hill.

———. 1973. "Judicial Enforcement of the Female Sex Role: The Family Court and the Female Delinquent." *Issues in Criminology* 8(2): 51–69.

Chesney-Lind, Meda, and Noelie Rodriguez. 1983 (October). "Women under Lock and Key: A View from the Inside." *Prison Journal* 63(2): 47–65.

Chesney-Lind, Meda, and R. G. Shelden. 2004. *Girls, Delinquency, and Juvenile Justice*, 3rd ed. Belmont, CA: Thomson/Wadsworth.

———. 1997. *Girls, Delinquency, and Juvenile Justice*. Belmont, CA: Wadsworth.

———. 1992. *Girls, Delinquency and Juvenile Justice*. Pacific Grove, CA: Brooks/Cole.

Christopher, Warren. 1991. *Report of the Independent Commission on the Los Angeles Police Department*. Los Angeles: Independent Commission on the LAPD.

Cleary, J. 2000. "Racial Profiling Studies in Law Enforcement: Issues and Methodology." St. Paul: Minnesota House of Representatives, Research Department.

Cohen, H. S., and M. Feldberg. 1991. *Power and Restraint: The Moral Dimension of Police Work*. New York: Praeger.

Comack, E. (Ed.). 2007. *Locating Law: Race/Class/Gender/Sexuality Connections*, 2nd ed. Halifax, NS: Fernwood Publishing.

Connell, R. W. 2005. "The Social Organization of Masculinity." In Carole R. McCann and Seung-kyung Kim (Eds.), *Feminist Theory Reader: Local and Global Perspectives*, 2nd ed. New York: Routledge, 232–43.

———. 1995. *Masculinities*. Cambridge, UK: Polity Press.

Cooley, Charles Horton. 1964, orig. 1902. "The Social Self." In *Human Nature and the Social Order*. New York: Charles Scribner's Sons.

Cops under Fire. 1996. A&E/History Channel Videos. VHS NTSC only.

Cordner, G. 1994. "Foot Patrol without Community Policing: Law and Order in Public Housing." In D. Rosenbaum (Ed.), *The Challenge of Community Policing: Testing the Promises*. Thousand Oaks, CA: Sage, 182–91.

Corsianos, Marilyn. 2011. "Responding to Officers' Gendered Experiences through Community Policing and Improving Police Accountability to Citizens." *Contemporary Justice Review* 14(1): 7–20.

———. 2009. *Policing and Gendered Justice: Examining the Possibilities.* Toronto: University of Toronto Press.

———. 2008. "Police Corruption." In Gregg Barak (Ed.), *Battleground: Criminal Justice.* Westport, CT: Greenwood Press.

———. 2004. "'Women' Detectives and Perceptions of 'Oppressive' Experiences: Exploring Experiential Essentialism and Phenomenology." *Critical Criminology* 12(1): 67–85.

———. 2003. "Discretion in Detectives' Decision Making and 'High Profile' Cases." *Police Practice and Research: An International Journal* 4(3): 301–14.

———. 2001. "Conceptualizing 'Justice' in Detectives' Decision Making." *International Journal of the Sociology of Law* 29(2): 113–26.

Council of State Governments; Eastern Kentucky University. 2006 (December). "The Impact of Terrorism on State Law Enforcement: Adjusting to New Roles and Changing Conditions." National Institute of Justice, Office of Justice Programs, U.S. Department of Justice.

Crank, John P. 1998. *Understanding Police Culture.* Cincinnati, OH: Anderson Publishing.

———. 1990. "The Influence of Environmental and Organizational Factors on Police Style in Urban and Rural Environments." *Journal of Research in Crime and Delinqency* 27(2): 166–89.

Crank, John P., and Michael A. Caldero. 2011. *Police Ethics: The Corruption of Noble Cause.* Burlington, MA: Elsevier, Inc.

———. 2004. *Police Ethics: The Corruption of Noble Cause.* Lexis Nexis: Matthew Bender.

———. 2000. *Police Ethics: The Corruption of Noble Cause.* Cincinnati, OH: Anderson Publishing Co.

Crank, John P., and L. Edward Wells. 1991 (June). "The Effects of Size and Urbanism on Structure among Illinois Police Departments." *Justice Quarterly* 8(2): 169–85.

Crawford, C., and R. Burns. 1998 (December). "Predictors of the Police Use of Force: The Application of a Continuum Perspective in Phoenix." *Police Quarterly* 1(4): 41–63.

Curran, D. J., and C. M. Renzetti. 2001. *Theories of Crime.* Boston: Allyn and Bacon.

Currie, Elliott. 2004. *The Road to Whatever: Middle-class Culture and the Crisis of Adolescence.* New York: Henry Holt and Co.

Daley, Robert. 1978. *Prince of the City: The True Story of a Cop Who Knew Too Much.* Boston: Houghton Mifflin.

Daly, Kathleen. 1987a. "Structure and Practice of Familial-Based Justice in a Criminal Court." *Law and Society Review* 21(2): 267–90.

———. 1987b. "Discrimination in the Criminal Courts: Family, Gender, and the Problem of Equal Treatment." *Social Forces* 66(1): 152–75.

Daly, Kathleen, and M. Chesney-Lind. 1988 (December). "Feminism and Criminology." *Justice Quarterly* 5(4): 497–538.

Dandeker, C. 1990. *Surveillance, Power and Modernity: Bureaucracy and Discipline from 1700 to the Present Day.* Cambridge: Polity Press.

D'Angelo, J. 2000. "Addicted to Violence: The Cycle of Domestic Abuse Committed by Patrol Officers." In D. C. Sheehan (Ed.), *Domestic Violence by Police Officers.* Washington, DC: U.S. Government, 149–61.

Daniels, Ron. 2000. "The Crisis of Police Brutality and Misconduct in America: The Causes and the Cure." In Jill Nelson (Ed.), *Police Brutality: An Anthology.* New York: WW Norton.

Dasgupta, P. 2001. *Human Well-Being and the Natural Environment.* Oxford: Oxford University Press.

Davis, K. C. 1975. *Police Discretion.* St. Paul, MN: West Publishing Company, 52–78.

———. 1969. *Discretionary Justice: A Preliminary Inquiry.* Baton Rouge: Louisiana State University Press.

Dean, G., P. Bell, and M. Lauchs. 2010. "Conceptual Framework for Managing Knowledge of Police Deviance." *Policing and Society* 20(2): 204–22.

DeKeseredy, Walter S. 2007. *Sexual Assault during and after Separation/Divorce: An Exploratory Study.* Report prepared for the U.S. Department of Justice. Washington, DC: National Institute of Justice.

DeKeseredy, Walter S., and Ronald Hinch. 1991. *Woman Abuse: Sociological Perspectives.* Toronto: Thompson Educational Publishing.

DeKeseredy, Walter S., and Martin D. Schwartz. 1998 (February). "Measuring the Extent of Woman Abuse in Intimate Heterosexual Relationships: A Critique of the Conflict Tactics Scales." VAWnet.org. http://new.vawnet.org/print-document.php?doc_id=388& find_type=web_desc_AR Delattre, Edwin J. 1996. *Character and Cops: Ethics in Policing*, 3rd ed. Washington, DC: AEI Press.

———. 1989. *Character and Cops: Ethics in Policing*, 1st ed. Washington, DC: Anderson Publishing.

De Lauretis, Teresa. 1987. *Technologies of Gender: Essays on Theory, Film and Fiction*. Bloomington: Indiana University Press.

Dick, Penny. 2005 (November). "Dirty Work Designations: How Police Officers Account for Their Use of Coercive Force." *Human Relations* 58(11), 1363–90, New York: Plenum Publishing Corporation.

Dietz, Steven A. 1997. "Evaluating Community Policing: Quality Police Service and Fear of Crime." *Policing: An Internal Journal of Police Strategies & Management* 20(1): 83–100.

Dixon, D. 1992 (December). "Legal Regulation and Policing Practice." *Social and Legal Studies* 1(4): 515–41.

Dobash, R. E., and R. P. Dobash. 1992. *Women, Violence and Social Change*. New York: Routledge.

Dobash, R. P. et al. 1992. "The Myth of Sexual Symmetry in Marital Violence." *Social Problems* 39(1): 71–91.

Dodge, M., and M. Pogrebin. 2001. "African-American Policewomen: An Exploration of Professional Relationships." *Policing: An International Journal of Police Strategies & Management* 24(4): 550–62.

Doig, J. W. 1978 (December). "Police Policy and Police Behavior: Patterns of Divergence." *Policy Studies Journal* 7: 436–42.

Donzinger, S. R. 1996. *The Real War on Crime: The Report of the National Criminal Justice Commission*. New York: Harper Collins.

Drummond, D. S. 1976. *Police Culture*. Thousand Oaks, CA: Sage Publications.

Eaton, M. 1987. *Justice for Women? Family, Court and Social Control*. Milton Keynes, England: Open University Press.

Eck, J. E. 1990 (July). "A Realistic Approach to Controlling Drug Harms." *Public Management*: 7–12.

Eck, J. E., and W. Spelman. 1987. "Who Ya Gonna Call: The Police as Problem-busters." *Crime & Delinquency* 33(1): 31–52.

Ehrenreich, Barbara. 2001. *Nickel and Dimed on (Not) Getting by in America*. New York: Metropolitan Books/Henry Holt.

Eigenberg, Helen M. 2001. *Women Battering in the United States: Till Death Do Us Part*. Prospect Heights, IL: Waveland Press.

Eigenberg, Helen M., and V. E. Kappeler. 2001. "When the Batterer Wears Blue: A National Study of the Institutional Response to Domestic Violence among Police." In Helen Eigenberg (Ed.), *Women Battering in the United States: Till Death Do Us Part*. Prospect Heights, IL: Waveland Press, 246–97.

Eigenberg, Helen M., K. E. Scarborough, and V. E. Kappeler. 2001. "Contributory Factors Affecting Arrest in Domestic and Non-Domestic Assaults." In Helen M. Eigenberg, *Woman Battering in the United States: Till Death Do Us Part*. Prospect Heights, IL: Waveland Press, 298–318.

Eng, S. 1997 (20–23 May). "Policies for Women in the Justice Field—Need or Necessity." A presentation made at the Women in Policing in Canada: The Year 2000 and Beyond—Its Challenges workshop, Canadian Police College, Ottawa, ON.

Engel, R. S., J. M. Calnon, and T. J. Bernard. 2002 (June). "Theory and Racial Profiling: Shortcomings and Future Directions in Research." *Justice Quarterly* 19(2): 249–73.

Engel, R. S., and Robert E. Worden. 2003 (February). "Police Officers' Attitudes, Behavior and Supervisory Influences: An Analysis of Problem Solving." *Criminology* 41(1): 1–20, Columbus: American Society of Criminology.

Ericson, R. V. 1994 (June). "The Division of Expert Knowledge in Policing and Security." *British Journal of Sociology* 45(2): 149–75.

———. 1989 (June). "Patrolling the Facts: Secrecy and Publicity in Police Work." *British Journal of Sociology* 40(2): 205–26.

———. 1982. *Reproducing Order: A Study of Police Patrol Work*. Toronto: University of Toronto Press.

———. 1981. *Making Crime: A Study of Detective Work*. Toronto: Butterworth.

Ericson, R. V., P. M. Baranek, and J. B. Chan. 1987. *Visualizing Deviance: A Study of News Organization*. Toronto, Ontario, Canada: University of Toronto Press.

Ericson, R. V., and K. Haggerty. 1997. *Policing the Risk Society*. Toronto: University of Toronto Press.

Faith, Karlene. 1993. *Unruly Women: The Politics of Confinement and Resistance*. Vancouver: Press Gang Publishers.

———. 1987. "Media, Myths and Masculinization: Images of Women in Prison." In Ellen Adelberg and Claudia Currie (Eds.), *Too Few to Count: Canadian Women in Conflict with the Law*. Vancouver: Press Gang.

Farkas, M., and P. Manning. 1997. "The Occupational Culture of Corrections and Police Officers." *Journal of Crime and Justice* 20(2): 51–68.

Feinman, C. 1986. *Women in the Criminal Justice System*. New York: Praeger.

Feminist Majority Foundation and National Center for Women and Policing. 2000 (September 5). "Gender Differences in the Cost of Police Brutality and Misconduct—A Content Analysis of LAPD Civil Liability Cases: 1990–1999." http://www.womenandpolicing.org/ExcessiveForce.asp?id=4516

Fielding, N. 1994. "Cop Canteen Culture." In T. Newburn and E. A. Stanko (Eds.), *Just Boys Doing Business? Men, Masculinities and Crime*. London: Routledge.

Fischer, B., and B. Poland. 1998. "Exclusion, 'Risk,' and Social Control: Reflections on Community Policing and Public Health." *Geoforum* 29(2): 187–97.

Fishman, M. 1981. "Police News: Constructing an Image of Crime." *Urban Life* 9(4): 371–94.

Fitzgerald, G. 1989. "Report of a Commission of Inquiry Pursuant to Orders in Council." Commission of Inquiry into Possible Illegal Activities and Associated Police Misconduct. Brisbane: Government Printer.

Flavin, J. 2001 (July–August). "Feminism for the Mainstream Criminologist: An Invitation." *Journal of Criminal Justice* 29(4): 271–85.

Fletcher, C. 1997. *Breaking and Entering*. New York: HarperCollins.

Fogelson, R. 1977. *Big City Police: An Urban Institute Study*. Cambridge, MA: Harvard University Press.

Forst, B., J. Lucianovic, and S. J. Cox. 1977. "What Happens after Arrest? A Court Perspective of Police Operations in the District of Columbia." Washington, DC: Institute for Law and Social Research.

Foucaut, M. 1979. *Discipline & Punish: The Birth of the Prison*. New York: Vintage Books.

Frank, J., S. G. Brandl, F. T. Cullen, and A. Stichman. 1996 (June). "Reassessing the Impact of Race on Citizens' Attitudes toward the Police: A Research Note." *Justice Quarterly* 13(2): 231–324.

Franzway et al. 1989.

Freedman, E. 1981. *Their Sisters' Keepers: Women's Prison Reform in America, 1830–1930*. Ann Arbor: University of Michigan Press.

Fridell, L. A., R. Lunney, D. Diamond, B. Kubu, M. Scott, and C. Laing. 2001. *Racially Biased Policing: A Principled Response*. Washington, DC: Police Executive Research Foundation.

Fridell, L. A., and A. M. Pate. 1997. "Use of Force: A Matter of Control." In M. Dantzker (Ed.), *Police Today and Tomorrow: Contemporary Personal Issues and Trends*. New York: Butterworth Heinemann Publishers, 217–56.

Friedan, Betty. 1963. *The Feminine Mystique*. New York: WW Norton.

Friedrich, F. J. 1977. "The Impact of Organizational, Individual, and Situational Factors on Police Behavior." Unpublished PhD dissertation. University of Michigan.

Friedrich, R. J. 1980 (November). "Police Use of Force: Individuals, Situations and Organizations." *Annals of the American Academy of Political and Social Science* 452(1): 82–79.

Fritsch, Jane. 2000 (February 26). "The Diallo Verdict: 4 Officers in Diallo Shooting Are Acquitted of All Charges." NewYorkTimes.com. http://www.nytimes.com/2000/02/26/ny-region/diallo-verdict-overview-4-officers-diallo-shooting-are-acquitted-all-charges.html?pagewanted=all&src=pm

Fyfe, J. J., J. Greene, W. Walsh, O. W. Wilson, R. McLaren. 1997. *Police Administration*, 5th ed. New York: McGraw-Hill.

Fyfe, J. J., D. A. Klinger, and J. Flavin. 1997 (August). "Differential Police Treatment of Male-on-Female Spousal Violence." *Criminology* 35(3): 455–73.

Fyfe, J. J., and J. Walker. 1990. "Garner Plus Five Years: An Examination of Supreme Court Intervention into Police Discretion and Legislative Prerogatives." *American Journal of Criminal Justice* 144: 167–88.

Fyfe, N. R. 1991 (September). "The Police, Space and Society: The Geography of Policing." *Progress in Human Geography* 15(3): 249–67.

Gadamer, Hans-Georg. 1976. *Philosophical Hermeneutics*. Berkeley: University of California Press.

Gaines, L. K. 2006 (June). "An Analysis of Traffic Stop Data in Riverside, California." *Police Quarterly* 9(2): 210–33.

Garcia, V. 2003. "'Difference' in the Policing Department: Women, Policing, and 'Doing Gender.'" *Journal of Contemporary Criminal Justice* 19: 330–44.

Garner, Joel, and Christopher Maxwell. 2002. *Understanding the Use of Force by and against Police*. Washington, DC: National Institute of Justice.

———. 2000. "What Are the Lessons of the Police Arrest Studies?" *Journal of Aggression, Maltreatment and Trauma* 4(1): 83–114.

Garner, Joel, Christopher Maxwell, and Cedrick Heraux. 2003a. "Patterns of Police Use of Force as a Measure of Police Integrity." In M. Hickman, A. Piquero, and J. Greene (Eds.), *Police Integrity and Ethics*.

———. 2003b. "Characteristics Associated with the Prevalence and Severity of Force Used by the Police." *Justice Quarterly* 19(4): 705–46.

Garner, Joel, T. Schade, J. Hepburn, and J. Buchanan. 1995. "Measuring the Continuum of Force Used by and against the Police." *Criminal Justice Review* 20 (2): 146–68.

Geller, William A., and Hans Toch (Eds.). 1996. *Police Violence: Understanding and Controlling Police Abuse of Force*. New Haven, CT: Yale University Press.

Gerber, G. L. 2001. *Women and Men Police Officers: Status, Gender and Personality*. New York: Praeger Publishers.

Gerber, T. P., and S. E. Mendelson. 2008. "Public Experiences of Police Violence and Corruption in Contemporary Russia: A Case of Predatory Policing?" *Law and Society Review* (42)1: 1–43.

Gilligan, J. 1996. *Violence: Reflections on a National Epidemic*. New York: Vintage.

Ginzberg, L. D. 1990. *Women and the Work of Benevolence: Morality, Politics, and Class in the Nineteenth-Century United States*. New Haven: Yale University Press.

Giroux, Henry A. 2004. "War on Terror: The Militarising of Public Space and Culture in the United States." *Third Text* 18(4): 211–21.

Glavin, A. P. 1986. *Acquaintance Rape: The Silent Epidemic*. Boston: Massachusetts Institute of Technology, Campus Police Department.

Glover, Scott, and Matt Lait. 2000a, February 10. "Police in Secret Group Broke Law Routinely, Transcripts Say." *Los Angeles Times*. http://articles.latimes.com/2000/feb/10/news/mn-62921

———. 2000b, April 27. "2 Women Say Rampart Squad Framed Them." *Los Angeles Times*. http://www.latimes.com/news/state/reports/rampart/lat_rampart 000427.htm

Goetz, Barry, and Roger Mitchell. 2003. "Community-Building and Reintegrative Approaches to Community Policing: The Case of Drug Control." *Social Justice* 30(1): 222–47, San Francisco: Global Options.

Goffman, Erving. 1959. *The Presentation of Self in Everyday Life*. Garden City, NY: Anchor Books.

Goldsmith, Andrew. 2005 (November). "Police Reform and the Problem of Trust." *Theoretical Criminology* 9(4): 443–70, Thousand Oaks, CA: Sage.

———. 1990. "Taking Police Culture Seriously: Police Discretion and the Limits of Law." *Policing and Society* 1(2): 91–114.

Goldsmith, H. H. 1983 (April). "Genetic Influences on Personality from Infancy to Adulthood." *Child Development* 54(2): 331–35.

Goldstein, H. 1990. *Problem-Oriented Policing.* New York: McGraw-Hill.

———. 1977. *Policing a Free Society.* Cambridge, MA: Ballinger.

———. 1963 (September). "Police Discretion: The Ideal vs. the Real." *Public Administration Review* 23: 140–48.

Goode, Erich, and Nachman Ben-Yehuda. 1994. *Moral Panics: The Social Construction of Deviance.* Cambridge, MA: Blackwell.

Goolkasian, G. 1986 (November). "Confronting Domestic Violence: A Guide for Criminal Justice Agencies: Issues and Practices, NCJ 101680." Washington, DC: U.S. Department of Justice, National Institute of Justice.

Gordon, David M. 1973 (April). "Capitalism, Class, and Crime in America." *Crime and Delinquency* 19(2): 163–84.

Gordon, P. 1987. "Community Policing: Towards the Local Police State?" In P. Scraton (Ed.), *Law, Order and the Authoritarian State.* Philadelphia: Open University Press, 121–44.

Gottesdiener, Linda. 2011 (May 12). "Newark Police Department under Federal Investigation for Years of Alleged Abuses." HuffingtonPost.com. http://www.huffingtonpost.com/2011/05/12/newark-police-department-investigation_n_861360.html

Gramsci, A. 1957. *The Modern Prince and Other Writings.* New York: International Publishers.

Grant, D. R. 2000. "Perceived Gender Differences in Policing: The Impact of Gendered Perceptions of Officer-Situation 'Fit.'" *Women & Criminal Justice* 12(1): 53–74.

Greene, J. R. 2004. "Community Policing and Police Organization." In Wesley Skogan (Ed.), *Community Policing (Can It Work)?* Stanford, CT: Thomson-Wadsworth.

Greene, J. R., and S. D. Mastrofski. 1988. *Community Policing: Rhetoric or Reality.* New York: Praeger.

Grennan, S. E. 1987. "Findings on the Role of Officer Gender in Violent Encounters with Citizens." *Journal of Police Science and Administration* 15(1): 78–85.

Griggs v. Duke Power Company, 401 U.S. 424 [1971].

Griswold, David B. 1994. "Complaints against the Police: Predicting Dispositions." *Journal of Criminal Justice* 22(3): 215–21.

Griswold, Wendy. 1986. *Renaissance Revivals: City Comedy and Revenge Tragedy in the London Theatre, 1576–1980.* Chicago: University of Chicago Press.

Grossman, J. 2002. "What Defines 'Business Necessity' in the Discrimination Context? A Federal Appellate Case Grapples with How Fast Transit Police Officers Must Run." FindLaw.com. http://writ.lp.findlaw.com/grossman/20021119.html

Grove, Casey. 2011 (February 24). "Officer Convicted of Rape Was Disciplined for On-duty Sex." *Anchorage Daily News.* http://www.adn.com/2011/02/23/1718930/convicted-police-man-had-been-investigated.html

Guarino-Ghezzi, S. 1994 (April). "Reintegrative Police Surveillance of Juvenile Offenders: Forging an Urban Model." *Crime and Delinquency* 40(2): 131–53.

Haar, R. N. 1997. "Patterns of Interaction in a Police Patrol Bureau: Race and Gender Barriers to Integration." *Justice Quarterly* 14(1): 53–85.

Haggerty, Ryan. 2011 (April 19). "Former Chicago Cop Admits Role in Robberies." *Chicago Tribune.* http://articles.chicagotribune.com/2011-04-19/news/ct-met-chicago-cop-guilty-0420-20110419_1_worst-misconduct-scandals-robberies-federal-felony-charges

Hale, D. C. 1989. "Ideology of Police Misbehavior: Analysis and Recommendations." *Quarterly Journal of Ideology* 13(2): 59–85.

Hale, D. C., and C. L. Bennett. 1995. "Realities of Women in Policing: An Organizational Cultural Perspective." In A.V. Merlo and J. M. Pollock (Eds.), *Women, Law and Social Control.* Boston: Allyn & Bacon, 41–54.

Hall, Stuart, C. Critcher, T. Jefferson, J. Clarke, and B. Roberts. 1978. *Policing the Crisis: Mugging, the State, and Law and Order.* London: Macmillan.

Haller, Mark H. 1976. "Historical Roots of Police Behavior: Chicago, 1890–1925." *Law and Society Review* 10(2): 303–23.

Hamilton, Brad. 2011 (February 20). "'Rape' Cop in 'Confession': Victim Wears Wire to Nab 'Fiend' after Cry to Pal: 'It Was the Police!'" NewYorkPost.com. http://www.nypost.com/p/news/local/manhattan/rape_cop_in_confession_H1vFwkDqjqFxqMnEcV1y3I/0

Harnden, Toby. 2011 (May 4). "Osama bin Laden Killed: CIA Admits Waterboarding Yielded Vital Information." Telegraph.co.uk. http://www.telegraph.co.uk/news/worldnews/al-qaeda/8491509/Osama-bin-Laden-killed-CIA-admits-waterboarding-yielded-vital-information.html

Harned, Melanie S. 2005 (March). "Understanding Women's Labeling of Unwanted Sexual Experiences with Dating Partners: A Qualitative Analysis." *Violence Against Women* 11(3): 74–413.

Harring, Sidney. 1983. *Policing a Class Society: The Experience of American Cities, 1865–1915.* New Brunswick, NJ: Rutgers University Press.

Harrington, P. E. 1999. *Triumph of Spirit: An Autobiography of Chief Penny Harrington.* Chicago: Brittany Publications Ltd.

Harrington, P. E., and K. A. Lonsway. 2004. "Current Barriers and Future Promise for Women in Policing." In Barbara Raffel Price and Natalie J. Sokoloff (Eds.), *The Criminal Justice System and Women: Offenders, Prisoners, Victims, and Workers*, 3rd ed. New York: McGraw Hill.

Harris, D. A. 2002. *Profiles in Injustice: Why Racial Profiling Cannot Work.* New York: New Press.

———. 1999. "Driving while Black: Racial Profiling on Our Nation's Highways." Washington DC: American Civil Liberties Union. http://www.aclu.org/racial-justice/driving-while-black-racial-profiling-our-nations-highways

———. 1997. "Driving while Black and Other Traffic Offenses: The Supreme Court and Pretextual Traffic Stops." *Journal of Criminal Law and Criminology* 87: 544–82.

Harrison, Bob. 1999. "Noble Cause Corruption and the Police Ethic." *FBI Law Enforcement Bulletin* 68(8): 1–7.

Hayden, G. A. 1981. "Police Discretion in the Use of Deadly Force: An Empirical Study of Information Usage in Deadly Force Decisionmaking." *Journal of Police Science and Administration* 9(1): 102–7.

Heffernan, W. C. 1985. "The Police and Their Rules of Office: An Ethical Analysis." In W. C. Heffernan and T. Stroup (Eds.), *Police Ethics: Hard Choices in Law Enforcement.* New York: John Jay Press, 3–24.

Heidensohn, F. M. 1992. *Women in Control? The Role of Women in Law Enforcement.* New York: Oxford University Press, Inc.

———. 1985. *Women and Crime: The Life of the Female Offender.* New York: New York University Press.

———. 1968 (June). "The Deviance of Women: A Critique and an Enquiry." *British Journal of Sociology* 19(2): 160–76.

Heidensohn, F., and J. Brown. 2000. *Gender and Policing: Comparative Perspectives.* New York: St. Martin's Press, LLC.

Henry, S., and D. Milovanovic. 1999. *Constitutive Criminology at Work: Applications to Crime and Justice.* Albany: State University of New York Press.

Herbert, S. 2006 (November 1). "Tangled up in Blue: Conflicting Paths to Police Legitimacy." *Theoretical Criminology* 10(4): 481–504.

Heumann, Milton, and Lance Cassak. 2003. *Good Cop, Bad Cop: Racial Profiling and Competing Views of Justice.* New York: Peter Lang, 739–41.

Hickman, M. J. 2008. "On the Context of Police Cynicism and Problem Behavior." *Applied Psychology in Criminal Justice* 4(1): 1–44.

Hickman, M. J., A. Piquero, and J. Greene. 2004. *Police Integrity and Ethics.* Belmont, CA: Wadsworth/Thomas Learning.

Hickman, M. J., and B. Reaves. 2006. "Local Police Departments, 2003." (NJC210118). Washington, DC: U.S. Department of Justice, Bureau of Justice Statistics.

———. 2001. "Community Policing in Local Police Departments, 1997 and 1999." BJS Special Report NCJ 184794. Washington, DC: U.S. Department of Justice.

Hoffman, P. 1993. "The Feds, Lies and Videotape: The Need for an Effective Federal Role in Controlling Police Abuse in Urban America." *Southern California Law Review* 66(4): 1455–1531.

Homant, R., and D. Kennedy. 1985. "Police Perceptions of Spouse Abuse: A Comparison of Male and Female Officers." *Journal of Criminal Justice* 13(1): 29–47.

Honig, A., and E. White. 1994. "Violence and the Law Enforcement Family." In *Law Enforcement Families Issues and Answers*, 2–9.

Hoover, L. 1995. "Education." In W. G. Bailey (Ed.), *The Encyclopedia of Police Science*, 2nd ed. New York: Garland, 245–48.

Hopkins, E. J. 1972. *Our Lawless Police: A Study in the Unlawful Enforcement of the Laws*. New York: DeCapo Press (first published in 1931).

Horvath, F. 1987. "The Police Use of Deadly Force: A Description of Selected Characteristics of Intrastate Incidents." *Journal of Police Science and Administration* 15: 226–38.

Huang, W., and M. S. Vaughn. 1996. "Support and Confidence: Public Attitudes toward the Police." In T. J. Flanagan and D. R. Longmire (Eds.), *Americans View Crime and Justice: A National Public Opinion Survey*. Thousand Oaks, CA: Sage, 31–45.

Hughes, Everett C. 1962. "Good People and Dirty Work." *Social Problems* 10(1): 3–11.

Huisman, Kimberly, Jeri Martinez, and Cathleen Wilson. 2005. "Training Police Officers on Domestic Violence and Racism: Challenges and Strategies." *Violence Against Women* 11(6): 792–821, Thousand Oaks, CA: Sage.

Humphries, Drew. 2009. *Women, Violence, and the Media: Readings in Feminist Criminology.* Boston, MA: Northeastern University Press.

Hunt, J. 1990. "The Logic of Sexism among Police." *Women and Criminal Justice* 1(2): 3–30.

———. 1984. "The Development of Rapport through Negotiation of Gender in Field Work among Police." *Human Organization* 43: 283–96.

Hurtado, A. 1989. "Relating to Privilege: Seduction and Rejection in the Subordination of White Women and Women of Color." *Signs* 14(4): 833–55.

Inciardi, J. 1987. *Criminal Justice*, 2nd ed. New York: Harcourt, Brace, Jovanovich.

Independent Commission on the Los Angeles Police Department. 1991. "Summary of Report." Unpublished manuscript.

International Association of Chiefs of Police. 1967. "Training Key 16: Handling Domestic Disturbance Calls." Gaithersburg, MD: IACP.

Itwaru, A. 1989. *Critiques of Power*. Toronto: Terebi Publications.

Jackson, L. D. 1997 (20–23 May). "Crossing the Thin Blue Line: A Study of Female Police Officers in Atlantic Canada." A presentation made at the Women in Policing in Canada: The Year 2000 and Beyond—Its Challenges workshop, Canadian Police College, Ottawa, ON.

James, J., and J. Meyerding. 1977. "Early Sexual Experiences and Prostitution." *American Journal of Psychiatry* 134(12): 1381–85.

Jernigan, A. S. 2000. "Driving while Black: Profiling in America." *Law & Psychology Review* 24: 127–38.

Jolin, A., and C. A. Moose. 1997. "Evaluating a Domestic Violence Program in a Community Policing Environment: Research Implementation Issues." *Crime and Delinquency* 43(3): 279–97.

Jurik, N. C., and S. E. Martin. 2001. "Femininities, Masculinities and Organizational Conflict: Women in Criminal Justice Occupations." In C. M. Renzetti and L. Goodstein (Eds.), *Women, Crime and Criminal Justice*. Los Angeles: Roxbury.

Kappeler, Victor E. 2006. *The Police and Society*, 3rd ed. Long Grove, IL: Waveland Press.

———. 1993. *Critical Issues in Police Civil Liability*. Prospect Heights, IL: Waveland Press.

———. 1989. "St. Louis Police Department." In W. G. Bailey (Ed.), *The Encyclopedia of Police Science*. New York: Garland.

Kappeler, Victor E., M. Blumberg, and G. W. Potter. 1996. *The Mythology of Crime and Criminal Justice*, 2nd ed. Prospect Heights, IL: Waveland Press.

Kappeler, Victor E., Richard D. Sluder, and Geoffrey P. Alpert. 2006. "Breeding Deviant Conformity: Police Ideology and Culture." In Victor E. Kappeler (Ed.), *The Police and Society*, 3rd ed. Long Grove, IL: Waveland Press, 277–302.

———. 1998. *Forces of Deviance: Understanding the Dark Side of Policing*, 2nd ed. Prospect Heights, IL: Waveland Press.

———. 1994. *Forces of Deviance: Understanding the Dark Side of Policing*, 1st ed. Prospect Heights, IL: Waveland Press.

Kasinsky, R. G. 1994. "Patrolling the Facts: Media, Cops, and Crime." In G. Barak (Ed.), *Media, Process, and the Social Construction of Crime*. New York: Garland, 203–36.

Kavanagh, John. 1994. "The Occurrence of Violence in Police-Citizen Arrest Encounters." *Criminal Justice Abstracts* 26: 319–30.

Kelling, George L. 1987a. "Acquiring a Taste for Order: The Community and Police." *Crime and Delinquency* 33: 90–102.

———. 1987b. "Juveniles and Police: The End of the Nightstick." In Francis X. Hartmann (Ed.), *From Children to Citizens, Vol. II: The Role of the Juvenile Court*. New York: Springer-Verlag.

———. 1983. "Reforming the Reforms: The Boston Police Department." Occasional Paper, Joint Center for Urban Studies of M.I.T. and Harvard, Cambridge.

Kelling, George L., and Mark H. Moore. 1988 (November). "The Evolving Strategy of Policing." Washington, DC: National Institute of Justice.

Kelling, George L., R. Wasserman, and H. Williams. 1988. "Police Accountability and Community Policing." National Institute of Justice. U.S. Department of Justice and Program in Criminal Justice Policy and Management, John F. Kennedy School of Government, Harvard University.

Kennedy, D., and R. Homant. 1983 (December). "Attitudes of Abused Women toward Male and Female Police Officers." *Criminal Justice and Behavior* 10(4): 391–405.

"Key West Police Department Called a 'Criminal Enterprise.'" 1984 (July 1). *New York Times*. http://www.nytimes.com/1984/07/01/us/key-west-police-department-called-a-criminal-enterprise.html

Klein, D. 1973 (Fall). "The Etiology of Women's Crime: A Review of the Literature." *Issues in Criminology* 8: 3–30.

Klockars, Carl. 1988. "The Rhetoric of Community Policing." In J. R. Greene and S. D. Mastrofski (Eds.), *Community Policing: Rhetoric or Reality*. New York: Praeger, 239–58.

———. 1983. "The Dirty Harry Problem." In Carl Klockars (Ed.), *Thinking about Police: Contemporary Readings*. New York: McGraw-Hill, 428–38.

———. 1980 (November). "The Dirty Harry Problem." *Annals of the American Academy of Political and Social Science* 452: 33–47.

Knapp Commission Report on Police Corruption. 1972. New York: George Braziller.

Koons-Witt, B. A., and P. J. Schram. 2003. "The Prevalence and Nature of Violent Offending by Females." *Journal of Criminal Justice* 31(4): 1–11.

Koss, Mary P. 1996 (March). "The Measurement of Rape Victimization in Crime Surveys." *Criminal Justice and Behavior* 23: 5–69.

Koss, Mary P., and C. J. Oros. 1982. "Sexual Experiences Survey: A Research Instrument Investigating Sexual Aggression and Victimization." *Journal of Consulting and Clinical Psychology* 50(3): 455–57.

Kozol, Jonathan. 1992. *Savage Inequalities: Children in America's Schools.* New York: HarperPerennial.

Kraska, P. B., and D. J. Paulsen. 1997. "Grounded Research into U.S. Paramilitary Policing: Forging the Iron Fist inside the Velvet Glove." *Police and Society* 7: 253–70.

Kurtz, Howard. 1994. *Media Circus: The Trouble with America's Newspapers*. New York: Random.

LaFave, W. 1965. *Arrest: The Decision to Take a Suspect into Court*. Boston: Little Brown.

Lane, R. 1971. *Policing the City: Boston, 1822–1885*. New York: Atheneum.

Langworthy, Robert H., and Lawrence F. Travis III. 2003. *Policing in America: A Balance of Forces*, 3rd ed. Upper Saddle River, NJ: Prentice Hall.

Lanning v. SEPTA, 308 F3d 286 [3rd Cir. 2002].

Las Vegas Metropolitan Police Department. 2004. "Procedural Order PO-03-04, 'Use of Force.'" Las Vegas: Las Vegas Metropolitan Police Department.

Lawrence, Regina Greenwood. 1997. *Defining Events: News Coverage of Police Use of Force.* Ann Arbor, MI: University of Microfilms International.

Lawson, G., and W. Oldham. 2006. *The Brotherhoods: The True Story of Two Cops Who Murdered for the Mafia.* New York: Simon and Schuster.

Lee, Joohee, Elizabeth C. Pomeroy, Seo-Koo Yoo, and Kurt T. Rheinboldt. 2005. "Attitudes toward Rape: A Comparison between Asian and Caucasian College Students." *Violence Against Women* 11(2): 177–96.

Leonard, E. B. 1982. *Women, Crime, and Society: A Critique of Theoretical Criminology.* New York: Logman.

Lersch, Kim Michelle. 2002. *Policing and Misconduct.* Upper Saddle River, NJ: Prentice Hall.

———. 1998a. "Exploring Gender Differences in Citizen Allegations of Misconduct: An Analysis of a Municipal Police Department." *Women and Criminal Justice* 9: 69–79.

———. 1998b. "Police Misconduct and Malpractice: A Critical Analysis of Citizens' Complaints." *Policing: An International Journal of Police Strategies and Management* 21(1): 80–96.

———. 1998c. "Predicting Officer Race in Internal and External Allegations of Misconduct." *International Journal of Comparative and Applied Criminal Justice* 22(2): 249–58.

Lersch, Kim Michelle, and Tom Mieczkowski. 2005 (July–August). "Violent Police Behavior: Past, Present, and Future Research Directions." *Aggression and Violent Behavior* 10(5): 552–68. New York: Elsevier Science Publishing Co., Inc.

———. 2004. "Armed and Dangerous: Exploring Police Drug Use and Drug Related Corruption." In Matthew Hickman, Alex R. Piquero, and Jack R. Green (Eds.), *Police Integrity and Ethics.* Belmont, CA: Thomas Learning.

———. 1996. "Who Are the Problem-Prone Officers? An Analysis of Citizen Complaints." *American Journal of Police* 15(3): 23–44.

Levitt, Len. 2011 (June 6). "Bronx Juries: More Woe for the NYPD." HuffingtonPost.com. http://www.huffingtonpost.com/len-levitt/bronx-juries-more-woe-for-nypd_b_871850.html

Logan, J., D. Oakley, and J. Stowell. 2008. "School Segregation in Metropolitan Regions, 1970–2000: The Impacts of Policy Choices on Public Education." *American Journal of Sociology* 113(6): 1611–44.

Lombroso, C., and W. Ferrero. 1895. *The Female Offender.* London: Fisher Unwin.

Lonsway, Kimberly A. 2003. "Tearing Down the Wall: Problems with Consistency, Validity, and Adverse Impact of Physical Agility Testing in Police Selection." *Police Quarterly* 6(3): 237–77.

———. 2000. "Hiring and Retaining More Women: The Advantages to Law Enforcement Agencies." Washington, DC: National Center for Women and Policing.

Lonsway, Kimberly A., M. Wood, and K. Spillar. 2002. "Officer Gender and Excessive Force." *Law and Order* 50(12): 60–66.

Lord, L. K. 1995. "Policewomen." In W. G. Bailey (Ed.), *The Encyclopedia of Police Science,* 2nd ed. New York: William Bailey.

Lord, V. B. 1996. "An Impact of Community Policing: Reported Stressors, Social Support, and Strain among Police Officers in a Changing Police Department." *Journal of Criminal Justice* 24(6): 503–22.

Los Angeles Police Department. 2000. "Board of Inquiry into the Rampart Area Corruption Incident: Public Report." Los Angeles: LAPD.

Loving, N. 1981. "Spouse Abuse: A Curriculum Guide for Police Trainers." Washington, DC: Police Executive Research Forum. United States National Criminal Justice Institute.

Lowe, Michael. 2011 (June 2). "Federal Judge Sam A. Lindsay Sick and Tired of Bad Cops Getting Cushy Sentences: Orders Former Mesquite Narc Officer to 15 Months in Fed Pen for Taking $2000." Dallas Criminal Defense Lawyer Blog—DWI Attorney. http://www.dallasjustice.com/dallascriminallawyerblog/federal-judge-sam-a-lindsay-sick-and-tired-of-bad-cops-getting-cushy-sentences-orders-former-mesquite-narc-officer-to-15-months-in-fed-pen-for-taking-2000

Lundman, R. J. 1980. *Police and Policing: An Introduction.* New York: Holt, Rinehart & Winston.

Lundman, R. J., and R. L. Kaufman. 2003. "Driving while Black: Effects of Race, Ethnicity, and Gender on Citizen Self-reports on Traffic Stops and Police Actions." *Criminology* 41(1): 195–220.

Lynch, G. W. 1999. *Human Dignity and the Police: Ethics and Integrity in Police Work.* Springfield, IL: Charles C. Thomas.

———. 1976. "Contributions of Higher Education to Ethical Behavior in Law Enforcement." *Journal of Criminal Justice* 4(4): 285–90.

Maas, Peter. 1973. *Serpico.* New York: Viking.

MacDonald, J. M. 2002 (October). "The Effectiveness of Community Policing in Reducing Urban Violence." *Crime & Delinquency* 48(4): 592–618.

Macionis, J. J. 2005. *Sociology,* 11th ed. New Jersey: Prentice Hall.

Maguire, E. 2001. "Context, Complexity and Control: Organizational Response to Gangs: An Examination of a 'Moral Panic' in Nevada." *Justice Quarterly* (15): 41–64.

———. 1997 (September). "Structural Change in Large Municipal Police Organizations during the Community Policing Era." *Justice Quarterly* 14(3): 701–30.

Main, Frank, and Natasha Korecki. 2011 (April 8). "Cops Charged in Thefts from Drug Suspects Expected to Plead Guilty." *Chicago Sun-Times.* http://www.suntimes.com/4715108-417/4-cops-charged-with-shaking-down-drug-dealers-for-600k.html

Malamuth, Neil M. 1981. "Rape Proclivity among Males." *Journal of Social Issues* 37(4): 138–57.

Manning, Peter K. 1997. *Police Work: The Social Organization of Policing,* 2nd ed. Prospect Heights, IL: Waveland Press, Inc.

———. 1992 (April). "The Police, Symbolic Capital, Class and Control (Bourdieu on the Beat)." Prepared for a conference on Class and Social Control, University of Georgia, Athens, Georgia.

———. 1990. "Policing and Technology: Technologies and the Police." Draft intended for *Modern Policing,* volume 5 of *Crime and Justice Annuals,* edited by Michael Tonry and Norval Morris. Chicago: University of Chicago Press.

———. 1978. "The Police: Mandate, Strategies, and Appearances." In P. Manning and J. Van Maanen (Eds.), *Policing: A View from the Street.* Santa Monica: Goodyear, 7–32.

———. 1977. *Police Work: The Social Organization of Policing,* 1st ed. Cambridge: MIT Press.

Manning, Peter K., and J. Van Maanen (Eds.). 1978. *Policing: A View from the Street.* Santa Monica: Goodyear.

Marks, Daniel, and Ivan Sun. 2007 (May). "The Impact of 9/11 on Organizational Development among State and Local Law Enforcement Agencies." *Journal of Contemporary Criminal Justice* 23(2): 159–73.

Martelli, T., J. Martelli, and L. Waters. 1989. "The Police Stress Survey: Reliability and Relation to Job Satisfaction and Organizational Commitment." *Psychological Reports* 64: 267–73.

Martin, Susan E. 1999 (January). "Police Force or Police Service? Gender and Emotional Labor." *Annals of the American Academy of Political & Social Science* 561: 111–26.

———. 1994 (August). "'Outsider within' the Station House: The Impact of Race and Gender on Black Women Police." *Social Problems* 41(3): 383–400.

———. 1992. "The Changing Status of Women Officers: Gender and Power in Police Work." In I. Moyer (Ed.), *The Changing Role of Women in the Criminal Justice System.* Prospect Heights, IL: Waveland Press, 281–305.

———. 1990. *On the Move: The Status of Women in Policing.* Washington, DC: Police Foundation.

———. 1980. *Breaking and Entering: Policewomen on Patrol.* Berkeley: University of California Press.

Martin, Susan E., and Nancy C. Jurik. 2007. *Doing Justice, Doing Gender: Women in Law and Criminal Justice Occupations,* 2nd ed. Thousand Oaks, CA: Sage Publications.

———. 1996. *Doing Justice, Doing Gender: Women in Law and Criminal Justice Occupations*, 1st ed. Thousand Oaks, CA: Sage.

Marx, Karl. Excerpt from "A Contribution to the Critique of Political Economy," 1859. In Karl Marx and Friedrich Engels, *Marx and Engels: Basic Writings on Politics and Philosophy*. Lewis S. Feurer, ed. Garden City, NY: Anchor Books.

Mathieson, Chris. 2006. "Woman Officer Goes 4000 Miles beyond the Call." In *Beyond the Call—Annual Report 2005*. Vancouver Police Department. http://www.vancouverpolicemuseum.ca/weblog/2006/05/woman-officer-goes-4000-miles-beyond-the-call/

Matthews, K. 2007 (October 8). "Abner Louima Remembers New York Police Torture Case on 10th Anniversary." *Brooklyn Daily Express*. www.brooklyneagle.com/categories/category.php?category_id=4&id=14753

Matulia, K. J. 1982. "A Balance of Forces: National Survey of Police Deadly Force." Gaithersburg, MD: International Association of Chiefs of Police.

McAlary, Mike. 1994. *Good Cop, Bad Cop: Detective Joe Trimboli's Heroic Pursuit of NYPD Officer Michael Dowd.* New York: Pocket Books.

McCormick, Chris. 1995. *Constructing Danger: The Mis/representation of Crime in the News.* Halifax: Fernwood Publishing.

McElvain, J., and A. Kposowa. 2004. "Police Officer Characteristics and Internal Affairs Investigations for Use of Force Allegations." *Journal of Criminal Justice* 32(3): 265–79.

McLaughlin, Eugene. 2007. *The New Policing.* Thousand Oaks, CA: Sage.

McLaughlin, Eugene, and John Muncie. 2001. *The Sage Dictionary of Criminology.* London: Sage Publications.

McLean, J. 1997 (20–23 May). "The Future of Women in Policing in Canada—Final Notes." A presentation made at the Women in Policing in Canada: The Year 2000 and Beyond—Its Challenges workshop, Canadian Police College, Ottawa, ON.

McMahon, J., J. Garner, R. Davis, and A. Kraus. 2002 (October). "How to Correctly Collect and Analyze Racial Profiling Data: Your Reputation Depends on It!" Final Project Report for Racial Profiling Data Collection and Analysis. Washington, DC: United States Department of Justice, Office of Community Oriented Policing Services.

McMahon, M., and E. Pence. 2003. "Making Social Change: Reflections on Individual and Institutional Advocacy with Women Arrested for Domestic Violence." *Journal of Violence Against Women* 9(1): 47–74.

McNamara, J. 1967. "Uncertainties in Police Work: The Relevance of Recruits' Background and Training." In D. J. Bordua (Ed.), *Police Work.* New York: Wiley & Sons, 163–252.

McNulty, E. W. 1994 (Fall). "Generating Common Sense Knowledge among Police Officers." *Symbolic Interaction* 17(3): 281–94.

Mead, George Herbert. 1962, orig. 1934. *Mind, Self and Society: From the Standpoint of a Social Behaviorist.* Charles W. Morris, ed. Chicago: University of Chicago Press.

Melton, Heather C., and Joanne Belknap. 2003. "He Hits, She Hits: Assessing Gender Differences and Similarities in Officially Reported Intimate Partner Violence." *Criminal Justice and Behavior* 30(3): 328–48.

Merminger, Dean. 2011 (April 29). "Judge Declares Partial Mistrial in Bronx Road Rage Case." NY1.com. http://www.ny1.com/content/news_beats/criminal_justice/138247/judge-declares-partial-mistrial-in-bronx-road-rage-case/

Messerschmidt, J. W. 2003. "Diversity in Blue: Lesbian and Gay Police Officers in a Masculine Occupation." *Men and Masculinities* 5(4): 355–85.

———. 1997. *Crime as Structured Action: Gender, Race, Class, and Crime in the Making.* Thousand Oaks, CA: Sage.

———. 1993. *Masculinities and Crime: Critique and Reconceptualization of Theory.* Lanham, MD: Rowman and Littlefield.

Meyer, M. 1980 (November). "Police Shootings at Minorities: The Case of Los Angeles." *Annals of the Academy of Political and Social Science* 452: 98–110.

Michigan.gov/mcoles. Michigan Commission on Law Enforcement Standards.

Miller, J. 1998 (February). "Up it Up: Gender and the Accomplishment of Street Robbery." *Criminology* 36: 37–66.

Miller, Matthew, and Peter Newcomb (Eds.). 2005. "The Forbes 400." http://www.forbes.com/forbes/2005/1010/089.html

Miller, N. 1997. "Domestic Violence Legislation Affecting Police and Prosecutor Responsibilities in the United States: Inferences from a 50-state Review of State Statutory Codes." Alexandria, VA: Institute for Law and Justice.

Miller, Susan L. 2001. "Gender and Policing Issues." Chapter 18 in Lynne Goodstein and Claire M. Renzetti (Eds.), *Women, Crime, and Justice: Contemporary Perspectives*. Los Angeles, CA: Roxbury.

———. 1999. *Gender and Community Policing: Walking the Talk*. Boston, MA: Northeastern University Press.

Miller, Susan L., Kay B. Forest, and Nancy C. Jurik. 2004. "Lesbians in Policing: Perceptions and Work Experiences within the Macho Cop Culture." In B. R. Price and N. J. Sokoloff (Eds.), *The Criminal Justice System and Women*. New York: McGraw-Hill, 511–26.

———. 2003 (April). "Diversity in Blue: Lesbian and Gay Police Officers in a Masculine Occupation." *Men and Masculinities* 5(4): 355–85.

Miller, Susan L., and J. Hodge. 2004. "Rethinking Gender and Community Policing: Cultural Obstacles and Policy Issues." *Law Enforcement Executive Forum* 44: 39–49.

Millman, M. 1975. "She Did It All for Love: A Feminist View of the Sociology of Deviance." In Marcia Millman and Rosabeth Moss Kanter (Eds.), *Another Voice: Feminist Perspectives on Social Life and Social Science*. Garden City, NY: Anchor/Doubleday, 251–79.

Mills, Kay. 1990. *A Place in the News: From the Women's Pages to the Front Page*. New York: Columbia.

Mohr, L. 1973. "The Concept of the Organizational Goal." *American Political Science Review* 67: 470–81.

Mollen Commission. 1994. "Commission Report of the Commission to Investigate Allegations of Police Corruption and the Anti-Corruption Procedures of the Police Department—Anatomy of Failure: A Path for Success. " Commission Report, New York: City of New York.

Molloy, D., T. Knight, and K. Woodfield. 2003. "Diversity in Disability: Exploring the Interactions between Disability, Ethnicity, Age, Gender and Sexuality." Department of Works and Pensions. Research Report 188, October. London.

Monk, R. C. 1993. *Taking Sides: Clashing Views on Controversial Subjects in Crime and Criminology*. Guilford, CT: Dushkin.

Monkkonen, Eric. 1981. *Police in Urban America, 1860–1920*. New York: Cambridge University Press.

Moore, M. 1997. Epilogue. In S. J. Gaffigan and P. McDonald (project managers), *Police Integrity: Public Service with Honor*. Washington, DC: U.S. Department of Justice, National Institute of Justice, 59–70.

Moran, Jon. 2005. "'Blue Walls,' 'Grey Areas,' and 'Cleanups': Issues in the Control of Police Corruption in England and Wales." *Crime, Law and Social Change* 43(1): 57–79.

———. 2002. "Anti-Corruption Reforms in the Police: Current Strategies and Issues." *The Police Journal* 75(2): 137–59.

Morash, M., and J. R. Greene. 1986 (April). "Evaluating Women on Patrol: A Critique of Contemporary Wisdom." *Evaluation Review* 10(2): 230–55.

Morash, M., and R. N. Haar. 1995. "Gender, Workplace Problems and Stress in Policing." *Justice Quarterly* 12(1): 113–40.

Morash, M., and A. L. Robinson. 2001. "Correctional Administrators' Perspectives on Gender Arrangements and Family-Related Programming for Women Offenders." *Marriage and the Family Review* 32(3/4): 83–109.

Moriarty, J. 2002. "Desert and Distributive Justice in a Theory of Justice." *Journal of Social Philosophy* 33(1): 131–43.

Morris, A. 1987. *Women, Crime and Criminal Justice*. New York: Blackwell.

Murphy, P. V., and D. G. Caplan. 1993. "Fostering Integrity." In R. G. Dunham and G. P. Alpert (Eds.), *Critical Issues in Policing: Contemporary Readings*, 2nd ed. Prospect Heights, IL: Waveland Press, 304–24.

Murray, J. 2005. "Policing Terrorism: A Threat to Community Policing or Just a Shift in Priorities?" *Police Practice and Research: An International Journal* 6(4): 347–61.

Myers, G. E. 1995. *A Municipal Mother: Portland's Lola Greene Baldwin: America's First Policewoman.* Corvallis: Oregon State University Press.

Myers, Kristen, Kay Forest, and Susan Miller. 2004. "Officer Friendly and the Tough Cop: Gays and Lesbians Navigate Homophobia and Policing." *Journal of Homosexuality* 47(1): 17–37.

Naffine, N. 1996. *Feminism and Criminology.* Philadelphia: Temple University Press.

———. 1987. *Female Crime: The Construction of Women in Criminology.* Sydney, Australia: Allen & Unwin.

National Center for Women and Policing. 2005a. "A History of Women in Policing in the United States." Feminist Majority Foundation. http://womeninpolicing.org/history/index.asp

———. 2005b. "Workplace Issues: Pregnancy Issues in Law Enforcement." Feminist Majority Foundation. http://www.womeninpolicing.org/workplace4~pregnancy.asp

———. 2003. "Under Scrutiny: The Effect of Consent Decrees on the Representation of Women in Sworn Law Enforcement." Feminist Majority Foundation. http://www.womeninpolicing.org/pdf/Fullconsentdecreestudy.pdf

———. 2002. "Men, Women, and Police Excessive Force: A Tale of Two Genders: A Content Analysis of Civil Liability Cases, Sustained Allegations and Citizen Complaints." Feminist Majority Foundation. www.womenandpolicing.org/PDF/2002_Excessive_Force.pdf

———. 2000 (December). "Recruiting & Retaining Women: A Self-Assessment Guide for Law Enforcement." Feminist Majority Foundation. http://www.womeninpolicing.org/sag.asp

National Research Council. 2004. "Fairness and Effectiveness in Policing: The Evidence." Washington, DC: National Academies Press.

Neidig, P. H., H. E. Russell, and A. F. Seng. 1992. "Interspousal Aggression in Law Enforcement Families: A Preliminary Investigation." *Police Studies* 15(1): 30–38.

Nelson, Jill. 2000. *Police Brutality: An Anthology.* New York: WW Norton and Company.

Ness, C., and R. Gordon. 1995 (August 13). "Beating the Rap." *San Francisco Examiner*, A11.

Neugebauer, R. 1999. "First Nations People and Law Enforcement: Community Perspectives on Police Response." In Marilyn Corsianos and Kelly A. Train (Eds.), *Interrogating Social Justice: Politics, Culture and Identity.* Toronto: Canadian Scholars' Press, 247–69.

———. 1996. "Kids, Cops and Colour: The Social Organization of Police-Minority Youth Relations." In Gary M. O'Bireck (Ed.), *Not a Kid Anymore: Canadian Youth, Crime, and Subcultures.* Toronto: Nelson.

Newburn, Tim. 1999. "Understanding and Preventing Police Corruption: Lessons from the Literature." *Policing: An International Journal of Police Strategies Management.* Research Development Statistics Directorate. London, 1–64.

Newell, Charldean, Janay Pollock, and Jerry Tweedy. 1992. "Financial Aspects of Police Liability." *Baseline Date Report* 24(2). Washington, DC: International City/County Management Association.

News Times. 2011 (February 25). "Former Deputy Gets 18 Months in Prison." LawEnforcementCorruption.blogspot.com. http://lawenforcementcorruption.blogspot.com/2011/02/former-deputy-gets-18-months-in-prison.html

New York Civil Liberties Union. 1993. "Civilian Review Agencies: A Comparative Study." New York: New York Civil Liberties Union.

Nichols, D. 1995 (Summer). "The Brotherhood: Sexual Harassment in Police Agencies." *Women Police* 29(2): 10–12.

Niederhoffer, A. 1967. *Behind the Shield: The Police in Urban Society.* New York: Doubleday.

Novak, K. 2004 (March). "Disparity and Racial Profiling in Traffic Enforcement." *Police Quarterly* 7(1): 65–96.

O'Connor, T. R. 2005 (February 11). "Police Deviance and Ethics." In part of web cited, MegaLinks in Criminal Justice. http://faculty.ncwc.edu/toconnor/205/205lect11.htm

Odem, M. E., and S. Schlossman. 1991 (April). "Guardians of Virtue: The Juvenile Court and Female Delinquency in Early 20th Century Los Angeles." *Crime and Delinquency* 37(2): 186–203.

Oliver, W. M. 2000. "With an Evil Eye and an Unequal Hand: Pretextual Stops and Doctrinal Remedies to Racial Profiling." *Tulane Law Review* 74(4): 1409–81.

Orban, C. 1998. "Badges, Bitches, Dykes and Whores: Women in the Occupation of Policing." In S. McMahon (Ed.), *Women, Crime and Culture: Whores and Heroes.* Toronto: Centre for Police and Security Studies at York University, 267–91.

O'Reilly, J. T. 2002. *Police Traffic Stops and Racial Profiling.* Springfield, IL: Charles C. Thomas.

Ostroy, Andy. 2011 (June 1). "Too Drunk to Remember, Not Too Drunk to Be Raped?" HuffingtonPost.com.   http://www.huffingtonpost.com/andy-ostroy/cops-acquitted-of-rape-wo_b_869432.html

Paoline, Eugene A. III, and William Terrill. 2004. "Women Police Officers and the Use of Coercion." *Women and Criminal Justice* 15(3/4): 97–119.

Pate, A. M., L. A. Fridell, E. E. Hamilton. 1993. "Police Use of Force: Official Reports, Citizen Complaints, and Legal Consequences." Washington, DC: Police Foundation.

Peak, Kenneth J., Grant Stitt, and Ronald W. Glensor. 1998 (September). "Ethical Considera-tion in Community Policing and Problem Solving." *Police Quarterly* 1(3), 19–34, Police Executive Research Forum.

Pelfrey, W. 2007. "Style of Policing Adopted by Rural Police and Deputies: An Analysis of Job Satisfaction and Community Policing." *Policing: An International Journal of Police Strate-gies and Management* 30(4): 2007.

Perlstein, G. R. 1972. "Certain Characteristics of Policewomen." *Police* 16(5): 45–46.

———. 1971. "Exploratory Analysis of Certain Characteristics of Policewomen." Ann Arbor: University of Michigan Microfilms.

Pessen, Edward. 1989. *Riches, Class, and Power: America before the Civil War.* New Bruns-wick, NJ: Transaction Publishers.

Platt, T., J. Frappier, G. Ray, R. Schauffler, L. Trujillo, L. Cooper et al. 1982. *The Iron Fist and the Velvet Glove.* San Francisco, CA: Synthesis Publications.

Pogrebin, M., M. Dodge, and H. Chatman. 2000. "Reflections of African-American Women on Their Careers in Urban Policing: Their Experiences of Racial and Sexual Discrimination." *International Journal of the Sociology of Law* 28(4): 311–26.

Police Advisory Commission. 1997. "Annual Report." Philadelphia: Police Advisory Commis-sion, 2–3.

Pollack, O. 1950. *The Criminality of Women.* Philadelphia: University of Pennsylvania Press.

Pollock, J. 2007. *Ethical Dilemmas and Decisions in Criminal Justice.* Belmont, CA: Wads-worth.

Porter, L. E., and C. Warrender. 2009. "A Multivariate Model of Police Deviance: Examining the Nature of Corruption, Crime and Misconduct." *Policing & Society* 19:1, 79–99.

Poulantzas, N. 1980. *State, Power, Socialism.* London: Verso.

Prenzler, Tim. 2009. *Police Corruption: Preventing Misconduct and Maintaining Integrity.* Boca Raton, FL: CRC Press-Taylor and Francis Group.

Price, B. R. 1974. "A Study of Leadership Strength of Female Police Executives." *Journal of Police Science and Administration* 2: 219–26.

Prokos, A., and I. Padavic. 2002 (August). "'There Oughtta Be a Law Against Bitches': Masculinity Lessons in Police Academy Training." *Gender, Work, and Organization* 9(4): 439–59.

Punch, M. 2003. "Rotten Orchards: 'Pestilence,' Police Misconduct and System Failure." *Po-licing and Society* 13(2): 171–96.

Rabe-Hemp, Cara E. 2008. "Female Officers and the Ethic of Care: Does Officer Gender Impact Police Behavior?" *Journal of Criminal Justice* 36(6): 426–34.

Radelet, L., and D. Carter. 1994. *The Police and the Community.* New York: Macmillian.

Rafter, N. H. 1985. *Partial Justice: Women in State Prisons, 1800–1935.* Boston: Northeastern Press.

Ramirez, Deborah, Jack McDevitt, and Amy Farrell. 2000. "A Resource Guide on Racial Profiling Data Collection Systems: Promising Practices and Lessons Learned." United States Department of Justice: Northeastern University.

Reckless, W. C. 1961. *The Crime Problem,* 3rd ed. New York: Appleton-Century-Crofts.

Reichel, Philip L. 1998. "Southern Slave Patrols as a Transitional Police Type." *American Journal of Police* 7(2): 51–78.

Reiman, Jeffrey, and Paul Leighton. 2010. *The Rich Get Richer and the Poor Get Prison: Ideology, Class and Criminal Justice*, 9th ed. Boston: Pearson/Allyn & Bacon.

———. 2007. *The Rich Get Richer and the Poor Get Prison: Ideology, Class and Criminal Justice*, 8th ed. Boston: Pearson/Allyn & Bacon.

Reiss, Albert J. Jr. 1972. *The Police and the Public.* New Haven, CT: Yale University Press.

Renzetti, C. M., and R. K. Bergen. 2005. "Introduction: The Emergence of Violence Against Women as a Social Problem." In Claire M. Renzetti and Raquel Bergen (Eds.), *Sourcebook on Violence against Women*. Lanham, MD: Rowman and Littlefield Publishers.

Richardson, James F. 1974. *Urban Police in the United States*. Port Washington, NY: National University: Kennikat Press.

Robinson, A. L., and M. S. Chandek. 2000. "Philosophy into Practice? Community Policing Units and Domestic Violence Victim Participation." *Policing: An International Journal of Police Strategies and Management* 23(3): 280–302.

Robinson, O. 1993. "Part-time Employment in the Economies of Ireland." *Review of Employment Topics* 1(1): 143–60.

Rockwood, Edith, and Augusta J. Street. 1932. "Social Protective Work of Public Agencies: with Special Emphasis on the Policewoman." Washington, DC: Committee on Social Hygiene—National League of Women Voters.

Rojek, J., R. Rosenfeld, and S. Decker. 2004. "The Influence of Drivers' Race on Traffic Stops in Missouri." *Police Quarterly* 7(1): 126–47.

Rosenbaum, D. P. 1986. *Community Crime Prevention: Does It Work?* Beverly Hills, CA: Sage.

Roth, J. A., J. Roehl, and C. C. Johnson. 2004. "Are Police Changing: Trends in Community Policing." In Wesley Skogan (Ed.), *Community Policing (Can It Work)?* Belmont, CA: Thomson-Wadsworth.

Russell, Diana E. H. 1990. *Rape in Marriage*. New York: Macmillan Press.

———. 1984. *Sexual Exploitation: Rape, Child Sexual Abuse, and Workplace Harassment.* Beverly Hills, CA: Sage.

Russell-Brown, Katheryn, Heather Pfeifer, and Judith Jones. 2000. *Race and Crime: An Annotated Bibliography*. Westport, CT: Greenwood Press.

Sacco, V. F. 1995 (May). "Media Constructions of Crime." *Annals of the American Academy of Political and Social Science* 539: 141–54.

Sanday, Peggy Reeves. 1996. *A Woman Scorned: Acquaintance Rape on Trial.* New York: Doubleday.

———. 1990. *Fraternity Gang Rape: Sex, Brotherhood, and Privilege on Campus.* New York: New York University Press.

Sanders, W. B. 1977. *Detective Work: A Study of Criminal Investigations.* New York: The Free Press.

Saunders, R. H. 1999 (February). "The Space Community Policing Makes and the Body That Makes It." *Professional Geographer* 51(1): 135–46.

Schuck, Amie M., and Cara Rabe-Hemp. 2005. "Women Police: The Use of Force by and against Female Officers." *Women and Criminal Justice* 16(4): 91–117.

Schulz, D. M. 2004. "Invisible No More: A Social History of Women in U.S. Policing." In Barbara Raffel Price and Natalie J. Sokoloff (Eds.), *The Criminal Justice System and Women: Offenders, Prisoners, Victims, & Workers*, 3rd ed. New York: McGraw Hill.

Schwartz, Martin D., and Walter S. DeKeseredy. 1997. *Sexual Assault on the College Campus.* Thousand Oaks: Sage.

Scott v. Hart (1976), No. 6-76-2395 (N.D. Cal. 1976).

Scripture, A. E. 1997. "The Sources of Police Culture: Demographic or Environmental Variables?" *Policing and Society* 7(3): 63–176.

Scully, Diana. 1990. *Understanding Sexual Violence: A Study of Convicted Rapists.* Boston: Unwin Hyman.

Segrave, K. 1995. *Policewomen: A History.* Jefferson, NC: McFarland.

Seron, Carroll, Joseph Pereira, and Jean Kovath. 2006 (November). "How Citizens Assess Just Punishment for Police Misconduct." *Criminology* 44(4): 925–60, Columbus: American Society of Criminology.

Shearing, C. 1981 (August). "Subterranean Processes in the Maintenance of Power: An Exam-
    ination of the Mechanisms Coordinating Police Action." *Canadian Review of Sociology and
    Anthropology* 18(3): 283–98.
Shelden, R. 1981. "Sex Discrimination in the Juvenile Justice System: Memphis, Tennessee,
    1900–1917." In M. Q. Warren (Ed.), *Comparing Male and Female Offenders*. Beverly Hills,
    CA: Sage Publishing Company.
Sherman, Lawrence W. 1982. "Learning Police Ethics." *Criminal Justice Ethics* 1(2): 10–19.
———. 1980. "Causes of Police Behavior: The Current State of Quantitative Research." *Jour-
    nal of Research in Crime and Delinquency* 17: 69–100.
——— (Ed.). 1974. *Police Corruption: A Sociological Perspective*. Garden City, NY: Anchor.
Sherman, Lawrence W., and R. A. Berk. 1984. "The Deterrent Effects of Arrest for Domestic
    Violence." *American Sociological Review* 49(2): 261–72.
Sibley, D. 1988. "Survey 13: Purification of Space." *Environment and Planning D: Society and
    Space* 6: 409–21.
Sigelman, Lee, Susan Welch, Timothy Bledsoe, and Michael Combs. 1997. *Race and Place:
    Race Relations in an American City (Cambridge Studies in Public Opinion and Political
    Psychology)*. Cambridge: Cambridge University Press.
Silbert, M. H., and A. M. Pines. 1981. "Sexual Child Abuse as an Antecedent to Prostitution."
    Child Abuse and Neglect 5(4): 407–11.
Simon, David, and Frank Hagan. 1999. *White Collar Deviance*. Boston, MA: Allyn & Bacon.
Simon, H. A. 1964 (June). "On the Concept of Organizational Goal." *Administrative Science
    Quarterly* 9: 1–22.
Simon, Rita James. 1975. *Women and Crime*. Lexington, MA: D.C. Heath.
Skogan, W. G. 2006. "Advocate: The Promise of Community Policing." In David L. Weisburd
    and Anthony A. Braga (Eds.), *Police Innovations: Contrasting Perspectives*. New York:
    Cambridge University Press.
——— (Ed.). 2004. *Community Policing (Can It Work)?* Belmont, CA: Thomson-Wadsworth.
———. 1996 (August). "The Community's Role in Community Policing." *National Institute of
    Justice Journal*: 31–34.
———. 1990. *Disorder and Decline: Crime and the Spiral of Decay in American Neighbor-
    hoods*. New York: Free Press.
Skogan, W. G., and T. Meares. 2004. "Lawful Policing." *Annals of the American Academy of
    Political and Social Science* 593: 66–83.
Skolnick, Jerome H. 2002. "Corruption and the Blue Code of Silence." *Police Practice and
    Research* 3(1).
———. 1994. *Justice without Trial: Law Enforcement in a Democratic Society*, 3rd ed. New
    York: Macmillan.
———. 1975. "A Sketch of the Policeman's Working Personality." In Jerome H. Skolnick
    (Ed.), *Justice without Trial*, 2nd ed. New York: John Wiley and Sons.
———. 1966. *Justice without Trial*, 1st ed. New York: Wiley and Sons.
Skolnick, Jerome H., and James J. Fyfe. 1993. *Above the Law: Police Abuse and the Excessive
    Use of Force*. New York: Free Press.
Smart, Carol. 1982. "Regulating Families or Legitimising Patriarchy? Family Law in Britian."
    International Journal of the Sociology of Law 10(2): 129–47.
———. 1976. *Women, Crime and Criminology: A Feminist Critique*. Boston: Routledge and
    Kegan Paul.
Smith, D. J., and J. Gray. 1985. *Police and People in London: The PSI Report*. London: Gower.
Southwestern Law Enforcement Institute. 1995. "Domestic Assaults among Police: A Survey
    of Internal Affairs Policies." Arlington, Texas, Police Department.
Spelman, W., and J. E. Eck. 1987. *Problem-Oriented Policing*. Washington, DC: National
    Institute of Justice (Research in Brief Series).
Spencer, Cassie C. 1987. "Sexual Assault: The Second Victimization." In L. L. Crites and W.
    L. Hepperle, *Women, the Courts, and Equality*. Newbury Park, CA: Sage, 54–73.
Stapinski, H. 1998. "Let's Talk Dirty." *American Demographics* 20, 50–56.
Steffensmeier, Darrell. 1979. "Sex Role Orientation and Attitudes toward Female Police."
    Police Studies 2: 39–42.

Steffensmeier, Darrell J., and E. A. Allan. 1988. "Sex Disparities in Arrests by Residence, Race, and Age: An Assessment of the Gender Convergence/Crime Hypothesis." *Justice Quarterly* 5: 53–80.

Steffensmeier, Darrell J., and M. J. Cobb. 1981. "Sex Differences in Urban Arrest Patterns, 1934–1979." *Social Problems* 29: 37–50.

Stenson, K. 1993 (August). "Community Policing as Governmental Technology." *Economy and Society* 22(3): 373–89.

Stoddard, E. 1979. "Organizational Norms and Police Discretion: An Observational Study of Police Work with Traffic Violators." *Criminology* 17(2): 159–71.

Stone, Sandra. 2000. "Barriers to Safety for Victims of Police Domestic Violence." Domestic Violence by Police Officers; U.S. Department of Justice, Federal Bureau of Investigation.

Storch, J., and R. Panzarella. 1996. "Police Stress: State-Trait Anxiety in Relation to Occupational and Personal Stressors." *Journal of Criminal Justice* 24(2): 99–107.

Strecher, Victor. 1995. "People Who Don't Even Know You." In Victor Kappeler (Ed.), *The Police and Society: Touchstone Readings*. Prospect Heights, IL: Waveland Press, 207–24.

———. 1991. "Revising the Histories and Futures of Policing." *Police Forum* 1(1): 1–9. Academy of Criminal Justice Sciences.

Sumner, C. 1981. "Race, Crime and Hegemony: A Review Essay," *Contemporary Crises* 5: 277–91.

Sykes, G., and D. Matza. 1957. "Techniques of Neutralization: A Theory of Delinquency." *American Sociological Review* 22(6): 664–70.

Tappan, P. W. 1947. *Delinquent Girls in Court: A Study of the Wayward Minor Court of New York.* New York: Columbia University Press.

Taylor, Verta, and Nancy Whittier. 1992. "Collective Identity in Social Movement Communities: Lesbian Feminist Mobilization." In Aldon Morris and Carol McClurg Mueller (Eds.), *Frontiers in Social Movement Theory*. New Haven: Yale University Press.

Temin, C. E. 1973. "Discriminatory Sentencing of Women Offenders." *American Criminal Law Review* 11(2): 355–72.

Tennessee v. Garner, 471 U.S. 1.

Terrill, R. J. 1990. "Alternative Perceptions of Independence in Civilian Oversight." *Journal of Police Science and Administration* 17(2): 77–83.

Terrill, William, and S. D. Mastrofski. 2002 (June). "Situational and Officer-Based Determinants of Police Coercion." *Justice Quarterly* 19(2).

Terrill, William, and John McCluskey. 2002 (March–April). "Citizen Complaints and Problem Officers: Examining Officer Behavior." *Journal of Criminal Justice* 30(2): 143–55, Tarrytown: Pergamon Press, Inc.

Thacher, David. 2001. "Conflicting Values in Community Policing." *Law & Society Review* 35(4): 765–98.

Thomas, W. I. 1966 (orig. 1931). "The Relation of Research to the Social Process." In Morris Janowitz (Ed.), *W. I. Thomas on Social Organization and Social Personality*. Chicago: University of Chicago Press, 289–305.

———. 1923. *The Unadjusted Girl.* Boston: Little, Brown.

Thurman v. City of Torrington, 595 F.Supp. 1521 (1984).

Tiffen, Rodney. 2004 (May). "Tip of the Iceberg or Moral Panic? Police Corruption Issues in Contemporary New South Wales." *American Behavioral Scientist* 47 (9): 1171–93.

Times-Picayune. 2011 (April 5). "New Orleans Police Capt. Michael Roussel Was a Consultant for Corruption: An Editorial." http://www.nola.com/opinions/index.ssf/2011/04/new_orleans_police_capt_michae.html

Tomaskovic-Devey, D., M. Mason, and M. Zingraff. 2004 (March). "Looking for the Driving While Black Phenomena: Conceptualizing Racial Bias Processes and Their Associated Distributions." *Police Quarterly* 7(1): 3–29.

Totten, M. 2000. *Guys, Gangs, and Girlfriend Abuse*. Peterborough, ON: Broadview Press.

Travis, Lawrence F. III, and Robert H. Langworthy. 2008. *Policing in America: A Balance of Forces*, 4th ed. Upper Saddle River, NJ: Pearson Prentice Hall.

Trojanowicz, R. J. 1983. "An Evaluation of a Neighborhood Foot Patrol Program." *Journal of Police Science and Administration* 11(4): 410–19.

Trojanowicz, R. J., and B. Bucqueroux. 1990. *Community Policing: A Contemporary Perspective.* Cincinnati, OH: Anderson Publishing Company.

UAW v. Johnson Controls, 499 U.S. 187 (1991).

Uchida, Craig D. 1997. "The Development of the American Police: An Historical Overview." In R. G. Dunham and G. P. Alpert (Eds.), *Critical Issues in Policing: Contemporary Readings*, 3rd ed. Prospect Heights, IL: Waveland Press.

———. 1989. "The Development of the American Police: An Historical Overview." In R. G. Dunham and G. P. Alpert (Eds.), *Critical Issues in Policing: Contemporary Readings*, 2nd ed. Prospect Heights, IL: Waveland Press, 16–32.

U.S. Census Bureau. 2008a (August 26). "Current Population Survey: Annual Social and Economic Supplement."

———. 2008b. "Housing and Household Economic Statistics."

U.S. Civil Rights Commission. 1981. "Who Is Guarding the Guardians? A Report on Police Practices." Washington, DC: The United States Commission on Civil Rights.

U.S. Department of Justice. 2001. "Principles for Promoting Police Integrity." Washington DC: Department of Justice. Available at www.ncjrs.org, NCJ 186189.

U.S. Department of Justice, Bureau of Justice Statistics. 2000. Census of State and Local Law Enforcement Agencies. Washington, DC: U.S. Government Printing Office.

U.S. Department of Labor, Bureau of Labor Statistics. 2008 (October). Highlights of Women's Earnings in 2007. Report 1008. http://www.bls.gov/cps/cpswom2007.pdf

Valverde, M. 1985. *Sex, Power and Pleasure.* Toronto: Canadian Scholars' Press.

Van-Maanen, J. 1984 (July–October). "Making Rank: Becoming an American Police Sergeant." *Journal of Contemporary Ethnography* 13(2–3): 155–76.

———. 1973. "Observations on the Making of Policemen." *Human Organization* 32(4): 407–18.

Van Wormer, K. S. 1981. "Are Males Suited to Police Patrol Work?" *Police Studies* 3(4): 41–44.

Van Wormer, K. S., and C. Bartollas. 2000. *Women and the Criminal Justice System.* Boston: Allyn & Bacon.

Van Wormer, K. S., and A. Roberts. 2009. *Death by Domestic Homicide: Preventing the Murders and the Murder-Suicides.* Westport, CT: Praeger.

Vedder, C. B., and D. B. Somerville. 1970. *The Delinquent Girl.* Springfield, IL: Charles C. Thomas.

Vera Institute of Justice. 2002 (March). "Racial Profiling." Police Assessment Resource Center.

Vicchio, Stephen. 1997. "Ethics and Police Integrity: Some Definitions and Questions for Study." Keynote address at the National Symposium on Police Integrity, July 1996. In S. J. Gaffigan and P. P. McDonald (Eds.), *Police Integrity: Public Service with Honor.* Washington, DC: U.S. Department of Justice.

Visano, L. 1998. *Crime and Culture: Refining the Traditions.* Toronto: Canadian Scholars' Press Inc.

Walker, Samuel. 2006. "Alternative Models of Citizen Oversight." In J. C. Perino (Ed.), *Citizen Oversight of Law Enforcement.* Chicago: IL: American Bar Association Publishing.

———. 2005. *The New World of Police Accountability.* Thousand Oaks, CA: Sage Publications.

———. 2001. *Police Accountability: The Role of Citizen Oversight.* Belmont, CA: Wadsworth.

———. 1981. *Popular Justice: A History of American Criminal Justice.* New York: Oxford University Press.

———. 1977. *A Critical History of Police Reform: The Emergence of Professionalization.* Lexington, MA: Lexington Books.

Walker, Samuel, and Geoffrey P. Alpert. 2004. "Early Intervention Systems: The New Paradigm." In Matthew Hickman, Alex R. Piquero, and Jack R. Green (Eds.), *Police Integrity and Ethics.* Belmont, CA: Wadsworth/Thomas Learning.

Walker, Samuel, and C. M. Katz. 2008. *The Police in America: An Introduction*, 7th ed. Boston, MA: McGraw-Hill.

———. 2005. *The Police in America: An Introduction*, 5th ed. New York: McGraw-Hill.

————. 1999. *The Police in America: An Introduction*, 3rd ed. New York: McGraw-Hill.

————. 1992. *The Police in America: An Introduction*, 2nd ed. New York: McGraw-Hill.

————. 1983. *The Police in America: An Introduction*, 1st ed. New York: McGraw-Hill.

Wards Cove Packing Co. v. Antonio, 490 U.S. 642 (1989).

Washington Post/Associated Press. 2005 (February 25). "Hearings for Balt. Officers in Corruption Case." http://voices.washingtonpost.com/crime-scene/baltimore/hearings-for-balt-officers-in.html

Websdale, N. 1999. "Police Homicide Files as Situated Media Substrates: An Exploratory Essay." In Jeff Ferrell and Neil Websdale (Eds.), *Making Trouble: Cultural Constructions of Crime, Deviance and Control*. New Brunswick, NJ: Transaction Publishers, 227–300.

West, C., and D. H. Zimmerman. 1987 (June). "Doing Gender." *Gender and Society* 1(2): 125–51.

Westley, W. 1953 (July). "Violence and the Police." *American Journal of Sociology* 59: 34–41.

Wexler, J. G., and D. D. Logan. 1983. "Sources of Stress among Women Police Officers." *Journal of Police Science and Administration* 11(1): 46–53.

White, Michael D. 2002. "Identifying Situational Predictors of Police Shootings using Multivariate Analysis." *Policing: An International Journal of Police Strategies and Management* 25(4): 726–51.

Whren et al. v. United States, 517 U.S. 806 (1996).

Williams, C. L. 1989. *Gender Differences at Work: Women and Men in Nontraditional Occupations*. Berkeley: University of California Press.

Williams, Huber, and Patrick V. Murphy. 1990 (January). "The Evolving Strategy of Policing: A Minority View." *Perspectives on Policing* 13, Washington, DC: National Institute of Justice.

Williams, Jimmy J., and Gary Hester. 2003. "Sheriff Law Enforcement Officers and the Use of Force." *Journal of Criminal Justice* 31(4): 373–81.

Wilson, J. Q. 1968. *Varieties of Police Behavior: The Management of Law and Order in Eight Communities*. Cambridge, MA: Harvard University Press.

Wilson, J. Q., and G. L. Kelling. 1982 (March). "Broken Windows: The Police and Neighborhood Safety." *Atlantic Monthly*, 29–38.

Wilson, Orlando W. 1950. *Police Administration*. New York: McGraw-Hill.

Wilson, William Julius. 1996. *When Work Disappears: The World of the New Urban Poor*. New York: Knopf.

Wiseman, Jane. 2011. "Strategic Cutback Management: Law Enforcement Leadership for Lean Times," a Research for Practice report published by the National Institute of Justice, National Criminal Justice Reference Service, NCJ 232077. https://www.ncjrs.gov/pdffiles1/nij/232077.pdf

Withrow, Brian L. 2006. *Racial Profiling: From Rhetoric to Reason*. Upper Saddle River, NJ: Pearson Education, Inc.

————. 2004 (September). "Driving While Different: A Potential Theoretical Explanation for Race-Based Policing." *Criminal Justice Policy Review* 15(3): 344–64.

Withrow, Brian L., and H. Jackson. 2002. "Race-Based Policing: Alternatives for Assessing the Problem." In W. R. Palacios, P. F. Cromwell, and R. Dunham (Eds.), *Crime and Justice in America: Present Realities and Future Prospects*, 2nd ed. Upper Saddle River, NJ: Prentice Hall, 183–90.

WKMG Orlando. 2011 (May 20). "Woman: Orlando Cop Broke My Teeth in Takedown; Orlando Police Investigate Downtown Incident." http://www.clickorlando.com/news/27952314/detail.html

Worden, A. P. 1993 (May). "The Attitudes of Women and Men in Policing: Testing Conventional and Contemporary Wisdom." *Criminology* 31(2): 203–37.

Worden, R. E. 1995. "The 'Causes' of Police Brutality: Theory and Evidence on Police Use of Force." In W. A. Geller and H. Toch (Eds.), *And Justice for All: Understanding and Controlling Police Abuse of Force*. Washington, DC: Police Executive Forum, 31–60.

Wyrick, P. A. 2000 (November). "Law Enforcement Referral of At-Risk Youth: The SHIELD Program." Office of Juvenile Justice and Delinquency Prevention, U.S. Department of Justice.

Young, J. 1992. "The Rising Demand for Law and Order and Our Maginot Lines of Defence against Crime." In N. Abercrombie and A. Warde (Eds.), *Social Change in Contemporary Britain*. Cambridge: Polity.

Young, M. 1993. *In the Sticks: Cultural Identity in a Rural Police Force*. Oxford: Oxford University Press.

Zahn, Margaret A., and Kevin J. Strom. 2003. "Terrorism and the Federal Social Science Research Agenda." In Mathieu Deflem (Ed.), *Terrorism and Counter-Terrorism: Criminological Perspectives*. London: Elsevier Science Press, 111–28.

Zdanowicz, M. 2001 (June). "A Shift in Care." *Community Links*, Community Policing Consortium, 3–5.

Zhao, J. 1996. "Why Police Organizations Change: A Study of Community Policing." Paper presented at Police Executive Research Forum, Washington, DC.

Zhao, J., N. He, and N. Lovrich. 2003. "Community Policing: Is It Changing the Basic Functions of Policing in the 1990s?" *Justice Quarterly* 20: 697–724.

Zimbardo, P. G. 2007. *The Lucifer Effect: Understanding How Good People Turn Evil*. New York: Random House.

Zorza, J. 1992 (Spring). "The Criminal Law of Misdemeanor Domestic Violence, 1970–1990." *Journal of Criminal Law and Criminology* 83(1): 46–72.

Index

ABC *20/20*, 126

Abuse of power: Against minorities, 18, 168; Benefits for family and friends, 88; Community policing and, 153, 173; Domestic violence and, 44, 45; Females and, 13, 43; Financial/material gain and, 21, 71, 102, 162, 175; Gender specific, 46, 47; Police corruption and, 25, 26; Police culture and, 4, 54, 23, 71, 61, 89, 114, 142, 179; Public/media and, 14, 130, 131, 127, 180; Wickersham Commission and, 8

Accountability mechanisms, 50, 38, 48, 53

Albany, NY, 19, 150

Affirmative action programs, 120

African American, 11, 18, 25, 66, 112, 150, 152, 168, 168, 173

American Civil Liberties Union (ACLU), 42, 48

Anchorage, AK, 127

Anchorage Daily News, 127

Anglin, Michelle, 147

Anthony, Casey, 132

Arm bar technique, 143

Assault, 19, 26, 28, 33, 43, 45–46, 47, 60, 68, 76, 79, 87, 90, 92, 95, 126, 134, 135, 137, 140, 147

Authoritarian policing, 37, 158

Automobiles, 6, 9

Baez, Anthony, 150

Baldwin, Lola Greene, 10

Baltimore, MD, 144

Baltimore Police Department, 127

Batista, Norman, 85

Beccaccio, Livio, 142–143

Berkeley, CA, 8

Bertillon system, 9

Beth Israel Hospital, 136

Bicycle units, 155

bin Laden, Osama, 171

Blankenship, Betty, 118

Bloomberg, Michael, 150

Blue collar crimes, 108, 164

Blue Ribbon Commissions, 51

Booker, Cory, 140

Bordellos, 5

Boss, Kenneth, 19

Boston, MA, 7

Boston Police Department, 3

Bowens, Matthew, 62

Branch, Joseph, 146

Bribes, 5, 75

Bronx, NY, 19, 147, 150, 152

Brothels, 6

Brotherhood: Hegemonic masculinity, xii, 134; Police corruption, xii, 59, 92, 99, 78, 109; Police culture, 26, 50, 56, 64–70, 61, 139, 149, 154, 176; Women, 65

Bruno v. Codd, 43, 45

"Buddy Boys", 17

207

Index

Bumpers, Eleanor, 150

California Highway Patrol, 18
Canada, 14, 137, 160
Car patrol, 10, 153
Caracappa, Stephen, 20
Carroll, Sean, 19
Casso, Anthony "Gaspipe", 20
CBS *60 Minutes*, 126
Central command, 3, 9
Cherry, Bob, 144
Chicago, IL, 16, 158
Chicago Alternative Policing Strategy
    (CAPS), 158
Chicago Police Department, 120, 149
Chicago Sun Times, 148
Chicago Tribune, 141
Chiseling, 23
Christopher Commission, 51
Cincinnati, OH, 7
Cincinnati Enquirer, 28
Cincinnati Police Department, 28
Citizen complaints, 17, 19, 28, 42, 47, 50,
    52, 54, 78, 96, 100, 101, 129, 157, 160
Citizen oversight agencies, 51–52
Civil lawsuits, 17, 40
Civil Rights Act (1964), 118
Civil Rights Act (1991), 119
Class: Bias, 54; Criminal offending and,
    100, 108, 164; History of policing and,
    70; Inequalities and, 14; Police recruits
    and, 61; Police response and, 93; Risky
    populations and, 33; Upper and middle,
    the, 6, 11, 13, 70, 130, 129, 166, 180;
    Working, the, 7, 11
Cocaine, 17, 49, 85, 168
Coercion, 2
Coffal, Elizabeth, 118
Collins, Gail, 150
Community policing: Building bridges
    and, 155, 156, 157, 162, 167;
    Challenges for integration of the CP
    model (*see* community police
    challenges); Criticisms of, 34;
    Definition of, 154, 155–156; Evaluation
    of police corruption and, 153; Flatter
    power structure, 156, 157, 159, 162;
    Identity categories and, 160, 161;
    Increased visibility and, 153, 154, 157;

Information exchange and, 158–159;
    Initiatives and, 4, 34, 35, 99, 154, 156,
    158, 162, 165, 167, 172, 177; Minimize
    police corruption, xiii, 153, 159–160;
    Officer attitudes and, 164; Philosophy
    of, 156, 158, 162; Police accountability
    and, 156, 157, 159, 160, 162, 173;
    Policing priorities and, 158; Proactive
    policing approaches and, 154, 155, 157;
    Service to communities and, 157
Community policing challenges:
    Community mistrust, 168–171;
    Hegemonic masculinity and, 163; Ethos
    of individualism, 166–167; Police
    attitudes and, 164–165; War on terror
    and, 171–173
Confessions, 6
Conspiracy, 17
CRASH, 19, 26, 29, 50
Crime: Investigation laboratories, 9;
    Reduction, 153; Scene analysis, 9;
    Statistics, 9, 31, 94, 126, 170
Crime control strategies/tactics/techniques,
    30, 31, 35, 61, 65, 70, 116, 135, 155,
    178
Criminal behavior, 29, 93, 108, 132, 170
Criminal justice system, 8, 30, 35, 135
Criminal law, 38, 108, 166
Criminal profiling, 47
Criminologist: Critical, 14, 125; Feminist,
    14, 93, 125; Mainstream, 4, 10, 25, 64,
    93, 40

Dabdoub, Louis, 146
Davis, Larry, 150, 152
Deadly force, 19, 25, 36, 40, 40, 42, 47,
    105, 168
Del Bosque, Stephen, 141, 148
Denver, CO, 16
Detective divisions, 6
Detroit, MI, 16, 47, 62
Detroit Police Department, 19
Diallo, Amadou, 19, 82, 150
District of Columbia Metropolitan Police
    Department, 49
Double marginality, 66
Domestic violence, 4, 25, 27, 40, 43,
    45–47, 60, 92, 95, 99, 105, 113, 116,
    122

Dow Chemical, 128

Early Intervention Systems (EI), 4, 41, 52
Elections, 4, 6
Embezzlement, 94, 145, 145, 164
English, 1, 3, 6
Eppolito, Louis, 20
Excessive force, 4, 15, 17, 18, 19, 27, 26, 28, 42, 47, 80, 96, 102, 105, 110, 135, 140, 142, 143, 152, 160, 168, 170, 178
Extortion, 23, 60, 92, 102, 144, 170

Favoritism, 23
Federal Bureau of Investigation (FBI), 8, 14, 134, 146, 172
Felony arrests, 35, 40
Female officers (*see* policewomen)
Fematt, Jose, 148
Feminist criminology, 93–95
Feminist inquiries, 64
Feminist Mystique, the, 93
Feminization of poverty, 97, 177
Fettig, Jennifer, 62
Fingerprinting, 8–9
Finnegan, Jerome, 141
Fishman, Paul, 140
Fixes, 23
Flanagan, Louise, 145
"Fleeing Felon Rule", 40
Florida, 17, 25, 29
Foot patrol, 10, 76, 80, 88, 89, 167, 155
Fourth Amendment, 40
Fraud, 94, 99, 164–165, 146

Galizia, Frank, 145
Gambling, 5, 7, 16, 23
Garner v. Memphis, 40
Gender: Abuse of power and, 47; Biases, 65, 46; Criminal offending and, 92, 100; Discrimination and, 66, 118; Force and, 27; Gender constructions, xii, 59, 69, 113, 115, 118; Media and, 132–133; Perceptions of risk and, 26, 98, 96, 99, 177, 178; Performance evaluations and, 120; Roles, 64, 68, 97, 177; Recruitment/promotion and, xii, 101, 120; Social constructions of, 93; Technology and, 69

Gender Configuring: Division of labor in, 122; Policies and practices in, 121
Ghraib, Abu, 55
Gillespies, Kevin, 150
Goris, Julissa, 150–151
Graft, 8, 39
Grass eaters, 16, 24
Griggs v. Duke Power Company, 118

Hakeem, Adam Abdul, 150
Hamilton, Torri, 148
Hegemony, 57, 109, 113
Herrera, Keith, 141, 148–149
Hispanics, 25, 48, 112, 168
Holfeld, Mike, 142
Homicide, 19, 47, 99, 168
Hopkins, Ernest Jerome, 111
Hoover, Herbert, 8
Huffington Post, 140, 150
Human Rights Watch, 13, 129

Identity: Collective, 104, 109; Conflict of, 80, 176; Construction, xii, 71, 101, 110, 103, 105, 107; Crisis of, 103, 104; Gender/categories, 26, 69, 113, 133, 140, 161, 164; Occupational, 103; Organizational, xii, 22, 101, 106, 108, 114; Police corruption and, 71; Police/officers, 11, 59, 61, 64, 69, 70, 80, 92, 101, 102, 103, 105, 104, 109, 112, 118, 134, 139, 154, 163; Self/Individual, xii, 22, 65, 80, 103, 106, 108, 114, 176; Socially constructed, 103
Ideologies: Crime control, xi, 1, 10, 21, 30, 34, 35, 42, 43, 48, 54, 55, 110; Dominant, 14, 34, 37, 42, 70, 95, 110, 112, 114, 128, 131, 178; "Equal but separate", 7, 11, 13, 115; Moral, 80, 102; Patriarchy, xiii, 61, 63, 70, 93, 109, 113, 138, 153, 154, 162, 175; Professional, 107; "Science of policing", 9; "Tough on Crime", 95; "Us versus them", 63, 106, 109, 135, 153, 170, 176; War on Drugs, 95
Image maintenance, 31
Immigration, 4
Indianapolis Police Department, 118
Industrial Revolution, 11
Industrialization, 7, 11

Innovative Response to Improve Safety
  (I.R.I.S.), 143
Internal Affairs, 17, 51, 53, 135, 144
International Association of Chiefs of
  Police, the, 7, 9
Intimidation, 4–5, 163, 170

Kansas City, MO, 47
Kansas City Police Department, 41
Kansas City Preventative Patrol
  Experiment, 154
Kelly, Ray, 150
Key West Police Department, 17
Kickbacks, 23, 60, 92, 144, 144
Kidnapping, 20
King, Rodney, 18, 51
Knapp Commission, the, 13, 16, 17, 24,
  129, 150–151

Labeling theory, 97
Lanning v. SEPTA, 119
Las Vegas Police Department, 41
Liberation theorists, 94, 125
Lie detectors, 9
Lindsay, Sam A., 14
Lippman, Jonathan, 150
Livoti, Francis X., 150
London Metropolitan Police, 2, 3
LoPresti, Stephen, 150
Louima, Abner, 19
Los Angeles, CA, 7, 18, 51
Los Angeles Police Department (LAPD),
  10, 18, 20, 29
Los Angeles Police Department (LAPD)
  Board of Inquiry, 29
Los Angeles Sheriffs Department, 50
Lucchese family, 20

Malice Green, 19
Manhattan, NY, 85, 135, 150
Marshal, Harrington, 150
Marshals, 1
Maryland, 48
Masculinity: Definition of, 65, 113, 116;
  "Doing", 70, 67; Hegemonic, xi, xii,
  xii–xiii, 20, 59, 64, 71, 92, 95, 101, 105,
  109, 112, 113, 115, 116, 125, 134, 163;
  Hypermasculinity, 135; Police culture
  and, 65, 69, 103, 116, 117, 178

Mata, Franklin, 135–136
McAllister, John David, 14
McMellon, Edward, 19
Meat eaters, 16, 24
Media: Corruption coverage, 125, 128,
  131, 135, 179, 180; Gendered offending
  and, 132–133; Females and, 95, 125,
  132–133; Ideological constructions of
  criminality, 147; Individual focus and,
  131; Infotainment, 126, 127; Legitimate
  victims and, 51, 102, 126, 140, 142,
  143, 144, 145, 147, 149, 180; Moral
  panic and, 125, 126, 130, 131;
  Newsworthy, 125, 130; Police
  criminality, 15–17; Public relations
  campaigns, 10; Random crimes and,
  128; Rape myths and, 137–138, 139;
  Role, 106; Sensationalizing crimes and,
  14, 32, 125, 133; Victim blaming and,
  45, 139; Violent crimes and, 133
Memphis, TN, 40
Mesquite Police Department, 14
Meyer, Louis, 148
Meyer, Michael, 150
Miami, FL, 17, 25, 29
Miami Police Department, 53
Michigan, 62, 118
Michigan Commission on Law
  Enforcement Standards (MCOLES),
  118
Millstone, Heather, 136
Mitchell, Neville, 147
Mollen Commission, the, 17, 29, 85
Moore, Matthew Dean, 134
Moore, Rasheed, 140
Money collectors, 5
Money laundering, 20
Mooching, 23, 24
Moral ambiguities, xii, 101, 110–111
Moral order, 80
Moral panic, 37, 94, 125, 126, 130, 131,
  180
Moreno, Kenneth, 135–136, 137, 139
Motor vehicle theft, 19
Morgenthau, Robert, 150
Mugging, 37
Municipalities, 3
Murder, 17, 19, 20, 26, 42, 126, 128, 132,
  141, 141

Murphy, Richard, 19

Narcotics trafficking, 16, 19, 23, 26
National Chiefs of Police Union, 9
National Crime Victimization Survey
(NCVS), 126
National Household Survey of Substance
and Drug Abuse, 168
NBC *Dateline*, 126
Neighborhood policing officers (NPOs),
157
New Bern, NC, 145
New Jersey, 47
New Orleans, LA, 19, 134, 146
New Orleans Police Department, 146
New Orleans Times Picayune, 146
New York, 5, 16, 19, 85, 137, 138
New York City, NY, 3, 19, 52, 165, 171
New York Police Department, 16, 17, 29
New York Post, 135
New York Times, 150
Newark, NJ, 140
Newark Police Department, 140
911 systems, 9

Obama, Barak, 173
Official Corruption Unit (OCU), 52
Olsen, Eric, 141, 148
Order maintenance, 8, 175
Orlando, FL, 142
Orlando Police Department, 142
Opportunistic thefts, 23
Osgoode Hall Law School, 14
Overseas Contingency Operation, 173

Parks, Bernard, 19
Patrolmen's Benevolent Association,
150–151
Payoffs, 5, 16, 23
Peacemakers, 43
Pendleton Civil Service Act, 7
Perez, Rafael, 19, 20
Perez, Thomas, 140
Perino, Christopher, 150
Perjury, 24, 60, 92, 102, 150, 152
Perlmutter, Adam, 150
Philadelphia, PA, 7, 16
Philadelphia Police Department, 50, 78

Physical strength, definition of, 65, 113,
118, 160, 178
Physical tests, 61, 65, 118, 160 .
Pittsburgh Police Department, 120
Polanco, Jose, 85
Police academy, 61, 114, 179
Police administrators, 6, 7, 29, 31, 175
Police agencies, 2, 17, 31–35, 42, 48, 66,
118, 120, 128, 166, 171, 179
Police biases, 6
Police brutality, 17, 18, 27, 36, 85, 106,
170
Police chiefs, 36, 69, 117, 168, 171
Police-citizen encounter(s), 28, 93, 96
Police conduct: Operating procedures, 40;
Policy manuals, 40
Police corruption: Bad apples (see also
rotten apple theory), 29–30, 34, 36,
106, 114, 127, 130, 144, 175, 180;
Categories of, 24; Definition of, 20, 22,
24; Dirty Harry Syndrome and, 71, 111;
Female officers and, 96–100; Forms of,
xii, 6, 21, 24–25, 39, 71, 127, 169, 175,
178, 180; Gender differences in, 27–28;
Illegal businesses and, 5, 6, 16;
Justifications/Rationalizations of, 71;
Measurement of, 129; Motivating
factors and, 96, 99; "Noble Cause", 24,
71, 85, 111; Proactive, 34, 106; Public
perceptions of, 13–15; Publicized cases
of, 1, 17–20, 21, 35, 134–152;
Subjective component of, 101;
Typology of, 22–24
Police criminality, xi, xii, 1, 15, 17, 24, 26,
30, 35, 59, 64, 125, 126, 131, 180
(*see also* police corruption)
Police culture, 64–70; Condoning
corruption, xii, 36, 71, 80, 101, 144,
176; Gender norms/roles and, 66, 68,
80, 97, 116, 177; Masculinity and, 65,
69, 103, 116, 117, 178; Sexual
orientation and, 113; Values, 46, 68, 61,
112
Police deviance, xi, 4, 24
(*see also* police corruption)
Police discretion: Application of rules, 38;
Definition of, 38; Limitations on, 40,
159; Policy, 39, 45, 49; Powers, 6, 9,
38–39, 42, 48, 57, 60, 69, 108, 126,

130, 135, 139, 142, 170
Police image, xi, 1, 9, 10, 13, 30, 31, 33, 34, 36, 66–67, 68, 69, 70, 80, 104, 106, 113, 116, 117, 160, 163, 176, 178
Police imagination, 33, 105, 160, 154
Police misconduct (*see* police corruption)
Police occupational themes, xii, 59, 92
Police officer: Assumptions of guilt and, 110; Cynicism and, 78; Front-line, 38, 53, 63, 114, 156, 160, 162; Guilty knowledge, 111; Perceptions, xi, xii, 45, 59, 62–63, 102–103, 108, 153, 164–165, 168, 179; Sense of entitlement, xii, 22, 26, 89, 109, 116, 125, 134, 138, 139, 154, 178; Stress, 61, 66; Supervision of, 6, 38, 63; tenure and, 7, 78
Police organizations: Appearance management, 10, 37, 107, 163, 167, 171, 175; Bad barrel maker, 34, 55–57; Enabler of corruption, as an, 38–49; Goals of, xi, 21, 29–37, 54, 57, 62, 99, 110, 114, 167, 176; Identities, xii, 22, 101, 106, 108, 114; Knowledge of insecurities, 35, 167, 176, 181; Policing methods and, 39; Popular cultural construction and (*see* policing); Priorities of, 31, 176; Social space and, 39, 60; Specialization, 9; Structure of, xii, 34, 57, 60, 96, 107, 126, 157, 159, 162; Survival of, xii, 31–35, 55, 56, 105, 107, 167, 171, 175, 179, 181; Response to corruption, 35–37
Police recruits, 8, 60, 61, 114, 179
Police surveillance, 3, 61, 173
Policewomen: Being proactive, 11; Child care and, 11, 65, 99, 120, 161, 177; Communication skills and, 99; Corruption and, 27–28; Education of, 11; Excessive force and, 27; Extreme controlling behaviors and, 28; Forms of exclusion and, 66; Gendered discrimination and, 66, 68, 118, 121, 163; Maternal duties and, 11; Moral crusaders and, 13; Negative attitudes of males, 66; Perceived threats of, 113; Personal identities of, 65; Policing morality, 12, 13; Pressures on, 28,

64–65, 66, 68; Sexuality of women and, 68; Social workers, as, 11, 68, 142; Specialized units and, 99
Policing: Complex social world, xii, 59; Dirty work, 102, 103, 107, 110, 112; Feminization of, 113; Gendered enterprise, xi, xii, 1, 12, 15, 101, 109, 115–117, 125; Institution, xi, 57, 34, 36, 129, 130–131, 139, 175, 176, 180; Knowledge of insecurities and, 33, 35, 167, 176, 181; Language, 56, 60, 65, 106, 108–109, 173; Legitimacy, 9, 10, 37, 157, 170, 180; Political influences in, 4, 38, 170; Popular constructions of, xii, xiii, 36, 101, 102, 105, 106, 107–112, 114, 153, 163, 176, 179; Site of contestation, xi, xii, 36, 101, 176; Order maintenance, 8, 175; Predatory, 24; Secrecy, xii, 61, 77, 103, 125, 130, 134, 154, 162, 176; Service, 164–165; Specialized units, 29, 59, 99, 122
Policing the Crisis, 37
Policing system, early formal, 1, 3, 6, 15–17
Policy: Continuum-Use-Of-Force, 40, 41–42; Domestic violence, 43, 46; Mandatory arrest, 4, 43, 45–46, 95; Mandatory sentencing, 95; Pro-arrest, 43; Racial profiling, 40, 47–49
Politicians, 3, 4, 6, 37, 173
Popolizio, Pasquale, 140
Portland, OR, 10
Precinct commanders, 9
Pregnancy Discrimination Act (PDA), 121
Prejudice, 23
Prince of the City, 17
Progressive Movement, the, 7
Prostitution, 12–13, 16, 33, 38, 23, 93, 105, 164
Protani, Paula, 144
Public imagination, 33, 35, 37, 112, 160, 176, 179

Race: Community policing and, 161; "criminal" identity and, 108, 164; Discriminatory practices and, 48, 119; Knowledge of insecurities and, 33; Media and, 37; Police and, 54, 61, 70,

93, 110, 112, 118, 140, 160, 166; Race-based policing, 25; Racial profiling, 4, 25, 47–49, 168; Racism; Riots, 16
Racketeering, 17
Radelet, Louis, 4
Racial oppression, 4
Rampart Area scandal, 29, 50, 102
Rampart Corruption Task Force, 19
Rampart Division, 19, 26, 34, 82
Rape myths, 14, 137–138, 139
Riots, 1, 4, 16, 18, 30
Risk discourse, 32
River Cops scandal, 17, 29
Riverside, CA, 50
Riverside Police Department, 50
Robair, Raymond, 134–135
Robbery, 19, 23, 33, 126, 141
Robinson, Koleen, 147
Rollins, Anthony, 127
Rosedale, CA, 141
Rotten apple theory, 30, 36, 176
Roussel, Michael, 146
Ruane, Matthew, 140

Safir, Howard, 150
Sanguinetti, Michael, 14
Schimenti, Richard, 138
Scott v. Hart 43, 45
Selective law enforcement, 20, 25, 60, 92, 108, 109, 128, 168, 170
Sergeants Benevolent Association, 150–151
Serpas, Ronal, 146
Serpico, 18
Serpico, Frank, 16
Sexism, 18, 66
Sexual assault, 19, 25, 27, 60, 92, 99, 113, 122, 136–138, 139
Sexual harassment, 68, 162
Sexuality, 12–13, 68, 70, 139
Shakedown, 23, 24, 148
Sheriff, 1, 117, 145
Shopping, 23
Sisters in Crime 94
Slave patrols, 2, 4
SlutWalk, 14
Smith, Marlon, 147
Social control, 1, 2, 5, 32, 33, 97, 99, 133, 158, 167, 177

Social justice, 33, 167
Social learning theory, 78
Social problems, 1, 11, 37, 128
Social stigmatization, 133, 177
Socialization, 60, 61, 97, 99, 112, 114, 177, 179
Southeastern Pennsylvania Transit Authority (SEPTA), 119
Southwestern Law Enforcement Institute, 44
Street Crime Unit, 19
Street justice, 85–86
Strikebreakers, 5
Summary punishment, 85

Tennessee v. Garner, 40, 42
Theft, 17, 19, 24, 60, 92, 94, 133, 164
Thin blue line, 37, 63, 61, 105, 179
Thomas' Theorem, 32
Thomas Jr., Ralph L., 145
Three Strikes Laws, 95
Thurman v. Torrington, 43, 45
Ticket fixing, 150, 150–151
Ticketgate scandal, 150–152
Title VII, 118, 140–141

UAW v. Johnson Controls, 121
Uniform Crime Reports (UCR), 8, 126, 170
United States Civil Rights Commission, 52
United States Congress, 172, 173
United States Court of Appeals, 119
United States Department of Defense, 172
United States Department of Jusice (DOJ), 42
United States Supreme Court, 40, 42, 49, 118–119, 121
Urbanization, 7, 11
USA PATRIOT ACT, 173

Vancouver Police Department, 160
Victimization, 3, 14, 31, 95, 108, 110, 128, 168
Vigilantes, 2
Violence against women (*see* domestic violence)
Vizcaino, Ramon, 150
Vollmer, August, 8–9
Volpe, Justin, 19

Wall Street, 81
War theory of crime control, 111
Wards Cove Packing Co v. Antonio 119
Wareham, Lisa, 142
Warner Brothers, 111
Washington, D.C., 48
Washington Post/ Associated Press, 127,
    144
Watchmen, 1
Welfare programs, 34
Wells, Alice Stebbins, 10
White-collar crimes, 12, 25, 92, 94, 164,
    168

Whren et al v. U.S., 49, 169
Wickersham Commission, 8, 111
Wilkins, Robert, 48
Williams, Melvin, 134
Women's Bureaus, 13
Women's Movement, 7, 10, 94, 133
Wuornos, Aileen, 132

York University, 14

Zelman, Andrew, 142

About the Author

Marilyn Corsianos (Ph.D. York University) is professor of criminology and sociology at Eastern Michigan University. She is the author of the CHOICE Outstanding Academic Title *Policing and Gendered Justice* (University of Toronto Press, 2009), coeditor of *Interrogating Social Justice* (Canadian Scholars Press, 1999) and has written numerous articles on policing, power and social inequalities.